ANGKOR

AN INTRODUCTION TO THE TEMPLES

Dawn F Rooney

Copyright © 1997, 1994 The Guidebook Company Ltd, Hong Kong
All maps copyright © 1997, 1994 The Guidebook Company Ltd, Hong Kong
Odyssey Guides, an imprint of The Guidebook Company Ltd,
G/F 2 Lower Kai Yuen Lane, North Point; Hong Kong
T 852 2856 3896, F 852 2565 8004   E-mail odyssey@asiaonline.net

Distribution in the United Kingdom, Ireland and Europe by
Hi Marketing Ltd, 38 Carver Road, London SE24 9LT, UK
ISBN: 962-217-419-1

This edition first published in North America in 1997 by
Passport Books, 4255 W. Touhy Avenue,
Lincolnwood (Chicago), Illinois 60646-1975,
USA T 847 679 5500   F 847 679 2494
ISBN: 0-8442-4766-9
Library of Congress Catalogue Card Number: 97-66479

PASSPORT BOOKS
NTC/*Contemporary Publishing Company*

Grateful acknowledgement is made to the following authors and publishers for permissions granted:
Oxford University Press for *The Land of the White Elephant: Sights and Scenes in South-East Asia 1871-
1872* by Frank Vincent, ©1988; Thornton Butterworth for *Cambodian Glory The Mystery of the Deserted
Khmer Cities and their Vanquished Splendour, and a Description of Life in Cambodia today* by H W Ponder,
©1936; H F & G Witherby for *Angkor: The Magnificent, The Wonder City of Ancient Cambodia* by H
Churchill Candee, ©1925; Oxford University Press for *The Straits of Malacca, Siam and Indo-China
Travels and Adventures of a Nineteenth-century Photographer* by John Thomson, ©1993

Editor: Adrian Bonds
Consultant Editor: John Sanday
Editorial Co-ordinator: Jane Finden-Crofts
Design: Bobby Chan
Map Design: Bai Yilang
Cover Concept: Aubrey Tse

Front cover photograph: the Bayon, built c.1177–1230, one of the most popular monuments at Angkor

Photography by Peter Danford, except for: Antiques of the Orient, Singapore, from the Garnier Plates
collection 23, 26-27, 36-37, 40-41, 50, 86, 87, 90, 142-143; Bibliothèque Nationale, Paris 140; Stefan
Cucos 99, 103, 112-113; Michael Freeman 63, 71-72, 98, 194-195; Dawn Rooney 2, 15, 48, 265; John
Sanday 19, 55, 75, 96, 106, 123, 201, 208, 243, 246, 250, back cover; Wattis Fine Art 44-45, 53

Production by Twin Age Limited, Hong Kong
Printed in Hong Kong

ANGKOR

Go to Angkor, my friend, to its ruins and to its dreams[1]

The Author

Dawn Rooney, who was born in America, has spent many years researching art history in southeast Asia. Awarded a Ph D in Art History in 1983, she has written several books on the region's culture, including *Khmer Ceramics* and *Betel Chewing Traditions in Southeast Asia,* as well as contributing articles to *Oriental Art* and other journals.

The Photographer

Born in Cleveland, Ohio and educated at Minnesota in computer science and east Asia studies, Peter Danford is a freelance photographer and multimedia developer based in Hong Kong. He works specifically in travel photography, Quicktime VR, 360 degree photography and computer programming to produce CD-Roms and content for the Worldwide Web.

Asparas — a ubiquitous design in Khmer art.

Special thanks to Kim and Andrew in Siem Reap.

Preface

—Amanda Reynolds

When the author, Dr Dawn F Rooney, first visited Angkor in 1969, she arrived as a tourist armed only with curiosity and enthusiasm to see one of the world's great cultural heritages.

The flight from Bangkok to Siem Reap passed over the temple complex allowing passengers a superb bird's eye view of Angkor Wat. Awestruck by its sheer size and complexity, Dr Rooney felt for the first time the mesmerising effect of the fabled temples. At dusk, on the terrace of the French-built Auberge des Temples, she gazed across at Angkor Wat, watching the majestic temple towers lit by the rays of a setting sun. That moment, she wrote, 'pierced my soul'.

A week-long exploration of the temples increased her fascination. The architecture, accentuated by exquisite decorative detail and powerful sculpture, she said, 'transcended the boundaries of anticipated beauty. I had never seen such mysterious, enigmatic yet human and harmonious art'.

Nevertheless, more than 20 years were to pass between the author's first and second trips to Angkor as the eruption of civil unrest led to the closure of the temples to tourists from 1969 to 1991. In that time, Dr Rooney devoted herself to the study of Khmer art and civilisation, especially the ceramics of the era which she has made her area of expertise. Travels to kiln sites in north-eastern Thailand, within the territorial boundaries of the Khmer Empire between the 11th and 13th centuries, yielded material for a Ph D dissertation and two books on Khmer ceramics.

A peace agreement in October 1991 led to the re-opening of Angkor. On her return that year, and many trips since, Dr Rooney found the hiatus had eroded none of the temples' mystique. Although the facilities for tourists are increasing all the time — more hotels, restaurants, food and cold drinks at the sites — the monuments remain mercifully unchanged. They continue, at least for the moment, to be easily accessible, uncrowded and in undisturbed surroundings. One major problem remains the depredations of looters who are depriving Angkor of archaeological evidence and selling the cultural relics on the international art market.

Angkor, she has noted, is most dramatic at sunset, sunrise and in the moonlight. Seeing the temples by the light of a full moon is still an unsurpassed experience. Her favourite time of year for visiting the complex is during the rainy season. 'To me, the background of the verdant vegetation against the grey sandstone and reddish brick of the temples is a magical combination.'

Travellers using this book as a guide to the monuments will find their experience heightened by its detailed scholarship, avid armchair tourists will discover in its pages an irresistible read. Above all, the author's enthusiasm will inspire many more people to visit this captivating place.

CONTENTS

Following pages: early European cartographers knew little of Cambodia. Angkor is Columpe, while the Tonle Sap is nowhere to be seen. Like much of south-east Asia, it was known but not understood.

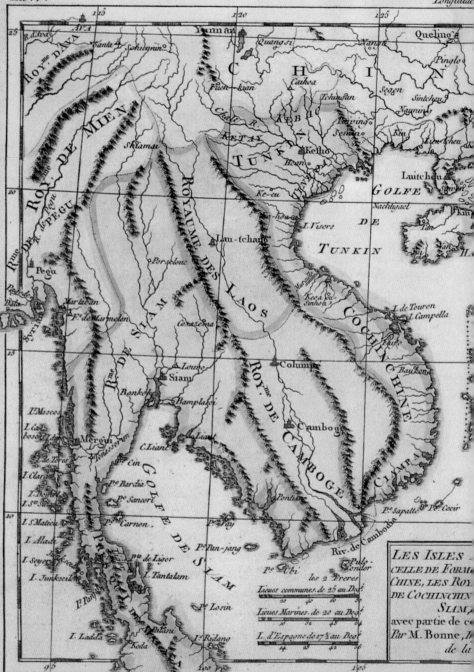

R. d'Ava
AVA
Yunnan
Queling
25
Nanta
Sakignin
Pinglo
ROY.me D'AVA
CHIN
Quangsi
Seogn
Sintcheu
Fuch-kian
Cauhoa
N
Naunino
KEBHO
Taiping
ROY. DE MIEN
Skiamar
Tchinfan
Semin
Kin
Lien-cheu
KETAY
Kelho
20
TUNKIN
Hean
Luitcheu
Rue. de. Pegu.
Ke-eu
GOLFE
Nachtigael
Pegu
Lau-tchang
Kan
DE
I. Visers
Por-selouc
TUNKIN
Martelle
Tan
Delta
Martaban
Keca su
I. de Touron
F. de Marmelon
Sinhon
I. Campella
Syriam
Corazema
Caifo
15
Rue. DE. SIAM
ROY.me DES LAOS
COCHINCHINE
I. Baydeus
Louro
Columir
Siam
ROY. DE CAMBOGE
Bankok
Bamplakoi
CIAMPA
I. Masceo
Camboge
L. au bossu
Liant
Mergui
C. Liant
Tanasserim
Cin
Po Cecir
I. Clara
Po Bardia
Pondiine
Po Sapatte
I. Dontel
Po Sancori
I. S.
GOLFE
10
I. S. Maticu
Po Carnon
Po Vey
Riv. de Camboda
I. Alada
DE SIAM
Pulo
I. Seyez
Po Pun-jang
Condor
LES ISLES
I. Junkseil
Po de Ligor
SIAM
les 2 Freres
CELLE DE FORM
L. Tantalam
Po Ubi
Lieues communes. de 25 au Deg.
CHINE, LES ROY.
I. Patit
DE COCHINCHIN
I. Losin
Lieues Marines. de 20 au Deg.
SIAM
I. Ladda
Patane
L. d'Espagne de 17½ au Deg.
avec partie de c
Keda
I. Ridang
Par M. Bonne, I
de la
95
100
105
Longi

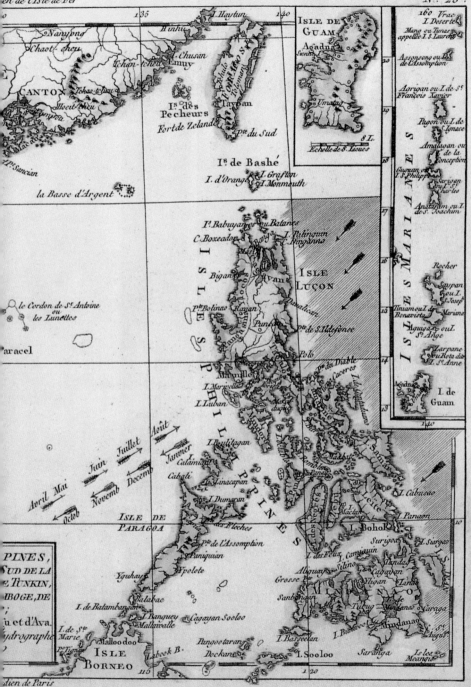

The Buddha is sheltered by the naga king.

Following pages: Angkor Wat — the world's largest religious construction in stone.

PART I

BACKGROUND

Introduction

The tale of it is incredible; the wonder which is Angkor is unmatched in Asia.[2]

The temples startle with their splendour and perfection, but beyond the emotions they evoke lie complex microcosms of a universe steeped in cosmology. While a thorough understanding may be out of reach for many, the monuments' profound beauty touches everyone. Even though there is little doubt the temples of India served as models for Angkor initially, there are concepts found in these Khmer structures that are rare on the sub-continent. Ideas such as the association of architecture with a capital, the link between the ruler and a divinity, the symbolism of the pyramid temple with Meru, a cosmic mountain, are prevalent throughout the Khmer monuments. The sculpture is equally as individualistic. Sensuous, yet never erotic, male and female forms stand in grandeur and dignity offering universal appeal, past and present.

What is Angkor? Many people who have not been to Angkor think it is only one monument — Angkor Wat. This erroneous idea probably arose because it is the most frequently visited and written about. Angkor, though, covers an area of 200 square kilometres (77 square miles) in north-western Cambodia. Many of the sites within this area have collapsed and only traces of some remain, and the grounds around others have not yet been cleared of mines. This guide includes descriptions of 40 accessible sites.

This book is both an introduction and a guide to Angkor. It aims to bring together in a single volume useful information to help you enjoy and appreciate your visit to Angkor. The text has been compiled from published sources, mainly works by Lawrence P Briggs and Maurice Glaize.[3]

The first part begins with the geography of Cambodia. Historical details follow, tracing the Khmers from early times through the period of Angkor and up to the 19th century. The next section includes a history of the restoration efforts at Angkor, describing preservation work on the monuments today. A hypothetical chapter follows on what daily life might have been like for the Khmer people. A chapter on religion describes the beliefs and practices of the Khmers and identifies their principal deities and mythical beings. The next chapter, on Khmer art and architecture, describes the building materials used in the monuments, the methods of construction, typical artistic and architectural features, stylistic periods and touches on the cosmological significance of the monuments.

Since the publication of the first edition in 1994, more sites have been cleared and more temples have been re-opened for visitors. Additional conservation projects involving international co-operation with the Royal Cambodian Government are in progress, and these have been described by John Sanday, who heads the World Monuments Fund team's restoration work at Preah Kahn, and who also collaborated on the art, architecture and temple itinerary sections.

The second part of the book is a series of ten tours, each one taking between three and four hours to complete. The tours can be taken in any order as can the temples within any one grouping. Each temple is described in detail giving the location, access, date of the monument, name of the king associated with the construction, prevailing religion at the time the site was built, art style, background and layout. A ground plan of the layout accompanies most of the descriptions.

The third and final part of the book gives practical information on Cambodia, including how to travel between Phnom Penh and Siem Reap and suggestions for accommodation and eating in both places.

Appendices include: a comparative chronology of Khmer and world history, a list of the kings, and a chronology of the monuments. There is also a general glossary and a list of books for further reading. Finally, a detailed index allows maximum use of the book.

Shiva commanded great respect from Khmer kings.

Measurements are in metric units with imperial units in parenthesis. The abbreviation 'BC' follows all dates before the Christian era. Dates of the Christian era have no abbreviation except where its absence would be confusing.

The use of foreign words has been avoided wherever possible and an English equivalent substituted. Technical terms have also been kept to a minimum. The spelling of names derived from Indian languages, such as those of deities, kings and geographical places, are the most commonly found usages and diacritical marks have been omitted for clarity. The phonetic system developed by the Royal Institute of Thailand has been followed for the spelling of Thai words.

The Pinyin system has been used for the transliteration of Chinese words except in quotations or captions where the original text has been retained. In those instances, the Pinyin equivalent is provided in parenthesis. Khmer words conform to a phonetic spelling, mainly that followed by the French. The spelling of foreign words is sometimes inconsistent with the conventions adopted for this book because each European country spelt Asian words according to its own interpretation of sound. Foreign words are italicised unless they are proper nouns or have been adopted into the English language.

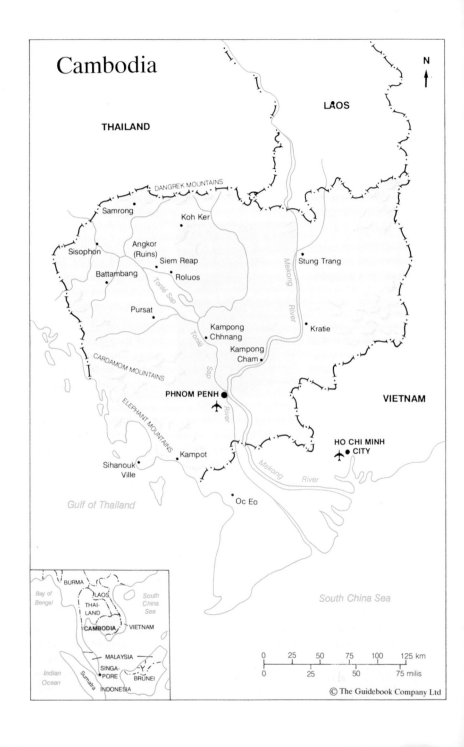

Geographical Setting

Kampuchea, Cambodia, Khmer and Angkor are all names associated with a single Asian civilisation renowned for its art and architecture. Kambujadesa or Kambuja is a Sanskrit name for the modern country of Cambodia. The word derives from a tribe in north India and is associated with Kambu Svayambhuva, the legendary founder of the Khmer civilisation. Kampuchea, a modern version of the name, was part of the official title of the country as recently as 1989. European transliterations of Kambuja became Cambodge in French and Cambodia in English, which is the name of this south-east Asian country today. The modern capital of Cambodia is Phnom ('hill') Penh, located in the southern part of the country. The inhabitants are Khmers or Cambodians; the national language is Khmer; and in the past the country has also been called Khmer.

The name Angkor derives from the Sanskrit word *nagara* ('holy city') which is *nakhon* in Thai and may have been pronounced *nokor* or *ongkor* in Khmer. Angkor was an ancient political centre situated 320 kilometres (199 miles) north of Phnom Penh in Siem Reap province. The town of Siem Reap ('the defeat of the Siamese'), the provincial capital, is six kilometres (four miles) south of Angkor Wat.

The core of the Khmer empire remained in the vicinity of Angkor for over 500 years, but the area of settlement and political domination fluctuated. At the height of territorial expansion, the Khmers claimed control over major parts of neighbouring areas. Evidence of a former Khmer presence in Thailand exists from as early as the seventh century. Control gradually spread to central and north-eastern Thailand and reached a peak in the 11th century under the leadership of Suryavarman I. Archaeological evidence can be seen today at Phimai, in Nakhon Ratchasima province, some 72 kilometres (45 miles) north of Korat. A laterite highway extending for 225 kilometres (140 miles) linked Phimai to Angkor.

TOPOGRAPHY

Angkor is situated in a large basin framed by the Tonle Sap (Great Lake) in the south and the Kulen hills in the north. This plateau is drained by tributaries of the Siem Reap River and intercepted by three hills — Phnom Bok, Phnom Bakheng and Phnom Krom, which became the sites of temples built by King Yasovarman I in the tenth century. Mountain ranges and internal water systems in other parts of Cambodia also formed large valleys where early settlements of the pre-Angkor period flourished.

The Cardamom Mountains (Chuor Phnom Kravanh) in the south-west with an elevation of 1,772 metres (5,814 feet) are the highest in the country. The Elephant

Range (Chuor Phnom Damrei) in the south has an elevation of 915 metres (3,002 feet). The lowest range is the Dangrek (Chuor Phnom Dangrek) which runs east-west across the north of Cambodia and has an elevation of 488 metres (1,601 feet). Between the western part of the Dangrek and the northern part of the Cardamom mountains, an extension of the delta connects with lowlands in Thailand and forms the southern edge of the Korat Plateau in Thailand. This is one of the few accesses by land between the two areas and, as such, it played an important role in Khmer history, providing a vital communication link to Angkor.

THE MEKONG RIVER

The Mekong River and its tributaries are dominant features of the waterways of Cambodia. From its northern source in the Himalayas, the Mekong flows southward, passing through China, Laos, Thailand, and in a south-eastern direction across Cambodia. Finally, the waters of the Mekong discharge into the South China Sea. At Phnom Penh, the Tonle Sap River, a major tributary, joins the Mekong at which an interesting phenomenon occurs. During the rainy season, between May and October, the silted channels of the Mekong River system are insufficient to accommodate the amount of water added to that sent forth by the melting mountain snows, so the river backs up.

The impact of the overflow forces the Tonle Sap River to reverse its course each year between July and October or November and feeds into the Tonle Sap or 'Great Lake'. This action more than doubles the size of the lake, which normally covers an area of approximately 2,600 square kilometres (1,000 square miles), and makes it a natural reservoir. When the flow reverses at the end of the monsoon the Cambodians traditionally hold a celebratory festival, Bon Om Tuk, that coincides with the full moon to give thanks to the spirits for bounteous waters. When the waters from the snows drain off, the course of the Tonle Sap River reverses once again to resume its normal flow.

Zhou Daguan, a Chinese envoy of the Mongol Empire who lived at Angkor for a year in the late 13th century, gave the earliest recorded account of this feature: 'From the fourth to the ninth moon there is rain every afternoon, and the level of the Great Lake may rise seven to eight fathoms. Large trees go under water, with only the tops showing. People living at the water-side leave for the hills. However, from the tenth moon to the third moon of the following year not a drop of rain falls; the Great Lake is navigable only for the smallest craft, and the depth of the water is only three to five feet'.[4]

The Great Lake was the lifeline of the Khmers. Its pattern of movement provided the structure and rituals of daily life and served as a source of fish and rice to an agrarian society. When the water doubled its volume the lake became an ideal feeding ground for spawning fish and, when it receded, the fish easily fell into the traps laid for them. This movement of the waters enabled the cultivation of floating rice, the earliest known form of Khmer agriculture. It is fast growing and germinates in deep water. The stems can grow up to 10 centimetres (4 inches) a day and reach a length of 6 metres (20 feet). The rice stays on the surface because its growth parallels the rise of the water level. Zhou Daguan recognised the unusual characteristics of floating rice and described 'a certain kind of land where the rice grows naturally, without sowing. When the water is up one fathom, the rice keeps pace in its growth. This, I think, must be a special variety', he noted 700 years ago.[5]

Villagers harvesting rice with the towers of Angkor Wat in the background.

Historical Background

PREHISTORIC PERIOD

Evidence suggests the presence of occupation in Cambodia in the prehistoric period. The earliest inhabitants are unknown. Neither their origins nor the dates they lived in the area can be traced. It is likely, though, that inhabitants throughout mainland south-east Asia — Cambodia, Burma, Laos, Thailand and Vietnam — developed basic skills such as the cultivation of rice, the domestication of the ox and buffalo and the use of metals, and practiced animistic worship at about the same time and in a similar way. The earliest settlement found so far at Loang Spean in Battambang province has produced evidence of occupation over 6,000 years ago.[6] The people lived in caves and knew the techniques of polishing stone and decorating pottery with cord-marked, combed and carved designs.

A second prehistoric site, Bas-Plateaux in Kompong Cham province, has yielded radiocarbon dates from the second century BC.[7] The inhabitants of this later site lived in groups resembling villages. Their level of domestication was similar to that of the people of Loang Spean. Samrong Sen in central Cambodia, a third prehistoric site, was occupied about 1500 BC. Opinions differ as to when the prehistoric period ended, but it is generally agreed it occurred sometime between 500 BC and AD 100.

FIRST CENTURY TO EIGHTH CENTURY AD

The succeeding period, known as protohistoric, lasted for about seven hundred years, from the first until the end of the eighth century. From then onwards sufficient historical records have survived to trace a continuous development of the people and places of Cambodia. The patterns of civilisation established in prehistoric societies may have continued to develop in the protohistoric period, although evidence of such a continuity is lacking.

But by the first century AD, the coastal and valley regions comprised settlements whose members grew rice and root crops, had domesticated pigs and water buffalo, made low fired earthenware for cooking food and storing liquids, and were adept at using metals. They practised animism, worshipping both the spirits of the land and their ancestors.

During the first centuries of the Christian era, the Chinese travelled by sea to the 'barbarian lands of the southern ocean' searching for new trade routes and commercial outlets to replace the formerly lucrative overland passages to India, which were blocked by nomadic tribes in Central Asia. Concurrently, India also ventured east for commercial purposes to establish trade with China by sea.

Trading ships sailed from the eastern coast of India across the Bay of Bengal to the upper western coast of the Malay peninsula. From there, goods were transported by land across the Isthmus of Kra to the western coast of the Gulf of Thailand. Then they followed the coastline around the gulf and on to the southern provinces of China. Mainland south-east Asia, ideally situated to offer the protection of an inland sea, developed as a mid-way station along this route.

Use of this seaway increased as maritime trade between India and China accelerated through better knowledge of shipbuilding, an understanding of the monsoon patterns, and improvements in navigational skills. It seems likely that religious and social ideas from India reached the shores of south-east Asia through these Indian-infiltrated areas and were transmitted by brahmin priests over a long period from the beginning of the Christian era. The phenomenon of elements of the Indian culture being absorbed by the Khmers is known as Indianisation.

As trade developed, groups of settlers emerged at ports along the coast. Archaeological evidence of one of these early habitation sites has been found at Oc-Eo, an ancient centre in the Mekong Delta used by traders in the early centuries of the Christian era.[8] Finds of Roman coins, Indian jewellery and Buddhist religious objects dating from the second and third centuries at Oc-Eo suggest it was a port along the vast maritime trading network that extended from the Roman empire and the Mediterranean region, eastward to India and the Spice Islands.

Chinese records of the third century name Funan as one of the earliest Indianised settlements in mainland south-east Asia. It was located in the area of the lower Mekong Delta of south Cambodia and south Vietnam. The inhabitants of this historic state are believed to have been a tribe which spoke a tongue from the Mon-Khmer family of languages, which provides a linguistic source for the Cambodians as early as the beginning of the Christian era. Thus Funan was linked to Cambodia geographically and linguistically and, as such, is the earliest recorded precursor of the Khmer empire. The name Funan may be a Chinese interpretation of *bnam*, an ancient Khmer word meaning 'mountain' and sounding like *phnom* ('hill' in modern Khmer).

Chinese texts describe the mythical founding of Funan, and later a variation of the same story was recounted in Sanskrit and Khmer inscriptions. Versions differ, but the main theme centres around a marriage between a foreigner from India, who was either a brahmin or a king of the Cholas, a dynasty in south India, and a daughter of the *naga* king, who inhabited the waters and ruled over the soil. An inscription from the third century in Champa names Kaudinya as the founder of the new kingdom and he travelled to the land where he met Princess Soma, daughter of the *naga* king, and married her. He carried with him a spear which he planted in the ground of the new land symbolising his authority.

The Khmer version has been linked to the nation's origins and the geneaology of the kings of Cambodia throughout history. According to the Khmer legend, the race is descended from Kamu, the mythical ancestor of the Khmers. His descendant, Preah Thong, left India and sailed for Cambodia after he was exiled for displeasing the king. One night he saw a beautiful *nagini* on the shore of the water. They fell in love and married. The girl's father, king of the *nagas*, drank the waters that covered the land, built a capital, gave the country to them and named it Kambuja.

Indian ideas were absorbed into the culture of Funan during the early centuries of the Christian era on an increasing scale. A new influence seems to have arrived in the fifth century which may have been due to the presence of a Hindu ruler at Funan. The main Indian concepts implanted in south-east Asia during that time include the introduction of formal religions — both Hinduism and Buddhism — and the adoption of the Sanskrit language at court level, which gave birth to a writing system and the first inscriptions. Other Indian ideas absorbed into the local culture were astronomy, a legal system, literature and universal kingship.

Civil wars undermined the stability of Funan and by the early sixth century the centre of political power had shifted inland. Chinese records mention the emergence of a new state called Zhenla (Chenla) in the latter half of the sixth century, situated on the Mekong in the area of modern-day, south-eastern Laos. Zhenla seems to have gained control of Funan and extended its territorial boundaries to the border of today's Vietnam in the north-east and as far as southern China in the north.

Some time in the eighth century, rivalry forced Zhenla to split into two parts, according to Chinese records. Upper Zhenla (of the land), situated on the upper reaches of the Mekong in south Laos and along the northern shore of the Tonle Sap, seems to correspond to the area of the original Zhenla. Lower Zhenla (of the Water) was situated east of the Tonle Sap with its capital at Isanapura (Sambor Prei Kuk). It comprised several small principalities, including the former one of Funan in the Mekong Valley. The time from the fall of Funan to the beginning of the ninth century is known as the pre-Angkor Period of Cambodian history.

Western historians have long held the view that Funan and Zhenla were kingdoms in south-east Asia and that they were predecessors to the Khmer civilisation. Knowledge of them, though, relies solely on Chinese sources and their existence is not supported by either archaeological or epigraphical evidence. Additionally the names of the two states are not mentioned in any existing inscriptions of the time and they are unknown in the Khmer language. A more plausible theory, according to some scholars, such as Claude Jacques, a French epigraphist, is that Cambodia consisted of numerous states and that Funan and Zhenla were only two of several, albeit perhaps the most important ones. They may have called themselves kingdoms for the purpose of offering tribute to China.[9]

Sketch of Angkor Wat by Louis Delaporte.

ANGKOR PERIOD: NINTH CENTURY TO FIFTEENTH CENTURY AD

The generally accepted dates for the Angkor Period are 802 to 1432. It began when Jayavarman II conducted a ritual that installed him as universal monarch and ended with the relocation of the Khmers from Angkor, first to Basan on the eastern side of the Mekong and to Phnom Penh in southern Cambodia in 1434. Neither date, though, is absolute as the area was occupied both before and after these years. The dates do, however, designate the period during which the Khmer empire reached its greatest territorial limits and its apogee in cultural and artistic achievements.

The history of this period has been reconstructed from the monuments and their reliefs, statuary, excavated artefacts and inscriptions in Pali, Sanskrit and Khmer — all found within the boundaries of the former empire. The inscriptions provide a genealogy and a chronological framework, describe the merits of the kings, give details about the temples such as the founding and inventories, and about the political organisation. Despite this seemingly large amount of information about the Angkor Period, there are areas such as daily life where information is scarce.

Little is known about Jayavarman II, the founder of Angkor, as no inscriptions from his reign have been found. Evidence of the achievements of this first king comes from the Sdok Kak Thom inscription, dating from the middle of the 11th century, some two hundred years after his reign. Uncovered in north-western Cambodia, this is the most important inscription on the history of the reign of Jayavarman II. It says that he spent some time at the court of the Sailendras dynasty in Indonesia before returning to Cambodia. According to a later account by an Arab merchant, the king of the Sailendras dynasty staged a surprise attack on the Khmers by approaching the capital from the river and the Great Lake. The young king, son of Rajendravarman I, was beheaded and the Khmer Empire became a vassal of the Sailendras dynasty.[10] So it could be that Jayavarman II was taken to Indonesia as a prisoner at the time of the attack.

The date that Jayavarman II returned to Cambodia from Indonesia is debated by historians, but most agree that he was back in the country by 790 if not earlier. He asserted his control and power through military campaigns to extend the area of his territorial jurisdiction and to consolidate small principalities before establishing a capital at Indrapura. He then moved his base three more times. The reasons for the changes are uncertain, but it may have been for a better source of food. One of the locations was Hariharalaya (present-day Roluos), an area that had been occupied in pre-Angkor times.

At the beginning of the ninth century Jayavarman II (reigned 802-50) moved his capital again, this time to another pre-Angkor site, Mount Mahendraparvata (today Phnom Kulen), 40 kilometres (25 miles) north-east of Angkor Thom, and it is at this site that the inscriptions say Jayavarman II proclaimed himself universal ruler. This historic event took place in 802 and marked the unification of the Khmer state, the declaration of its independence from Indonesia, and the beginning of the Angkor period. At the same time, Jayavarman II established a new religious belief, the devaraja god-king cult. Soon afterwards he moved the capital back to Roluos where he ruled until his death in 850.

Successive kings after Jayavarman II continued to unify and expand the Khmer Empire. The inscriptions give the names of 39 kings from the Angkor period. Seven of these, selected for worthy achievements and the mark they left on Khmer civilisation, are described in this guidebook.

Indravarman I (reigned 877-89) set a precedent for future kings by building a temple-mountain (Bakong), honouring his ancestors with a temple (Preah Ko), and building a *baray*, the Indratataka, at the capital of Hariharalaya. These elements became *de rigueur* as a means for successive rulers to display their omnipotence.

His son, Yasovarman I, (reigned 889-900) built the temple of Lolei at Roluos on an island in the middle of the large *baray* constructed by his father and he dedicated it to his ancestors. Then he moved the capital to Yasodharapura (Angkor) which served as the Khmer centre for the next 500 years, except for a brief time in the first half of the tenth century. Yasovarman I built Bakheng as his temple-mountain on a natural hill and smaller temples on the hills known as Phnom Bok and Phnom Krom. To the east of his temple-mountain he constructed a large *baray*, the Yasodharatataka (East Baray).

Two sons succeeded Yasovarman, then Jayavarman IV (reigned 928-944), a usurper, set up another capital at Koh Ker, north-east of Angkor in 928, and ruled for some 20 years. Colossal stone sculptures were produced during his reign and fine examples are on view at the National Museum in Phnom Penh.

His nephew, Rajendravarman II (reigned 944-68), brought the capital back to Yashodharapura in 944 and consolidated the empire. He built the two great temple-mountains of East Mebon and Pre Rup and staged a successful military campaign against Champa.

He was succeeded by his son, Jayavarman V (reigned 968-1001) who was a child when he ascended the throne. He left two significant architectural legacies: the temple of Banteay Srei, dedicated to him by an official who later became the king's tutor, and the majestic temple-mountain of Ta Keo.

Suryavarman I (reigned 1002-50) was the next significant king. He claimed dynastic lineage to a family at Nakorn Sri Thammarat in the south of peninsular Thailand, but his origins are obscure. He strengthened the organisation of the government, established internal security, and achieved political acclaim for extending the territorial boundaries southward to the Gulf of Thailand through a series of wars. He conquered the Mon kingdom of central and south Thailand, sometime

Following pages: the library at Angkor Wat is built in a symmetrical plan in the shape of a cross.

around 1025, and established a Khmer centre at Louvo (Lopburi), a move that strengthened the empire's economic control and extended it to include the Lower Menam. During Suryavarman I's reign the Khmer empire reached its greatest degree of territorial expansion.

After a series of minor kings and short reigns, Suryavarman II took the throne around 1113 and reigned until 1150. He was one of the most brilliant of the Khmer rulers and the builder of the great temple of Angkor Wat. He also established relations with China and sent embassies to the Song Emperor. Near the end of his reign he engaged in several wars against the Chams. In 1145, he attacked, defeated the king, and sacked the royal capital. He appears twice in the bas-reliefs of Angkor Wat (South Gallery). At one point he is shown standing on the back of an elephant reviewing his troops and accompanied by his field marshals, and at another he is seated on an elaborately carved throne.

The last major king was Jayavarman VII (reigned 1181–1220). He undertook a massive building programme and is accredited for constructing more monuments, roads, bridges, and resthouses than all the other kings put together. He was a devout follower of Mahayana Buddhism and this spiritual dedication permeated every aspect of his reign. He lived outside of Angkor for several years before he became king and then returned, perhaps to prepare to assert his claim to the throne some years later.

Before he took power, the Chams launched a naval battle in 1177 that destroyed the royal capital — the Khmers' worst defeat in history. The Chams launched a brilliantly planned and unexpected attack by sailing their fleet around the coast from central Vietnam and up the Mekong River to the Great Lake, then ravaging the city and setting it on fire. Following the attack, the Chams occupied Cambodia for the next four years until Jayavarman VII staged a war, regained the capital and ascended the throne at the age of 55. He then ruled for about 40 years more.

During his reign, he invaded Champa and took its king as prisoner to Angkor in 1190, claiming a major military victory. The annexation of Champa to Cambodia followed, and lasted from 1203 to 1220, after which Jayavarman VII died. The victories of the Khmers over the Chams in battles under the direction of Jayavarman VII are depicted on the historic bas-reliefs at the Bayon. Besides being a military leader of excellence, he extended the boundaries of the empire from the coast of Vietnam to the borders of Pagan in Burma and from the vicinity of Vientiane in Laos to much of the Malay Peninsula.

Several descendants of Jayavarman VII reigned after his death and, although they built no major monuments, we know that the capital was flourishing to some extent as late as the end of the 13th century because Zhou Daguan described several opulent monuments which he said, 'caused merchants from overseas to speak...of "Cambodia the rich and noble" '. At approximately the same time, a shift from Buddhism to a revival in Hinduism may have been responsible for the defacement of some Buddhist images at Angkor.

Under the rule of Indravarman III (1295-1307), Theravada Buddhism became the state religion of Cambodia. In 1350, the Thais established their capital at Ayutthaya and became a great threat to Angkor. The names and dates of the kings who ruled during the remainder of the Angkor period are obscure and dependent on unreliable chronicles composed at a later date. Angkor remained the capital until 1432, but from then onwards the Khmers moved, by degrees, southward to Phnom Penh, where the capital still stands today.

During the Angkor period several kingdoms rose to power in the region and threatened the supremacy of the Khmer Empire. Champa, located in the Mekong delta north of the Funan in an area corresponding to modern central and south Vietnam, was founded at the end of the second century, according to Chinese records. Indian influences penetrated Champa two or three hundred years later and Hinduism became the dominant religion. It is possible the Indian influence reached Champa by way of Indonesia as comparative decorative elements are found in the monuments of both cultures dating from the late ninth and early tenth centuries.

Natural geographical barriers restricted the development of Champa into a centralised state. The Chams concentrated on maritime activities and became a strong naval power. After the collapse of Funan in the sixth century, the Chams extended their influence southward. They came under the rule of the Khmers for a short time in the beginning of the 13th century, but otherwise Champa remained an independent state until the last half of the 15th century when it was absorbed by Vietnam.

Name	Period of Power (centuries)	Area
Champa	2nd-15th	central Vietnam
Dvaravati/Mon	6th/7th-11th	Thailand
Pyu	6th-11th	Burma
Srivijaya	6th-13th	Indonesia (Sumatra);
(9th-13th: ruled by Sailendras)		Malay Peninsula; south Thailand
Sailendras	8th-9th	Indonesia (central Java)
Pegu/Mon	9th-11th	Burma
Pagan	11th-13th	Burma
Sukhothai	13th-14th	Thailand (north-central)
Lan Na	13th-16th	north Thailand
Ayutthaya	mid-14th-mid-18th	Thailand (central plain)

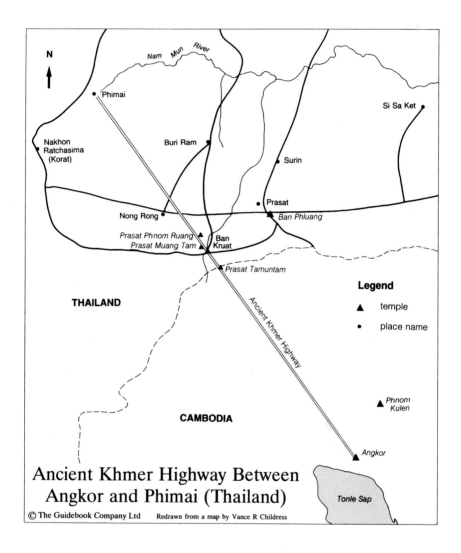

Ancient Khmer Highway Between Angkor and Phimai (Thailand)

© The Guidebook Company Ltd   Redrawn from a map by Vance R Childress

The Mons established several centres in mainland south-east Asia. The kingdom of Dvaravati controlled the Menam Valley, in central Thailand, from the sixth or seventh century to the eleventh century. The Pyu established a centre in the sixth century situated in the valleys of the central Irrawaddy and Sittang rivers in Burma. Pegu, another Mon site, was founded in the ninth century. The Burmese emerged from the north in the 11th century and took over the Pyus in the central valleys and established a capital at Pagan. The Burmese extended their territorial boundaries southward and conquered the Mons at Pegu.

Two states situated in the Indonesian islands emerged following the demise of Funan and grew to become powerful empires in the region. The south-east coast of Sumatra gained importance in the fifth century because of the development of a direct sea route from Indonesia to China and also because it served as a trans-shipment point between India and China. The Srivajayan empire became a centre in Indonesia of this trade. Its origins probably date to the sixth century and by the late seventh century it was a strong commercial power that had extended its territorial boundaries to the coasts of west Java, Malaysia and Chaiya in southern Thailand.

Although the capital of the Srivijaya dynasty has not yet been found, the south-east coast of Sumatra at Pandalembang and the Malay peninsula have been suggested as possibilities. Details of the decline of Srivijaya are sketchy. It was besieged by piracy in the Straits of Sunda and Malacca in the 11th century, and, during the Southern Song period (1127-1278) when China allowed its own vessels to conduct trade with south-east Asia, Srivijaya's importance decreased.

A second dynasty, the Sailendras, rose in Indonesia in central Java. Its origins and identity are not clear, but one theory is that survivors of Funan went to Java and, after some time, appeared as the Sailendra dynasty. Both Funan and Sailendra are known as the 'kings of the mountain'. The dynasty was well established in the eighth and ninth centuries when it undertook the construction of the great Buddhist monument Borobudur and others in central Java. Shortly afterwards, the Sailendras lost control of the central area and the capital moved to east Java.

Thailand was a persistent invader of Khmer territory. Sukhothai, the first organised Thai settlement, was established in the 13th century in north-central Thailand. About the same time, the Thai principality of Lan Na was founded with its capital at Chiang Mai. The Thais also controlled the area around the mouth of the Chao Phraya River which became the Ayutthaya kingdom in the middle of the 14th century. Within a hundred years, the Thais had gained control of a large part of the area corresponding to modern-day Thailand. Ayutthaya became the dominant power in the region until it was sacked by the Burmese in 1767.

The Thais seem to have made repeated raids on Angkor in the 14th century, and battles continued between the two rivals for almost another century until a final siege in 1431 which lasted, according to the Ayutthaya chronicles, for seven months. The Thai invasions, however, did not lead to permanent occupation of Khmer territory. Some time after the brutal attack on the city of Angkor Thom, the Khmers gradually retreated and shifted their capital southward to Phnom Penh, with Lovek and Udong briefly serving as capitals in the 16th and 18th centuries respectively.

Exactly how long this change took is unknown, but it probably occurred over several years and Angkor was never completely abandoned. Some temples, such as Angkor Wat, were maintained by monks even in the 15th and 16th centuries. The court returned to Angkor briefly in the late 16th century and again intermittently in the 17th century, but it never regained its former glory.

The evidence is inconclusive, but it seems likely that several forces acted as catalysts leading to the decline of the Khmer Empire. The most important reason was the increasing pressure brought about by the encroachment of the Thais, rendering Angkor unsuitable as a capital because of its proximity to the enemy. The loss of manpower through the ensuing wars further meant that maintenance of the hydraulic system was neglected. Not surprisingly, the Khmer people also revolted against harsh conditions in the empire, against Jayavarman VII's extravagant building and against his opulent lifestyle which exhausted the kingdom's resources. As central control weakened, the vassal states gradually asserted their independence.

In addition, ecologists point out that by the 13th century forests may well have become depleted. Sustaining the large population probably put pressure on the agricultural system, and drought, or other climatic factors, may well have contributed to the weakening of the state's authority. Increased missions from Cambodia to China in the late 14th and early 15th centuries suggest an interest in developing maritime trade in south-east Asia, and Phnom Penh would have been a more suitable base from which it could be developed.

A new religion, Theravada Buddhism, spread from Sri Lanka across south-east Asia in the 13th century eclipsing former beliefs. In summary, the Khmer rulers probably shifted south-east early in the 15th century and established a base at Phnom Penh and when this shift occurred the character of the kingdom changed.[11] It required new ways of unifying and administering the country and its people.

Sixteenth Century to Nineteenth Century AD

The ruins of Angkor were reported by many foreigners as early as the 16th century. Portuguese refugees forced out of Sumatra by the Dutch in that century sought asylum in Cambodia and were among the earliest Europeans to see Angkor. Numerous overseas traders from China, Japan, Arabia, Spain and Portugal resided in the Cambodian capitals of Phnom Penh and Lovek in the 16th century and were joined briefly by the Dutch and the English in the following century. At about the same time, Portuguese and Spanish missionaries arrived from Malacca.

The earliest and most detailed account of Angkor was by the Portuguese writer Diego do Couto, who described how, in the middle of the 16th century, a king of Cambodia came upon the ruins while hunting elephants. Although he never saw Cambodia it is believed that Antonio de Magdalena, a Capuchin friar, who visited Angkor about 1585, was his main source of information. He described a Cambodian

king who went on an elephant hunt and came upon a 'number of imposing constructions' enshrouded in vegetation.

Other published reports by Spanish visitors in the early 17th century seem to
have been based on Couto's account. Marcelo de Ribadeneira in a description of
Angkor published in 1601 wrote: 'There are in Cambodia the ruins of an ancient
city, which some say was constructed by the Romans or by Alexander the Great'.[12]
Gabriel Quiroga de San Antonio, a Spanish missionary, wrote in 1603: 'In 1570 a
city was brought to light that had never been seen or heard of by the natives'.[13]
Christoval de Jaque also mentioned visitors at the ruins in 1570 and, in a book published on his travels in Indo-China in 1606, he called the site 'Anjog' and described
the wall surrounding the city of Angkor Thom.[14]

Spanish missionaries in Cambodia in the 1580s heard of a city of ancient ruins
and prayed that the ruins 'may be rehabilitated to become an outpost of Christian
missions outside the Philippines....'[15] In 1672 Pere Chevruel, a French missionary,
wrote: 'There is an ancient and very celebrated temple situated at a distance of eight
days from the place where I live. This temple is called Onco, and it is famous among
the gentiles as St Peter's in Rome'.[16] Few reports of Dutch visitors have come to
light, which is surprising given their strong commercial presence in south-east Asia
in the 16th and 17th centuries. Gerard van Wusthoff described Angkor in 1641 and
15 years later Hendrick Indjick, a merchant, wrote: 'The king paid a visit to a lovely
pleasant place known as Anckoor, which the Portuguese and Castilians call Rome,
and which is situated an eight or ten-day journey from here [Phnom Penh]'.[17]

Evidence of the Japanese at Angkor in the 17th century is carved in sandstone at
Angkor Wat. Calligraphic characters corresponding to the date of 1632 can be seen
on a pillar on the second level of Angkor Wat. The oldest known plan of Angkor
Wat was drawn by Kenryo Shimano, a Japanese interpreter from Nagasaki, who
journeyed to Angkor some time between 1632 and 1636 and drew a remarkably
accurate diagram of the temple. Even though he called it Jetavana-vihara, a Buddhist site in India, and Angkor is not named on the diagram, other facts such as the
unusual layout and the orientation to the west confirm the identity of Angkor Wat.
The most telling reference is a note on the diagram that says 'sculptures in
relief...four gods pull the rope', which clearly refers to the Churning of the Ocean of
Milk in the gallery of bas-reliefs at Angkor Wat. Shimano's son, Morimoto Ukon-
dayu, visited the great temple some time later in the 17th century to pay tribute to
his father and purportedly carved the calligraphic characters which can be seen
today.

Other foreigners published accounts of Angkor, but they received little recognition in the west. For example, Dr A House, an American missionary and long-time
resident of Siam, wrote a lively and interesting description of Angkor in 1855.

Charles-Emile Bouilleaux, a French missionary, saw Angkor in 1850 and published an account of his travels eight years later. DO King, an Englishman who travelled in Indo-China in 1857-8, detailed his journey in a paper read to the Royal Geographical Society in London in 1859. He pointed out the ruins and the existence of a map of Angkor in a French work. 'The Temple stands solitary and alone in the jungle, in too perfect order to be called a ruin, a relic of a race far ahead of the present in all the arts and sciences', he wrote.[18]

Despite these published accounts by foreigners who saw and wrote about Angkor, they seem to have gone mainly unnoticed in the West. European interest in the ruins was not aroused until Henri Mouhot, a French naturalist, reported on his visit. At the time he planned his trip to the East he was living in Jersey with his Scottish wife. He was fortunate to gain the support of the Royal Geographical Society in London. Mouhot departed for Singapore in April 1858 and arrived in Siam in September.

Three months later he set off on a journey that continued until April 1860. During that time he spent two months in Cambodia, including three weeks at Angkor. He surveyed and measured the temple of Angkor Wat and kept detailed notes on his observations of the ruins. His last journey in the region was an exploration of uncharted territory in north-eastern Siam and a survey of the Mekong in Laos designed to fill in the blanks on maps made in the 17th century. Mouhot continued his work until November 1861 when he contracted a fever and died at Luang Prabang in Laos at the age of 35. His notes were taken to Bangkok by his faithful servants and later sent to his widow and brother in Jersey where they were published in 1864.

By the time of the publication of Mouhot's diaries, France had a presence in Indo-China. In 1864 a French Protectorate over Cambodia was in place except for Battambang and Siem Reap provinces, which were under the jurisdiction of Siam. A treaty between Siam and France in 1907 ceded these territories to France where they remained except for a brief period during the Second World War when they were returned to Siam.

The temple of Banteay Srei, north-east of Angkor, was disputed because it was located in the territory granted to Thailand. In 1941 the Japanese served as mediators in negotiations between Thailand and France and it was decided the temple should belong to Cambodia.

A History of Restoration Efforts at Angkor

In June 1866, a French expedition led by Ernest Doudart de Lagrée, who was formerly the French representative to the court of Cambodia, was undertaken to survey the northern reaches of the Mekong River in search of a trade route to China. As only Doudart de Lagrée had visited Angkor before, a side trip was planned which provided the catalyst for a systematic study of the ruins at Angkor.

The Mekong Exploration Commission set out from Saigon, Vietnam, and reached Angkor on 23rd June 1866. The team of six Frenchmen spent one week systematically recording their observations and surveying the area. Although Doudart de Lagrée died in 1868 in Yunnan, China, prior to the publication of the expedition's findings, two other members of the team, Francis Garnier and the artist Louis Delaporte completed the work and are recognised today as pioneers in France's research at Angkor. Garnier's findings were published in 1873 in *Voyage d'Exploration en Indo-Chine, Effectué Pendant le Années 1866, 1867 & 1868* and Delaporte's impressions appeared in 1880 in *Voyage au Cambodge: L'Architecture Khmer*. Delaporte's engravings of the ruins of Angkor are well known today and reflect the condition of the monuments in the mid-1860s. His widely published works no doubt perpetuated the idea of 'mysterious Angkor' noted in the writings of many early travellers.

John Thomson, a renowned Scottish photographer, who was travelling extensively in Asia at the same time, happened to meet the Doudart de Lagrée mission at Angkor. Thomson published the first photographic account of the ruins of Angkor. Descriptions of the bas-reliefs at Angkor Wat and at the Bayon, and plans of Angkor Wat based on his own survey, can all be found in his publication *The Straits of Malacca, Siam and Indo China or Ten Years Travels, Adventures and Residence Abroad*.

In 1879, the Dutchman Hendrik Kern was the first to decipher Sanskrit inscriptions found in Cambodia and two Frenchmen, Auguste Barthe and A Bergaigne, are credited with furthering the field of Khmer epigraphy which led to the translation of some 1,200 inscriptions relating to the genealogy of the Khmer kings. Etienne Aymonier, a representative of the French Protectorate, produced the first archaeological inventory of Cambodia at about that time.

The Ecole Francaise d'Extreme Orient (EFEO)

Even though France had made Cambodia a protectorate in 1864, it was only in 1898 that the EFEO, which was founded to study the history, language and archaeology of Indo-China in an effort to protect the ancient sites, was established in Cambodia.

Following pages: the 1866 French expedition was the first to systematically publicise Angkor to the outside world.

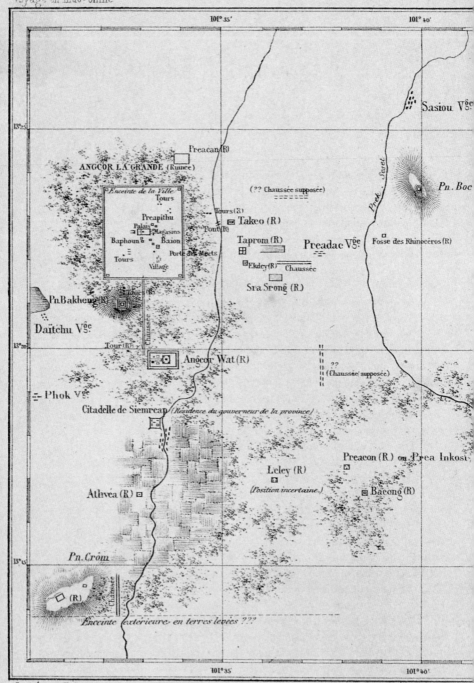

Pl. I

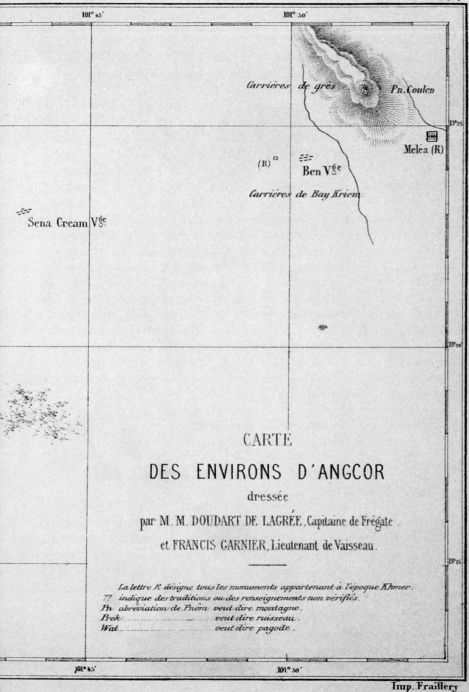

101° 45' 101° 30'

Carrières de grès Pn. Coulen

13° 25'

Meléa (R)

(R) Ben Vᵍᵉ

Carrières de Bay Kriem

Sena Cream Vᵍᵉ

13° 20'

CARTE
DES ENVIRONS D'ANGCOR
dressée

par M. M. DOUDART DE LAGRÉE, Capitaine de Frégate

et FRANCIS GARNIER, Lieutenant de Vaisseau.

13° 15'

La lettre R désigne tous les monuments appartenant à l'époque Khmer.
?? indique des traditions ou des renseignements non vérifiés.
Pn abréviation de Phôm veut dire montagne.
Prek................................. veut dire ruisseau.
Wat................................. veut dire pagode.

101° 45' 101° 30'

Imp. Fraillery

Since then, the EFEO has undoubtedly been the most dedicated and influential body to study Angkor. It started to document the Angkor sites by preparing measured surveys and inventories after disengaging them from the jungle. Later the EFEO began a systematic programme of consolidation and restoration of the monuments and the development of plans to present the sites to visitors. The EFEO, for example, created the road network and developed the visitation programme, which is still used by some guides today, following the 'Grand Circuit' or the 'Little Circuit.'

In 1908, the EFEO assisted in the setting up in Siem Reap of the Conservation d'Angkor or Angkor Conservation Office, the archaeological directorate of the Cambodian Government, which became responsible for the maintenance and protection of the monuments. The Conservation d'Angkor was formerly the nerve centre for all work relating to the conservation and protection of the monuments and sites of Angkor and efforts are being made for it to re-establish these responsibilities.

The Angkor Conservation Office is a short way from the centre of Siem Reap on the main road to Angkor and is in a secluded two-hectare enclosure close to the Siem Reap River. It houses the offices and the depot where most of the significant collection of sculptures brought to safety are kept under guard. In the near future, the Cambodian government plans to open a cultural centre in the compound for the use of all those contributing to the conservation and protection of Angkor and to bona fide researchers. At present, the Angkor Conservation Office is not open to the general public and those who wish to visit the collection require special permission in advance from the authorities.

Through their involvement, either directly or indirectly, with the Conservation d'Angkor, several Frenchmen have made significant contributions to its direction and programme of research. Its first French curator, Jean Commaille served from its inception until his untimely death at the hands of bandits in 1916. He started the laborious task of *dégagement* or clearance of the sites from the jungle and wrote the first guidebook to Angkor.

Commaille was succeeded by the great Henri Marchal, 'the father of Angkor', who spent most of his adult life in Cambodia. He served as curator until his retirement in 1933. He returned to take up the same position twice again. First, between 1935 and 1937, and, second, in 1947 (at the age of 61) to 1953. After serving later in Vietnam and Laos, he returned to Cambodia in 1957, where he remained until his death in Siem Reap in 1970. Marchal undertook an enormous amount of work including the clearance and restoration of large areas of Angkor Thom, Preah Khan and Ta Prohm. He was the first to introduce the system of anastylosis, the method of recording, dismantling, and reconstructing whole structures. It was a system he had learned from the Dutch in Borobudur, Indonesia.

In his book, *Angkor*, Malcolm Macdonald, the then British Commissioner for south-east Asia and a great champion of Angkor, recalls a meeting with Marchal: 'Almost eighty years old, his venerable age did not prevent him from walking with youthful briskness for hours on end as he conducted me on lightning tours through the monuments.... His fund of information about the ancient tombs, his genius as a raconteur of history and his charming, philosophical and witty personality made him a perfect guide amongst his beloved temples. One of my most fortunate experiences at Angkor was my introduction to them by him.'

Georges Trouvé, who took over from Marchal as curator between 1932 and 1935, was a 'chubby faced' man who had a knack for locating special treasures at Angkor and he was greatly missed by his colleagues following his sudden and tragic disappearance in 1935.

Another of the great champions of Angkor was Maurice Glaize who was curator from 1937 until 1946. Glaize contributed greatly to promoting Angkor with the preparation of his definitive guidebook *Les Monuments Du Groupe D'Angkor*, published in 1943 with three subsequent editions, the last one being in 1993, at which time it required only minimal updating. Henri Parmentier, chief of the archaeological services of French Indo-China, also wrote a comprehensive guidebook to Angkor, published in 1959.

Bernard Philippe Groslier, the son of Georges Groslier, Director of Khmer Art at the EFEO, was the last of the French curators at the Conservation d'Angkor. He took over as curator in 1960 and was forced to leave his post with most of the other French researchers in 1972.

After the EFEO's departure from Angkor in 1972, a noble group of its local staff continued to work on the monuments until 1975 when they were ordered by the Khmer Rouge to work in the fields. Subsequently, the monuments were once more abandoned and for nearly 20 years the jungle gradually reclaimed the structures. It was only in the early 1990s that a concerted effort was made to uncover the monuments and commence once more the never ending task of repairing, maintaining and presenting the sites to the world.

Fortunately the great archives of the EFEO were copied and kept in Paris and in Phnom Penh. The French copy has survived and recently drawings have been recorded on microfiches and the handwritten site notes and journals have been transcribed on computer disks and are available to those researching or working at Angkor.

Except for a brief period during the Second World War, the French worked continuously at Angkor from the beginning of this century until 1972 when they were forced to leave due to the civil war in Cambodia. Their presence at Angkor for over seven decades and the contributions of some devoted French archaeologists have earned the country a respected niche in the history of the protection of the monuments of Angkor.

Following pages: the members of the Mekong Exploration Commission.

M. GARNIER. M. DELAPORTE. M. JOUBERT.

M. Thorel.   M. de Carné   M. de Lagrée.

CIVIL WAR AND AFTER

During the period of civil strife, the monuments of Angkor became stores for supplies and occasionally a refuge, but, despite constant turmoil, it has always remained a national symbol. Also contrary to rumours and erroneous press reports, Angkor was never wantonly attacked for political ends. One stray American bomb is said to have exploded in Angkor Wat and there is evidence of gunfire on the odd sandstone image but, in general, the temples have survived the wars largely unscathed. It was more the people who had carefully tended the monuments that suffered torture, deprivation and death at the hands of the Khmer Rouge. Many among the work force were executed, leaving only a few to recommence the task of repair and maintenance at Angkor.

One exception at this time was the work of the Archaeological Survey of India at Angkor Wat. Following an agreement in the mid-1980s between the Peoples Democratic Republic of Kampuchea and Indira Gandhi, then India's premier, a six-year project to clean and restore Angkor Wat using Indian consultants and a Cambodian work force was begun. Their work has been greatly criticised by journalists and foreign experts who have condemned the methods and materials used. The Indian team, though, was working under extreme conditions, with difficulty in obtaining the necessary materials and in using untrained labourers and without the benefit of any past records and under continual threat of Khmer Rouge attack.

Another project in the 1980s comprised a small team of archaeologists from the Ateliers for the Conservation of Cultural Property of Poland undertaking research and some exploratory excavation at the Bayon complex. Their work was limited and hampered by lack of funds, as they were also involved in the restoration of early 20th-century murals of the Silver Pagoda in Phnom Penh.

THE ARRIVAL OF THE UNITED NATIONS AT ANGKOR

Following the United Nations' recognition of the Kingdom of Cambodia, international support and direction was offered to a country that had been devasted by grief and destruction, and had almost lost its will to survive. With the arrival of the United Nations Transitional Authority in Cambodia (UNTAC), UNESCO (United Nations Educational, Scientific and Cultural Organization) in 1991 established a regional office and assisted the new Royal Cambodian Government in seeking international support to safeguard Angkor.

In an historic declaration during a visit to Angkor Wat in November 1991, Federico Mayor, Director General of UNESCO, declared: 'Angkor, city of the Khmer kings, is waiting to become once more the symbol of its country. Vestiges, which bear witness to a rich and glorious past, reflect all those values that are a source for the Khmer people of hope reborn and identity recovered. Yet this symbolic city is in peril. The ravages of time, the assaults of nature and the pillaging of man further its decline with every passing day. It must be saved!'

THE LOOTING OF ANGKOR

While looting at the monuments in the past two decades has escalated, looting itself is not new to Angkor. In the 13th century a wave of Hindu iconoclastic fervour led to the destruction of all Buddhist images. Some historians claim that the Siamese carried off much of the cultural treasure of Angkor in the 15th century following their final raids on the Khmer capital. Since then, neglect and the advancing tropical jungle enshrouding the monuments have provided, in a less obvious way, protection against theft. There was a period when the monuments were ransacked for materials such as metal stone clamps, as is evident in the retaining walls of the Bakong at Roluos, or the decorative metal panelling, which is believed to have covered the walls of the central shrines of temples such as Ta Prohm and Preah Khan. Yet, it was at the beginning of the 20th century, however, that Angkor really became a target for art thieves.

Perhaps the most notorious case of a well planned expedition of looting in the early 20th century involved André Malraux, who was later to become France's Minister of Culture in the cabinet of Charles de Gaulle. Malraux and his accomplices located Banteay Srei, deep in the jungle, and removed large sections from the temple and shipped them to Phnom Penh where his misdeeds were discovered and he was arrested and tried.

During the Vietnamese army's occupation of Cambodia, an enormous number of artefacts disappeared over the border, many of which were sold for a few dollars in the bazaars. Later, the plundering became more organised, increasing at an alarming rate over the past two decades; robbing the temples of irreplaceable statues and lintels, leaving indelible scars where pieces have been hacked from the structures. Often, free-standing statues of great weight have been carried off and in many cases abandoned en route and left broken in pieces a few hundred yards from their original location. Other equally large pieces have also been smuggled into Thailand where they are acquired by antique dealers in Bangkok and sold on the international art market at great profit. Illegal excavation is now rife in the more out of the way temples of Cambodia, if to a lesser extent at Angkor, and is depriving the country of unique historical evidence and valuable artifacts.

It is reassuring to see that the Royal Cambodian Government, with assistance from UNESCO, has succeeded recently in taking positive measures to curb this illicit traffic in cultural property. A mobile cultural heritage police unit has been created and equipped with motorcycles and short wave radios linked to a central office. The EFEO is in the process of computerising an updated inventory of the entire collection of sculptures and other artefacts in safekeeping at the Angkor Conservation Office and most of the loose sculptures targeted by thieves have been brought into the custody of that office. The government has recently become signatories to the 1970 UNESCO Convention on the Illicit Import, Export and Transfer of Ownership of Cultural Property. Efforts at government, local and international levels continue to help strengthen security at the monuments, museums and borders and to ˌestablish a greater awareness of the ramifications of theft.

THE ROYAL UNIVERSITY OF FINE ARTS

Fourteen years after the Khmer Rouge forced its closure, Phnom Penh's University of Fine Arts reopened in 1989. Originally known as L'Ecole des Arts Cambodgiens (the School of Cambodian Arts) it was established as a co-educational institution for training students in the arts and crafts of Cambodia. Today it offers diploma courses in

Scenes of Judgement by Yama and torturers delivering punishments i

architecture, archaeology and the plastic arts as well and its students are becoming actively involved in the various international programmes related to the research and repair of the monuments of Angkor.

THE REVIVAL OF NATIONAL AND INTERNATIONAL ACTIVITIES AT ANGKOR

Following peace negotiations which commenced in the latter part of 1989 and the establishment of the coalition government after the national elections in 1993, international participation in saving Angkor became more active. The signing of the political settlement known as the Paris Agreement in 1991 lifted the embargo on international development in Cambodia, and foreign aid and investment started to return as did an increasing number of foreign visitors curious to experience the mysticism of Angkor.

Interest in assisting with the major challenge of safeguarding and maintaining Angkor came from around the the world. Following the archaeological survey of India's involvement, the World Monuments Fund was the first non-governmental foundation to arrive at Angkor in 1989 with offers of assistance. The EFEO soon returned to re-establish itself, and Japan, initially represented by the Institute of Asian Cultures from Sophia University in Tokyo and later by the Japanese government, together with France, took a lead in creating international awareness, as well as pledging millions of dollars to support the campaign to safeguard Angkor.

Gallery of Bas-reliefs at Angkor Wat.

Initially, UNESCO tried to co-ordinate the disparate international efforts by formulating a Zoning and Environmental Master Plan (ZEMP) for Angkor and the surrounding region which had an impact on the monuments. The area covered by the study was the province of Siem Reap, which covers more than 5,000 square kilometres (1,900 square miles), extending from the Kulen Hills to the shores of the Tonle Sap. The study was designed to collect data on archaeological sites dating from prehistory to the post-Angkor period and its geology as well as the present day land use, forest resources, population and ecology.

Using this information, abetted by satellite imagery and aerial photography, the data was analysed and a cultural and natural resources plan conforming to human and environmental needs was developed. The technical studies resulting from ZEMP have been assessed by the government and this plan together with the bi-lateral programmes and the individual conservation and restoration projects are being implemented through the International Co-ordinating Committee for the Safeguarding and Development of the Historic Site of Angkor (ICC). Software developed by Canada, the computerised Geographical Information System (GIS), was initiated in 1992 as part of the ZEMP project and is now the keeper of a wide range of technical data relating to the Angkor site.

Images obtained in various ways including radar, infra-red satellite, magnetic, aerial photographs and others are being used to give added dimension to the research of Angkor. Each of these techniques yields information that is not visible to the naked eye, and of particular interest are those methods that reveal details of features below the ground. Space radar, yet another type of imaging, is one of the latest geographical mapping techniques employed for research. Archaeologists, historians and historic city planners are excited by the information recently brought back by the American NASA space shuttle *Endeavour*, which will assist them in delving deeper into the terrain of the Angkor region. The information obtained from radar imagery will be the most detailed and up-to-date information available and it will be published and readily accessible to all those undertaking research at Angkor.

In December 1992, the historic site of Angkor was included on the UNESCO World Heritage List of over 400 sites; meeting stringent criteria set up by the International Convention on Monuments and Sites. Inclusion on the list, recognises Angkor as one of mankind's most significant cultural heritage sites and the international symbol of Cambodia and its people. Once on the World Heritage List, a site must comply with conservation principles and undertake the conservation management plan set out in its application. In this way, it is hoped the fate of Angkor and its environs will be adequately protected. It is anticipated that the government will put forth the Tonle Sap for possible inclusion on the World Heritage list as an endangered natural site as it represents one of the most important examples of wet land development in the world.

The New Royal Government of Cambodia elected in 1993 is assuming the responsibility of protecting and maintaining the historic monuments and realising their earning potential as tourist attractions. This has given protection and presentation a high priority in the government's plans to redevelop Cambodia. With UNESCO's assistance and financial support from France and Japan the ICC has been established. This committee, co-chaired by the French and Japanese ambassadors to Cambodia, was set up to assist the Cambodian government in the co-ordination of an international campaign and to advise it on technical matters.

His Majesty King Norodom Sihanouk is honorary president and a great advocate

Pilgrimage to Angkor

Frank Vincent, Jr, a frail young American who dropped out of university because of illness at the age of seventeen, was determined '…to make a systematic tour of the most interesting parts of the world'. In 1872, he visited Cambodia and the ancient ruins of Angkor. Vincent describes his journey overland from Bangkok to Siem Reap, the village closest to the ruins, in vivid detail. 'The total distance we travelled from Bangkok was 175 miles; of this 30 miles was by canal in boats, 30 miles on the Bang pa Kong river in boats, and the remainder—215 miles—was performed upon horses and elephants, in bullock-carts, and on foot; the greater part of the journey, however, was accomplished on horseback. The time consumed in making this trip was seventeen days.

'The governor of Siamrap having provided us with three elephants, on the 13th inst, we started for the ruins of Angkor, three and a half miles distant, to the north. We took but little baggage with us, being rather impatient now that we were nearing the main object of the expedition— the ultima Thule of our desires and hopes—and so we passed quickly and silently along a narrow but good road cut through the dense, riant forest, until, in about an hour's time, on suddenly emerging from the woods, we saw a little way off to the right, across a pond filled with lotus plants, a long row of columned galleries, and beyond—high above the beautiful cocoa and areca palms—three or four immense pagodas, built of a dark-grey stone. And my heart almost bounded into my mouth as the Cambodian driver, turning towards the howday, said, with a bright flash of the eye and a proud turn of the lip, "Naghon Wat"; for we were then at the very portals of the famous old "City of Monasteries", and not far distant was Angkorthom—Angkor the Great.'

Frank Vincent, Jr, The Land of the White Elephant:
Sights and Scenes in Southeast Asia 1871–1872
(*Oxford University Press, rep, Singapore, 1988*)

and supporter of the campaign to save Angkor. In Article 69, the new Constitution of Cambodia specifies that 'The State shall preserve ancient monuments, artifacts and restore historical sites.' The government has proposed a Five-year Emergency Plan, which includes the management of Cambodia's cultural heritage; the restoration and preservation of Angkor; the development of human resources; the education of the Cambodian people about their heritage and the implementation of a tourism master plan that is economically viable yet compatible with preserving the environment.

The Royal Cambodian Government has the support of the outside world and several international organisations have responded to the government's requests for assistance. At the administrative level, UNESCO's opening of its office in 1991 provided an international co-ordinator for contributions. Finding the most suitable way of providing international assistance that is the most beneficial to Cambodia still remains a great challenge. Terms such as 'controlled development' and 'cultural tourism' have been suggested as paths to pursue, but the final decision of the plan and its implementation for the future survival of Angkor rests with the national government.

The projects are monitored by APSARA, a non-governmental organisation set up specifically to administer the conservation and protection of Angkor, through the ICC. The international organisations provide the government with technical assistance, and help with the training of professional and local staff and craftsmen to enable them to care for their monuments in the future. Students from the University of Fine Arts are undergoing basic training on many of the sites.

Documentaries for television have been produced for the Discovery Channel in America and by Austrian and Polish television also. Angkor has featured in an archaeological series on the BBC World Service and Voice of America radio stations.

Base of a pillar decorated with geometric bands, lotus petals and rosettes, illustrated in Voyage au Cambodge, Delaporte, 1880.

Daily Life During The Khmer Empire

Reliefs carved in stone on the walls of the temples provide a glimpse of daily life at Angkor. From the scenes depicted we know something about what the people ate, what clothes they wore, their domesticated animals, flora and fauna; their means of transport, the games they played, the vessels they used for cooking, and the houses they lived in. There are striking similarities between the activities revealed on the bas-reliefs and those seen in rural Cambodia today. The suffering and devastation of the modern people notwithstanding, life in the countryside is probably quite similar to the past with little change in the basic methods and means of agrarian life.

One first-hand account survives from the 13th century and serves as an invaluable source by someone who actually experienced life at Angkor. The Chinese emissary, Zhou Daguan, gives a detailed description of daily life covering everything from his arduous journey on the Mekong to reach the capital, to childbirth and hygiene practices. This record gives insight on aspects of life for which we have no other information, but it has its limitations as the author was a foreign observer and thus excluded from activities within the palace. Just as many early western accounts were written from a European perspective, Zhou's journals reveal a distinctly Chinese outlook.

The ancient Khmers had physical characteristics similar to the modern Cambodians. They were of medium height with black, often curly hair and had square-shaped faces with a broad forehead, a long straight nose with wide nostrils, and deep-set eyes: characteristics that can be seen in the faces of the warriors in the bas-reliefs around the Bayon.

Similarities in dress between the ancient and modern Cambodians are also apparent. A single, rectangular piece of cloth, about two metres in length and one metre wide, is worn by both men and women today in the same manner as is depicted on the reliefs. The practical and versatile garment, a *sampot*, is of woven cotton, although a *sampot* worn by royalty in the Angkor period was made of embroidered silk woven with gold and imported from China, Champa (Central Vietnam), or Siam. A woman wraps a cloth around her body in a manner that looks like a floor-length skirt and ties it gracefully in front or secures it with a belt at the waist. A man, on the other hand, draws the ends of the cloth up between his legs to form a pant-like garment. Today the male *sampot* is checked or striped whereas a woman wears a patterned one, often in a brightly coloured floral design.

Zhou Daguan noted, however, that only the king could wear an 'all-over pattern,' probably referring to embroidered fabrics. A woman ties her hair back, off the face,

and may secure it with fresh jasmine. In ancient times, both sexes wore elaborate jewellery consisting of necklaces, bracelets, and arm and ankle bands. The quantity and material of the jewellery depended on the status of the person wearing it. The ultimate wearers of elaborate jewellery and exotic hairdos were the *apsaras*. Some of the finest examples of these celestial nymphs and all their finery stand beatifically on the interior of the second level of Angkor Wat. Sometimes they are alone, other times in twos or threes, but always richly dressed and bejewelled.

The monsoonal and lunar cycles governed daily life in the Khmer Empire. Alternating wet and dry seasons and the waxing and waning of the moon set the pattern for harvesting rice and catching fish, the two staples of the economy. To help nature provide the right balance of rain and to ensure abundant and fruitful harvests, the spirits had to be propitiated. Rites and festivals coinciding with the full moon were held in ancient times just as today. The year begins in April with a New Year Festival. This raucous event drives away evil spirits and concurrently invokes good ones with parades, boat-races, dances, and, above-all, merit-making, offering food, lustral water, and other beneficient things to the spirits, the gods, and the Buddha.

Zhou Daguan described the joyous New Year festivities at Angkor. 'In front of the royal palace a great platform is erected, sufficient to hold more than a thousand persons, and decorated from end to end with lanterns and flowers. Opposite this, some one hundred and twenty feet rises a lofty scaffold, put together of light pieces of wood, shaped like the scaffolds used in building stupas [temples], and towering to a height of 120 feet. Every night from three to six of these structures rise. Rockets and firecrackers are placed on top of these — all this at great expense to the provinces and the noble families. As night comes on, the king is besought to take part in the spectacle. The rockets are fired, and the crackers touched off. The rockets can be seen at a distance of thirteen kilometres: the fire-crackers, large as swivel-guns, shake the whole city with their explosions. Mandarins and nobles are put to considerable expense to provide torches and areca-nuts [used for betel chewing]. Foreign ambassadors are also invited by the King to enjoy the spectacle, which comes to an end after a fortnight.'[19]

When the rainy season begins in late May or early June a ceremony takes place to propitiate the spirits of the fields and to bless and sow the seeds before the rice is planted. On the auspicious day and hour the ritual of sowing rice is enacted. A sacred plough, ornately decorated with fresh, fragrant flowers, is drawn by buffaloes to the designated site, sacred rice is sowed, and the soil is ceremoniously furrowed, then the yokes are removed from the buffaloes. They are then free to seek out one of two previously placed bowls filled with water and rice; a third bowl is empty. If the

A late 19th century sketch of Angkor Wat.

buffaloes go to the bowl with water, then an adequate rainfall will follow. The bowl of rice ensures a bountiful harvest, and, conversely, the empty bowl signifies a poor harvest.

Just as the advent of the rainy season is recognised with fanfare, the end of it is celebrated with a rite to give thanks to the water spirits and offer a tribute to the *naga* king, god of the waters. The festival is a poignant one, even for those of other cultures and religions. Devotees solemnly lower boat-shaped offerings made of banana leaves and filled with candles, incense sticks, and fresh flowers into the water, either a river, canal, or pond. If you watch your boat until the candle extinguishes then all your wishes will be granted. This ceremony was celebrated on the River (*stung*) Siem Reap in November 1994 for the first time in over two decades.

Singing, dancing, music, and games are a spontaneous part of village life and the reliefs at the Bayon show some of this entertainment. You can see musicians playing drums, trumpets, cymbals, gongs, bells, conches, and flutes; a game of chess; and a cock fight.

From depictions on reliefs we know that a typical house for a Khmer family of the farmer class at Angkor was much the same as can be seen in rural Cambodia today. It is one-storey, built of wood, and stands on stilts with a stairway leading up to the door. The open space underneath the house on ground level is multi-purpose. It provides room for storing household goods, is an area where the women weave cloth, and at night it serves as a corral for domesticated animals such as water buffalo, chickens, and pigs. Farming implements such as ox carts used for transporting materials and people, ploughs, sickles and hoes are all shown on the reliefs.

Central markets serviced a nucleus of villages and took place only in the morning. Trade was conducted almost entirely by women. Prices were negotiable and, according to inscriptions, barter was the form of payment in Angkorian times. Honey, for example, was exchanged for oil; cloth for syrup, and cotton for ginger conserve.

The inscriptions give some understanding of the organisation of Khmer society and the structure of the state. A large corps of officials administered the nation. Revenue was collected in the form of taxes, usually paid in barter such as grain or other commodities. Various courts existed to hand out justice and the inscriptions suggest that harsh physical penalities were imposed on those found guilty. Flogging and the amputation of hands or feet are among the punishments mentioned.

Although the Khmers never adopted the caste system of India they did have classes of society. The king was at the top of the echelon. A successful king ensured the prosperity of the kingdom and passed it on to his ancestors. His protective power was omnipotent and encompassed the people, state, law and soil. This factor was so important that the reign-names of successive kings included the honorary suffix *varman* ('armour') which was later extended to mean 'protection' or 'protector'. Each king built a state temple, other monuments dedicated to his ancestors, a palace, and a *baray* — all as physical expressions of his power and protection over his people and his kingdom.

The territory that the Khmers controlled was divided into areas and districts, each administered by a team of officials, appointed by the king. From time to time, a provincial area increased its local autonomy and halting such threats to his rule was always a concern of the king. Priests were close to nobility in the class structure and occupied a revered position. Scholars, poets, astrologers and astronomers were privileged members of the intelligentsia, whereas teachers and sacrificers were hereditary appointments.

Warriors and farmers formed the largest classes. Armies were conscripted depending on the need for troops to protect the capital and to wage battles with enemies. Hand-to-hand combat is depicted in the reliefs and massive armies can be seen using shields, lances, swords, and spears in fierce battle. The slave class ranked the lowest in Khmer society and consisted of debtors, prisoners of war, and hill tribesmen. Slaves undoubtedly maintained the temples and comprised the massive work force that would have been required to build the monuments.

Women have held a position of respect and equality in Cambodian society throughout history. Inscriptions recount the hereditary lineage of the ruler often passing matriarchally with the inheritance of property also being transmitted through the female line. Women figured in the government during the Angkor period and were also prominent in the economic structure of the empire.

Early photograph of the ascent to the third level, Angkor Wat.

Religion

Your appreciation of Angkor will be greater if you have background to the religious traditions of the Khmers which both inspired and governed the concept and execution of all their art and architecture. The earliest form of worship in Cambodia was a widespread primitive belief in animism or spiritual forces. Patronage to it was potent and enduring, and spirits are still worshipped in modern Cambodia. Spirits reside everywhere, it is believed—in the trees, rivers, mountains, stones and the earth.

These supernatural forces are both revered and feared as they can be protective or destructive. Because of this duality, widespread superstitions surround them.[20] Rituals are conducted to either invoke or appease the spirits with attention to those who govern the earth such as the *naga*, guardian of the waters, and other forces that have control over man's survival. Ancestral spirits or *nak ta*, are another large and powerful group that resides in nature's habitats such as hills and trees. They require nurturing and pacifying because, according to tradition, when a person dies his soul is reincarnated and his spirit becomes free.

In the early centuries of the Christian era formal practices from India reached Cambodia and artistic interpretations of India's two religions, Hinduism and Buddhism, became the main themes of Khmer art. The foundations of these religions, though, are based on earlier beliefs of the Indo-Aryans, expressed mainly through the *Vedas*, a text compiled from oral traditions.

While the practices from India were adopted in principle, they were not accepted without modification. Instead, aspects were adapted to suit the ideological and aesthetic ideals of the inhabitants of mainland south-east Asia. Worship of nature's spirits was never abandoned and tenets from animism and the Indian-influenced religions were synthesised. During the Angkor period, even though the religion favoured by the reigning king predominated, worship of local spirits was always part of the prevailing religious practices. Buddhism, for example, absorbed animistic beliefs into its doctrines and borrowed a few of the Hindu deities, while Hinduism embraced gods from several ancient traditions. This amalgamation of beliefs is also reflected in Khmer art, and it is not uncommon to see scenes on bas-reliefs that incorporate aspects of Hinduism and Buddhism.

Legacies of Brahmanism, an earlier tradition, are found in later religious practices. Its principles were formulated between 900 and 500 BC and expressed in the *Brahmanas*, a group of texts used by priests or brahmins to conduct rituals. They also evolved from an earlier text, the *Vedas*, subscribed to by the Indo-Aryans, who settled in northern India during the second millennium BC. You can see reflections of this ancient religious practice in dramatic depictions of the Vedic gods, Agni (fire),

Religious monument (stupa) in the central sanctuary of Preah Khan.

Indra (thunder) and Surya (sun), at Angkor Wat in the gallery of bas-reliefs (northwest side).

Brahmanism derived its name from the brahmins, who were considered mediators with the gods. Brahmanism retained Vedic rituals and sacrificial practice, and supported the belief in a universal god, but also modified the gods of Vedic times. Besides a series of divine beings, Brahmanism embraced animistic spirits, demons and several other mythical beings that are found later in the Khmer art of the Angkor period. It also adopted the concept of the cosmology of the world with Mount Meru situated at the axis of the universe.

Sometime in the early centuries of the first millennium BC another group of texts, the *Upanisads*, was composed. It reacted against the sacrificial practices of Brahmanism and focused on philosophical thought. An important idea carried over to later religious practices was the relationship between the individual being and the Universal Being, a theme that recurs in both Hinduism and Buddhism. It recognised a common belief in rebirth or the idea that one is born again and again in different forms with the ultimate goal being unity and release from the infinite chain of rebirths. This idea was adopted by all the later formal religious practices in Cambodia.

Around the beginning of the Christian era the early beliefs of the Vedic traditions and Brahmanism fused with ideas from the *Upanisads* and other oral traditions and gave birth to Hinduism, the dominant religion in India today. Hinduism accepts the existence of many sects and schools of thought. Followers believe in a universal principle and they worship, among others, the deities Brahma, Shiva and Vishnu.

Hinduism inspired several religious cults that became dominant forms of worship at Angkor. Shivaism was the earlier of the two and prevailed in the ninth and tenth centuries. Vishnuism supplanted it in the 11th century. The *devaraja*, (meaning 'the king of the gods' in Sanskrit) was yet another cult that developed in Cambodia during the Angkor period. Despite the translation of the term, research by leading modern epigraphists and historians argues that there is no evidence of the ruler's consecration as a god-king.[21] Further debate amongst scholars centres on the importance of the cult in Cambodia during the early Angkor period in a political context, as evidence has shown that the cult was not unique as it existed in the pre-Angkor period at Zhenla. The *devaraja* cult did exist at Angkor, but its importance and function are still being determined.

The *Puranas*, another religious text, followed the *Upanisads* in chronology, although their present form did not materialise until around the fourth or fifth century AD. It contains mainly legends about the gods, particularly Krishna, the cowherd, who was one of the most popular Hindu deities in early Khmer art. You can see sculptures of Krishna holding up Mount Govardhara in many of the frontons of temples at Angkor.

The *Mahabharata*, a great Hindu epic, served as the source of inspiration for many narrative scenes depicted in Khmer art. It is written in stanzas and is longer than the *Illiad* and the *Odyssey* combined. The main event of this text is the Battle of Kurukshetra involving the Pandava clan and their cousins, the Kauravas, which probably took place between 900 and 650 BC. This event is dramatically depicted in an action-packed scene at Angkor Wat in the gallery of bas-reliefs (south-west side).

Another Hindu epic, the *Ramayana* (*Reamker* is the Cambodian version), has penetrated the art and culture of all south and south-east Asian countries and influenced Khmer art throughout the Angkor period. It was vividly transposed on the bas-reliefs. Later, tales of the *Ramayana* were depicted in mural paintings, shadow plays, theatre and dance. Episodes from the epic are being revived today in performances by the Cambodian Royal Ballet. It is generally accepted that the composition of the *Ramayana* took place between 200 BC and AD 200. The early date, long evolution, wide distribution and complexities in translations have resulted in numerous changes, additions and variations. Thus, the legacy of the *Ramayana* consists of many versions and sources differ.

This lengthy epic is written in grand heroic style and the theme centres on a series of adventures and ordeals of Rama and the abduction of his wife, Sita, by the demon Ravana. Laksmana, Rama's brother and Hanuman, the demi-god who leads the monkey warriors, figure prominently in the story and assist in the rescue of Sita. The drama of this much-loved story is portrayed in the Battle of Lanka at Angkor Wat in the gallery of bas-reliefs (north-west side).

Buddhism began in India as a reform movement against Hinduism. A main difference is that it centred on a historical figure known as the Buddha (the 'Enlightened One') who was born as Prince Siddhartha in Lumbini, in the lowlands of present-day Nepal, about 623 BC and died around 543 BC, although these dates are regularly disputed by experts. His surname was Gautama. Because he was born into the princely warrior clan of the Sakyas he is often called Sakyamuni. His parents were King Suddhodana and his first wife, Queen Mayadevi. Several key events in the historical life of the Buddha from childhood through his attainment of enlightenment provided themes for Khmer artists and are depicted in several bas-reliefs at Angkor.

By the first centuries of the Christian era two branches of Buddhism were defined—Mahayana and Theravada. Both of these were transmitted to Cambodia at various times, but it is Mahayana Buddhism that is of the most relevance to the art and architecture at Angkor, as Theravada Buddhism was introduced only in the 13th century, after all the major monuments had been built. Both schools give importance to the act of offering and recognise that giving frees the giver from all attachments.

Mahayana Buddhism, known as the 'Greater Vehicle', may have reached Cambodia by way of the Kingdom of Srivijaya (Indonesia) and Funan where it was practised in the

fifth century. Although Mahayana Buddhism had some following during the early Angkor period, it reached a peak of popularity in the late 12th and early 13th centuries during the reign of Jayavarman VII. It is practised today in Nepal, Tibet, Bhutan, Mongolia, China, Korea, Japan and Vietnam. The principles of this sect are expounded through the Sanskrit language. Followers of Mahayana Buddhism believe in the attainment of 'Buddhahood' and the removal of all ignorance. They recognise that there were others before the Buddha who had gained enlightenment and that there would also be others in the future.

The religious ideal of Mahayana Buddhism is a Bodhisattva and it was widely portrayed in Khmer art, especially during the late Angkor period. A Bodhisattva ('Enlightenment Being') is one who has performed enough merit to enter Nirvana, but renounces attainment of enlightenment to return to earth and help the sufferings of all humanity. Several Bodhisattvas appear in Khmer art, particularly in stone sculptures, but the one most frequently represented in reliefs is the Avalokiteshvara, 'the lord who looks down from above', known in Cambodia as Lokeshvara, 'Lord of the World'. A small figure of the Buddha seated in meditation on the head of an image, above the forehead, signifies an Avalokiteshvara. This figure, in Khmer art, is a four-armed deity who carries a flask, book, lotus and rosary.

If the Bodhisattva has eight arms, he holds additional objects — a thunderbolt, an elephant goad, a conch, discus and sword. The Avalokiteshvara appears in several forms in art during Jayavarman VII's reign. Some believe the faces on the towers of the Bayon represent this. And the temple of Neak Pean with pools filled with water with curative powers was a place of pilgrimage where the sick could invoke healing from Lokeshvara. In the middle of the central pond, the focal point is a sculpture of the horse Balaha with figures clinging to it which depicts the episode when Lokeshvara changes into a horse to rescue the people who were victims of a shipwreck.

The development of the cults of the Bodhisattvas and those of the Hindu gods parallelled each other in the early centuries of the Christian era, and, thus, it is not surprising to see Hindu features such as hair style or attributes in the Avalokiteshvara. Further merging of the two is seen in the ninth incarnation of the Hindu god Vishnu which is the Buddha.

The Theravada School of Buddhism spread gradually from Sri Lanka to mainland south-east Asia by way of Burma, Thailand and Cambodia between the 11th and 15th centuries and is practised in those areas today. Theravada Buddhism, known as the Lesser Vehicle, adhered to conservative principles preserving the original doctrines and expressed them through the Pali language.

HINDU DEITIES
Gods and goddesses from the Hindu pantheon depicted in Khmer art are eternally

One of the ubiquitous, majestic faces on a gopura at Angkor Thom.

youthful, yet have a noble air of elegance. They appear sitting, standing or reclining without eroticism or nakedness. Identification is not revealed in their faces as they show no emotion except for an expression of serenity.

So how is a Hindu deity recognised in Khmer art? Each deity is associated with specific symbols or attributes, that represent his powers and he often holds these in his hands, which help to identify him. A deity often rides a mount or vehicle, which is another distinguishing feature. The presence of a wife or consort, representing the god's female energy, or *sakti*, who often carries the symbols of her spouse is yet another clue to the identity of a deity.

Keep in mind that many of the Hindu pantheon of gods and goddesses had their origins in ancient Vedic times. When they reappeared later in Hindu iconography they had often changed, and had different identities, characteristics, functions, influence and prominence—all of which were introduced to suit the new concepts of Hinduism. The descriptions that follow are of gods, goddesses and other mythical beings, as they appeared in the Hindu pantheon. References to their earlier forms are only mentioned if needed for identification.

■ GODS

Shiva was one of the earliest and most popular of the Hindu gods represented in Khmer iconography. He appeared in the pre-Angkor period (fifth to eighth century) in the form of a composite figure Hari-Hara and in the early Angkor period when several temples—Phnom Bakheng, Baksei Chamkrong, Banteay Srei, and the Roluos group (Bakong, Lolei and Preah Ko) — were dedicated to him.

Early representations of Shiva were in the form of a *linga*, shaped like an erect phallus and usually made of polished stone. The vertical shaft may be divided into three parts symbolising gods that were often worshipped simultaneously. The lower, square portion represents Brahma; an octagonal section in the middle relates to Vishnu; and the upper, cylindrical part with a rounded tip is associated with Shiva. The base of the *linga* is anchored in a square pedestal with a hollow channel on one side, out of which the waters of ablution flow, symbolising a *yoni*, the vulva-shaped female emblem of power. The phallic meaning associated with the *linga* in India is less pronounced in Khmer iconography, where it was more a symbol of the 'creative energy of the powers of nature.'

Although Shiva as a *linga* was widely represented at Angkor, he also appears in some human forms in Khmer art. He is most often depicted as a benevolent god and his fierce aspect, so popular in India, is seldom found at Angkor. Shiva lives on Mount Kailasha in the western Himalayas with his wife Parvati (Uma) and two sons — Skanda (Karttikeya), the God of War, and Ganesha, the God of Knowledge.

A fine relief at Banteay Srei shows Shiva holding a frightened Parvati on his knee as the demon Ravana tries to topple Mount Kailasha (south library, east face). Shiva's vehicle is the bull, popularly known as Nandi, who is as 'white as the Himalayan peaks'. Images of a crouching Nandi are commonly found facing the entrance of temples dedicated to Shiva such as Preah Ko. Shiva's main attribute is a trident, an indestructible weapon that represents absolute truth. Shiva has a chignon separated into strands of loops in tiers, a brahmin cord over his shoulder, and has a third eye in the middle of his forehead near his brow. It is in a vertical position and is always closed because, according to legend, if it opens the whole universe will be destroyed by a great fire.

Another human form, depicting Shiva as 'Lord of the Dance', is rare at Angkor, but one example is a superb fronton at Banteay Srei (east *gopura*) which shows Shiva in a lively dance with his ten arms fully extended in a joyful rendition. Sometimes in one of his human forms Shiva is shown as an ascetic meditating on a mountain with hermits. Thin with matted hair tied up on top of his head; he carries a water pot and wears a rosary of 108 beads around his neck.

Vishnu was a popular Hindu god in Khmer art, widely depicted both in sculpture and reliefs. Images of Vishnu as a young man wearing a *sampot* and a belt are sublimely beautiful. Vishnu's headdress in pre-Angkor art is cylindrical, whereas, later in the Angkor period, he wears a diadem. In his typical posture, Vishnu is standing with four arms and holds a conch shell, a ball representing the Earth (a lotus in Indian iconography) and two weapons—the club and the discus. You can see a dramatic portrayal of this posture of Vishnu at Prasat Kravan (central tower). Vishnu is riding his mount the *garuda*, the mythical king of birds, with a human body, and his spouse Laksmi is with him.

Known as the preserver, Vishnu has *avataras*, literally 'descents' or reincarnations. Whenever the world is threatened by evil, he assumes the role of saviour and descends to earth in a suitable form. He is reincarnated as a human or animal and guides mankind through the dissemination of his love, which eventually triumphs over the forces of evil. Descriptions of the ten major *avataras* follow. The first four incarnations are of animal forms, then heroic acts and finally two with 'saviour-qualities'. Rama amd Krishna are the most popular *avataras* in Khmer art.

(1) **Matsya** (a fish). Vishnu saved mankind from a flood in the form of a fish;

(2) **Kurma** (a tortoise). This incarnation figures prominently in Khmer art, where it is associated with creation and the churning of the cosmic ocean. Vishnu, in the form of a tortoise, serves as a pivot for the pole that churns the ocean;

(3) **Varaha** (a boar). This form is uncommon in Khmer art. It is another creation myth, and Vishnu is usually depicted with a human body and an animal's head. He held the world above the waters of chaos to prevent its destruction;

(4) **Narasimha** (a lion). Vishnu took the form of part-human and part-lion to over-

come Hiranyakashipu, king of the demons, who was invulnerable to man or beast;
(5) **Vamana** (a dwarf). This is a human form that can easily be recognised, because of its diminutive size and by the objects he carries — a water-pot and an umbrella;
(6) **Parashurama** (a human); 'Rama with the Axe' is an incarnation of Vishnu as a martial hero;
(7) **Rama** (a human). Rama is the ideal king who performs heroic deeds;
(8) **Krishna** (a human). The complex personality of this figure reveals several stages in Krishna's life: childhood, when he performed great feats such as uprooting trees along with a stone he is tied to; youth, when he was a cow herd and dallied with young girls; manhood and middle age, when he became a charioteer. In his youthful forms he is easily recognisable by the flute he carries;
(9) the **Buddha** (a human). In this incarnation Vishnu takes the form of the historical Buddha;
(10) **Kalki** (a horse or a human figure with a horse head). Vishnu's last incarnation has not yet happened. Kalki will emerge at the end of our present time-cycle.

Agni was known as the god of fire in Vedic times, but later his power diminished. As a Hindu god he is the purifier of sarificial offerings and rides a ram.

Brahma was more important as a Hindu god than in Vedic times, but he was never as widely worshipped in Cambodia as Shiva and Vishnu. From the *Puranas*, he is known as the Creator. Brahma is easily identified by his four faces, each one looking in a cardinal direction. In his four hands he holds a rosary, a vase, a ladle and a book. According to legend, Brahma was born from a golden lotus that emerged from the navel of Vishnu, who was reclining during a cosmic sleep on the serpent, Ananta, on the waves of the ocean. His mount is the *hamsa*, a sacred goose, and his consort is Sarasvati.

Ganesha is a son of Shiva and Parvati. Depictions of Ganesha on reliefs at Angkor are uncommon, but he was a popular deity as a sculpture. According to one of the many legends, Ganesha was actually born with a human head. Shiva was away at the time of his birth and when he returned he encountered an unfamiliar young man guarding Parvati's quarters. Shiva tried to enter, but Ganesha forbade him. Shiva was so angry he could not enter his wife's quarters that he beheaded Ganesha, not knowing it was his son. Parvati pleaded with Shiva to save Ganesha's life, so Shiva gave him the head of the next creature he encountered, which was an elephant. Besides his elephant-shaped head, Ganesha has a corpulent, human-shaped body. He is usually depicted with four arms which carry three attributes—an elephant goad, a noose and a bowl of sweetmeats; his fourth arm is held in a gesture of fearlessness.

Hari-Hara is a composite deity with its origins in Brahmanism. It was immensely popular in early Khmer art and some superbly beautiful stone sculptures remain today, notably a standing example in the National Museum in Phnom Penh. The

Female divinities on the interior of the second level gallery, Angkor Wat.

figure bears characteristics of two deities — Shiva on the right and Vishnu on the left. On the right he displays the plaited locks of an ascetic, symbolising Shiva, and, on the left, the cylindrical headdress of Vishnu. Shiva's third eye appears on the forehead of the image.

Hevajra also known as Heruka, is one of the so-called inner divinities of Mahayana Buddhism derived from mystical elements of the Tantric strain. Often shown in a dancing posture with eight heads and sixteen arms. Bronze images are the most common in Khmer art.

Indra is another god from Vedic times, and, thus, has several aspects to his character. In his early form, he was a warrior and god of storms, who possessed power over the heavens and all its elements such as rain and thunder. He hurled lightning and thunderbolts and used the rainbow as his bow. In Hindu iconography, his importance was diminished and his main function was as guardian of the eastern quarter of the compass. He remained, though, a popular god in Khmer Iconography. His vehicle is a magnificent three-headed, white elephant known as Airavata and he lives in a palace of gold at the summit of Mount Meru in paradise. Befitting his splendid surroundings, he wears a high tiara or turban and is dressed in elaborate clothes and jewellery. The main weapon of Indra is a thunderbolt. He sits prominently atop an elephant holding a thunderbolt at the gates of the city of Angkor Thom.

Kama In Hindu times Kama is known as the god of love, and is concerned with creation, particularly sexual desire. He is one of the most handsome of the Hindu deities. His vehicle is a parrot and his attributes are a bow made of sugar cane, strung with a line of humming bees and arrows with floral tips. Kama likes to shoot his arrows so as to inspire passion in others, especially in the spring. His consort is Rati. Kama is portrayed in a popular relief at Banteay Srei.

Kubera An ugly dwarf and chief of the *yakshas* (attendants of Kubera who guard the wealth buried beneath the earth) in the Vedic period, Kubera was reborn as the god of wealth in Hindu times. He became guardian of the north and resides high in the Himalayas, where he watches over the treasures of the earth. He retains his physical characteristics of a dwarf from Vedic iconograpy, but flaunts his riches by covering himself in jewels and wearing a crown. Money bags, symbolising wealth, are often seen nearby Kubera. His vehicle and his attributes vary.

Skanda (Kartikeya) is one of the sons of Shiva and Parvati. From early times Skanda had been depicted as a young god of war, but his more popular form in Khmer art was as an adult deity still associated with battle and easily identified by at least six heads and riding a peacock. His attributes vary, but they often include a thunderbolt. Skanda showing his prowess as an archer with an arrow, made by Surya from the heat and energy of the sun, is a popular theme for reliefs.

Surya was an important deity in Vedic times and known as god of the sun, an association he carried into Hindu iconography. He often appears with another cosmic symbol, the moon. Surya rides a golden chariot drawn by seven horses, each one representing a day of the week. A variation is one horse with seven heads. His symbol is a *swatika* , 'swastika', and he sometimes holds a lotus in each hand.

Yama In Hindu iconography, Yama presides over the gloomy realm of punishment located in the lower regions. All souls must pass by Yama's throne of supreme judgement. As the Lord of Law, Yama keeps a register in which each man's life span is recorded. He allots seats after death in accordance with an individual's performance in the world. This deity rides a buffalo and, in his multiple arms, carries a heavy club to judge the dead and to determine their fate and a noose to put around the necks of his victims.

■ GODDESSES

Devi, the Great Goddess, is a complex and powerful being. In ancient times she was the great mother goddess connected with fertility of the earth and female reproduction. She was also the consort of Shiva. She has several different names, roles and characteristics. Some forms are fierce and others are mild. Despite her many forms, some features are recurring. Devi rides a lion or a tiger; at other times the mount is simply beside her. She often carries several weapons including a sword, a 'sacrificial chopper' and a trident.

Ganga A goddess associated with the Ganges River and one of Shiva's wives, although less important than Parvati. According to legend, Ganga descends from heaven and Shiva catches her in his hair to break her fall to earth. Thus, she is often depicted as a small figure in the matted hair of Shiva with a river flowing from her mouth.

Laksmi is the consort of Vishnu and the goddess of good fortune and abundance from early times. She is also kown as Sri and symbolises prosperity. Laksmi was born of the Churning of the Ocean of Milk. She is often depicted on a lotus (her symbol) pedestal and attended by two elephants sprinkling lustral water on her with their trunks. The number of her arms and attributes vary, but they usually include a lotus and a conch.

Parvati ('daughter of the mountain'), Shiva's consort, is the daughter of the god of the Himalayas. She was a goddess in Vedic times, and, thus, has several names and personalities. She is also known as Uma and the Great Goddess, Devi; in her fierce aspect she is Durga. Parvati sometimes carries the trident of Shiva, is often on a lotus pedestal and rides a tiger.

Sarasvati was a water deity in Vedic times, but in later iconography she is identified with holy rituals and believed to have influenced the composition of hymns. She is the goddess of creative arts, learning and science. Sarasvati is generally considered the consort of Brahma, but her connection with him is tenuous. This graceful goddess rides a peacock.

■ MINOR DIVINITIES AND MYTHICAL BEINGS

Ananta ('Endless') The serpent upon which Vishnu sits or reclines when he is in a cosmic sleep. Also called Sesa ('Remainder').

Apsaras (female minor divinity) A celestial nymph, a dancer and a courtesan of the sky. An *apsaras* has perfect beauty and evokes irresistible seduction.

Asura (demon) A class of gods who were adversaries of the *devas* in Vedic times. Later the term referred to a type of demon that represented the forces of darkness or evil and is the enemy of the gods.

Deva (*devata* in Sanskrit) A generic term that refers to a god or deity that is often a guardian. The feminine form is *devi* .

Dvarapala (Guardian of the Gate) This large figure is also known as the protector of shrines and is often found standing at the entrance to a temple holding a club.

Garuda is the mount of Vishnu and the enemy of the *nagas*. He is a gigantic mythical bird with a human body and bird-like wings, legs and a thick curved beak with bulging eyes; his lower body is covered with feathers and he has the claws of an eagle; he wears a diadem and jewellery. He appears in magnificent form on the enclosure wall at Preah Khan, with arms stretched above his head, grasping the tails of serpents whose heads curl up at his feet. Another good example of the *garuda* is seen around the base of the royal terrace at Angkor Thom.

Kala is a mask-like creature commonly found in both Hindu and Buddhist temples, who serves as a protector for the temples, and, as such, is found above the doorways. A *kala* has round bulbous eyes, a human or lion's nose, two horns, claw-like hands, and grins. According to legend, the *kala* had a voracious appetite and asked Shiva for a victim to satiate him. Shiva was angered by the request and ordered the *kala* to devour itself. The *kala* consumed its body but not its head. When Shiva heard that the *kala* had followed his order he had its head placed over the doors of temples as a reminder of its 'terrible and beneficient' powers. Fine examples of the *kala* are found on the lintels of the Roluos group.

Makara A large sea animal with the body of a reptile and a big jaw and snout that is elongated into a trunk; often depicted spewing another creature or plant motif from its mouth. This mythical creature appears on the lintels of the temples at Roluos.

Naga ('snake') A semi-divine being and a serpent-god of the waters who lives in the underworld beneath the earth or in the water. It is easily identified by its scaly body and multiple heads spread in the shape of a fan. In Khmer art, the *naga* always has an uneven number of heads, usually seven or nine. The *nagas* are ruled by Vasuki and are the enemy of the *garuda*. The *naga* controls the rains and the prosperity of

A powerful garuda spreads its wings on the enclosure wall at Preah Khan.

the region where they reside. *Nagas* often marry humans in mythology and the Khmers claim their descent from the union of a foreigner and the daughter of the *naga* king. The Khmer's obsession with the *naga* is reflected in its omnipresence at the temples of Angkor. A typical rendering of this mythical being is a balustrade formed by the body of the serpent that flanks the long causeways leading to the monuments and can be seen at Preah Khan, Bakong, Angkor Wat, and in front of the gates at Angkor Thom.

Nandi A white bull and the vehicle of Shiva.

Rahu A demon who rides through the sky in a silver chariot. According to legend, he causes eclipses by seizing and swallowing the sun and the moon. They eventually reappear from inside his throat, thus ending the eclipse, but he then resumes the task. Like the *kala*, Rahu has no body, just a head, arms and hands. Even today, the Cambodians make tremendous noise before an eclipse to keep Rahu from consuming the moon.

Rishi A Sanskrit term which refers to a sage, an ascetic or a hermit. A *rishi* in Khmer art is seated cross-legged in meditation and has a goatee.

Vasuki The serpent upon which Vishnu reclines or sits and whose body served as a rope when the Ocean of Milk was churned by the gods and demons.

Yaksha A male nature spirit and a deity who often serves as a guardian. This mythical being has a ferocious appearance and is gigantic in size with bulging eyes, fangs and a leering grin. In the *Ramayana*, the *yakhsa* is a demon giant who lives on the island of Lanka.

LEGENDS DEPICTED IN KHMER ART

Ramayana This ancient poem centres around two characters—Rama and his wife Sita—and unfolds in a series of adventurous tales that are packed with action. Violent battles rage. Heroes fight bravely and take on their enemies single-handedly. They go to battle in grand style, magnificently attired and bejewelled. Miracles happen and magical spells are cast. Arrows turn into snakes, then to mythical beings, then to fire. Monkeys lift mountains, and gods and demons shrink and expand in size to suit the scene. Even though the episodes are carved in stone, you can detect emotions in the characters—pain, fear, sadness, grief, and tears.

The story told in this guide is based mainly on the *Reamker*, the Cambodian version of the *Ramayana*, although the spellings of the names from the Indian version have been retained because of their familiarity to the general reader.[22] The characters and places that appear in this version of the *Ramayana* are:

Ayodhya: a city and kingdom
Dasarath: King of Ayodhya; father of Rama
Hanuman: white monkey-headed demi-god

Indrajit: conquerer of Indra; son of Ravana
Laksmana: brother of Rama
Lanka: Ravana's kingdom
Marica: a demon disguised as a golden stag
Rakshasa: a demon with fierce fangs
Rama: the hero; eldest son of Dasarath
Ravana: chief of the *rakshasas*; demon king; abductor of Sita
Sita: the heroine; wife of Rama
Sugriva: king of the monkeys; brother of Vali
Vali: brother of Sugriva
Viradha: a *rakshasas*; abductor of Sita

The story begins with the gods approaching Vishnu in a cosmic sleep with the request that he return to earth in human form to help them rid the world of the demon king Ravana. So Vishnu descends to earth as Rama, the eldest of four sons of the King of Ayodhya (in India), destined to succeed his father.

According to the *Reamker*, the Ploughing Ceremony is underway with the king presiding when a golden maiden of extraordinary beauty appears in a lotus. She is 'pure and beautiful, she glows like the full moon'. The maiden captivates the king and he takes her back to his kingdom as his daughter and names her Sita. When it is time for her to marry, the king looks for the finest man in the land and he puts forth the condition that anyone who is strong enough to lift his magic bow will be rewarded with Sita's hand in marriage. All the men are eager to win Sita and each one tries to lift the bow, but no one succeeds.

Then Rama steps forward and with his supreme strength raises the bow easily. The king rejoices and a wedding feast takes place. Meanwhile, Rama's father prepares to hand the Kingdom of Ayodhya over to his son, but his wife, Rama's stepmother, persuades him instead to send Rama into exile so that her own son can be successor to the throne. Rama and his beautiful wife, Sita, depart for the forest, accompanied by Laksmana, Rama's brother.

When the king eventually dies, Rama refuses to return to Ayodhya, but remains with Sita and Laksmana in the forest where they live as ascetics and encounter many strange adventures. One such episode is depicted at Angkor Wat in the gallery of bas-reliefs (west side) where Viradha, a demon, seizes Sita and, just as he is about to devour her, Rama and Laksmana appear and slay the monster.

Ravana, the demon king (whom Vishnu had taken earthly form to destroy), is the ruler of the *rakshasas* in the neighbouring kingdom of Lanka (Sri Lanka). His terrifying form is easily recognised by his huge size, and his 10 heads and 20 arms.

Following pages: a scene from the Judgement of Yama, South Gallery of Bas-reliefs, Angkor Wat.

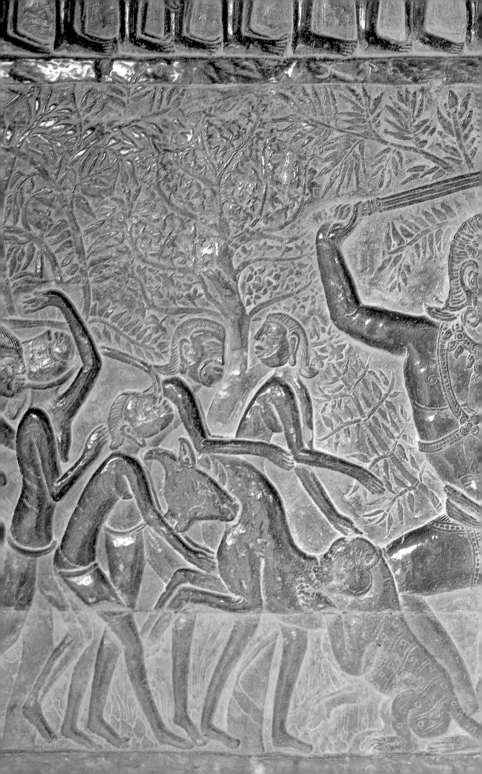

Captivated by the beauty of Sita, one day he uses his power to have her kidnapped. He enlists the demon, Marica, to help him separate Sita from the two brothers. Marica appears before them in the form of a golden deer.

When Sita sees the beautiful illusion she urges Rama to capture the deer for her. Rama follows it and manages to shoot the deer with an arrow, and, as Marica is dying, he takes his true form and imitates the voice of Rama and calls to his brother for help. Laksmana hesitates, but Sita persuades him to go to Rama's aid. Ravana, disguised as a brahmin, waits for the moment when both brothers have left and Sita is alone, then he approaches and praises her beauty. He returns to his true form and carries her off to his palace on the island of Lanka. (This episode is depicted at Angkor Wat in the gallery of bas-reliefs, west side.) En route, Sita appeals to an egret to fly to Rama and plead with him to rescue her. Ravana and Sita arrive at Lanka where she is held captive in the park of Asoka trees.

Meanwhile, Rama and his brother return home and find Sita gone. When they set out to look for her, they meet the egret who tells them about Sita's capture. A series of battles and adventures centred on the rescue of Sita follows. Hanuman, the white monkey, and his army of monkeys help in the search. He allies them to Sugriva, the great monkey king, who is battling with his brother Vali. (This fight between the two brothers is portrayed in a powerful stone sculpture in the National Museum in Phnom Penh.) Rama intervenes in support of Sugriva and shoots Vali with an arrow.

In return, Sugriva and his army join Rama and Laksmana, and together they prepare to invade Lanka to retrieve Sita. Rama sends Hanuman to Lanka to find out where Sita is hidden and gives Laksmana his ring to prove his identity. With a mighty bound Hanuman flies to the island and, when he arrives, he magically makes himself smaller so that he can enter the palace and enter Sita's quarters. He gives Rama's ring to Sita and assures her that she will soon be free. Sita, in turn, gives the ring to Hanuman for Rama. He leaves, climbs to the top of the Asoka trees, then leaps on to the golden rampart and breaks it before killing the entire demon army. When Ravana hears of this he sends his son, Indrajit, who attacks Hanuman's army.

The battle which ensues is a long one. Hanuman is captured and taken to Ravana who orders him to be executed. Hanuman, though, requests that he be wrapped in cloth and set on fire. The demons comply and after this is done, Hanuman uses the fire to set one of his own and burns the Kingdom of Lanka to the ground, then returns to Rama who praises him for his brave deed.

They prepare to take Sita by force and plan how to cross the ocean with armies. Both Sugriva and Hanuman offer to magically turn into a bridge, but Rama's plan is faster. He merely shoots one of his powerful arrows to make the sea dry up and the forces cross. As they move towards the palace they encounter various enemies and fierce battles ensue. In the bloody fight which follows, a poisonous weapon strikes

Laksmana's foot and a gigantic strychnine plant emerges. Hanuman travels to the Himalayas with lightning speed and brings back potent herbs to cure Laksmana. Then he flies to Lanka to get a stone needed to grind the herbs, but which is kept under Ravana's head when he sleeps. The medicine cures Laksmana.

The battles continue. Hanuman and the rejuvenated Laksmana fight Indrajit, whose powerful magical arrows turn into a web of *nagas* that entangle themselves with Laksmana and his army. But eventually Laksmana kills Indrajit. The armies of Rama and Ravana finally battle each other and good is victorious over evil as Rama defeats his enemies.

Rama returns to the Kingdom of Ayodhya and takes his rightful place on the throne and is reunited with Sita. But all is not well, as he suspects his wife of infidelity after she has spent 14 years with Ravana and, after an argument over a portrait of Ravana, Rama orders Laksmana to kill Sita. He takes her to the forest, but hesitates about carrying out Rama's orders as Sita is pregnant. Sita pleads with Laksmana to kill her. He lifts his sword, but a miracle occurs. When he lowers it to strike Sita the sword turns into a garland. The god Indra helps Laksmana fool Rama by preparing the liver of a dead deer to present to him, hoping he will think it is Sita's. Then he sends his wives to help her with the birth of her son. She leaves her son in the care of a sage, but later returns and takes him away. When the sage discovers the boy is missing he creates another one, similar in age and character. These two boys are the sons of Rama.

At last, after many years, Rama meets the boys and prays they are of his own lineage. They tell Rama that Sita is their mother and that she is still alive. He asks them to take him to her so he can bring her back to the Kingdom of Ayodhya. When they meet, Sita refuses to return with Rama and blames him for thinking she was unfaithful. He finally accepts that he cannot convince Sita to return, but he pleads with her to let him take his sons back and she reluctantly agrees. They return to Ayodhya where Rama hosts a feast in their honour and everyone rejoices.

The boys, though, are unhappy without their mother and worry about her being lonely. Rama decides to send the boys to see her. They beg Sita to return with them to Ayodhya, but she says she will only go back if Rama dies. So the boys return and relay this condition to Rama who then tries to trick Sita into thinking he is dying by building a funeral pavilion and an urn. Then he dispatches Hanuman to bring Sita back to Ayodhya. As she laments beside the pavilion Rama walks up to her. She flees from him and is terrified that she cannot escape. She prays the earth will open for her and, as it does, she descends to the land of the *nagas*, where she is offered refuge by their king.

Rama is desolate without her. 'From this day onwards I shall never be able to see you, who are so dear to my heart....From now on there will be nothing — only the sound of your name.'[23] He writes Sita a message and sends it attached to his powerful arrow which flies like a 'hundred thousand thunderbolts' through the earth and then falls into the kingdom of the *nagas*.

The Buddha is always represented in Khmer art with great composure and supreme sensitivity. Artists achieved a sublime balance between the human and spiritual aspects of the Buddha which resulted in ethereal images. This ideal expression of the Buddha in Khmer art was noted by Georges Groslier: 'My impression is that no country his worship reached, nor even in his own native land, has any image of Gautama embodied the idea of Buddhism more intelligently. No one has so perfectly epitomized his doctrine, his meditation, his renunciation, his profound benevolence.'[24]

The most frequently depicted episodes of the Buddha at Angkor centre around his historical life before he attains enlightenment, when he was known as Prince Siddhartha, or Gautama. They begin after he marries a young maiden named Yasodhara at the age of 16. The first event is the 'Great Departure', seen, for example, on the north fronton of the central sanctuary at Neak Pean. During childhood his father had tried to shelter Gautama from seeing the suffering of others by creating pleasure gardens to provide him with everything he needed. But one day on his way to the gardens he encounters an old man, then a sick one, and then a funeral procession.

Another time he meets an itinerant monk. Having seen the suffering of old age, illness and death contrasted with the inner peace of the monk he decides to renunciate the world and to pursue a religious life to help others. Gautama departs secretly from the palace on the night of his 29th birthday, leaving his wife and son behind. He goes on horseback accompanied by his faithful groom Chandaka. The gods help him by making sure everyone is deeply asleep, and by opening the town gates, and carrying the hooves of the horses to muffle the sound.

Gautama's departure leads to another major passage in his life that provided a theme for artistic expression — the 'Cutting of the Hair'. An interpretation of this episode appears on the east fronton of the central sanctuary at Neak Pean. The prince and his groom are travelling through a kingdom and they come to a river where they stop. Gautama removes his royal attire and hands it to the groom. Then with one stroke of his sword he cuts off his long hair, renouncing his worldly life. Gautama bids farewell to his beloved groom and horse. Later, the horse dies of grief over the departure of his master. This scene is depicted on a lintel in the west tower at Ta Prohm.

After his renunciation, the prince assumes the life of the monk Gautama. He follows the teachings of several masters and then sets out to discover the path of salvation himself. He stays in north India for six years practising the life of an ascetic, becoming emaciated and weak. Mara ('death', 'destroyer', 'killer') appears to try to thwart Gautama from finding salvation and from achieving enlightenment.

The inner causeway of the western entrance to Angkor Wat.

This episode is the prelude to the 'Attack of Mara' and another source for artistic interpretation in reliefs at Buddhist temples at Angkor. It begins with Gautama meditating beneath the bodhi tree, as seen on the west fronton of the central sanctuary at Neak Pean. Mara and his army arrive and harrass him and dispute his right to reign over the world. Gautama replies by telling Mara how much merit he accumulated in previous existences. He says that each time he made merit he poured water over the hands of recipients. The result was that his merit is so great it fills the waters of the earth with his virtues. Mara requests proof of these deeds. Then the goddess of the earth appears and vouches for Gautama. As witness to this conversation, she seizes her hair, wrings it and the waters of ablution pour forth as offerings from Gautama. The act creates a flood that drowns the army of Mara. This event is depicted at Preah Palilay on a large fronton standing on the ground in front of the central sanctuary. It originally filled the space above the door at the east.

The god Indra appears and convinces Gautama that in order to achieve his goal he must avoid all excesses. So Gautama leaves his life as an ascetic and abandons his austere practices. He assumes the role of an itinerant monk, continues to meditate, and gradually regains his strength. At last Gautama knows he is ready to attain enlightenment. But before he does, Mara interferes again and tries to stop Gautama from achieving his goal. Gautama, though, sends an army of demons to frighten him and Mara admits defeat.

Gautama became the Buddha on his 35th birthday. From this time onward, he appears in Khmer iconograpy wearing a simple monastic robe with the right shoulder bare. In some images, this robe is only suggested by a faintly incised line. He has several other easily recognisable characteristics, all centred on his head. The most common hair arrangement is that of tight curls that look like a snail shell. A cranial protuberance on top of the head that looks like a chignon is typical. And the Buddha has elongated ear lobes. Sometimes the Buddha is dressed in princely garments with jewels and a diadem. An example of this can be found on the crowned headdress of images of the Buddha under the *naga* of the 12th and 13th centuries. The crowned Buddha of this period symbolised both a royal and a religious significance.

The moment that Gautama's spiritual quest climaxes in the achievement of enlightenment is one of profound beauty. It takes place on the night of a full moon beneath the bodhi tree at Bodhgaya in the modern state of Bihar in India. Near dawn, he looks up and sees the morning light, not as Gautama, but as the Buddha. You can imagine this moment by looking at the south fronton of the entry tower to Preah Palilay in the morning light. He sits under the bodhi tree meditating for seven weeks enjoying the blissfulness of his enlightenment.

An unseasonal thunderstorm followed by torrential rains occurs, but the Buddha is in such deep meditation that he is unaware of the storm. The *naga* king, Mucalinda, appears to shelter the Buddha and coils his body forming a seat that lifts the Buddha off the ground and, thus, keeps him dry. Then Mucalinda unfurls his multiple heads to make a hood protecting the Buddha from the rain. This event in the Buddha's life is recorded with skill and beauty by Khmer sculptors. It is seen most vividly in several remarkable stone images, carved in the round from the 12th and 13th centuries, that are on display in the National Museum in Phnom Penh.

The assaults of Mara and his ultimate defeat by Gautama provide an allegory for the triumph of virtue over evil, and are depicted in a scene known as the 'Victory Over Mara', which can be seen on a lintel to the right of the central sanctuary at Banteay Kdei. The Buddha is in a posture of meditation, seated with his legs crossed; his left hand rests in his lap and his right hand extends over his knee and points to the ground, in a symbolic gesture of touching the earth.

The Buddha then goes to Benares, on the bank of the Ganges River, and announces that he will teach his doctrines. 'The First Sermon', expounding the Four Noble Truths is sometimes called 'Setting the Wheel of the Law in Motion'. You can recognise this episode at the fronton on the west entrance of Ta Som by deer crouching beside the Buddha with their heads turned back to hear his words.

For the next 45 years, the Buddha travels through the Ganges basin with his disciples teaching his doctrines. This period is shown in Khmer art with the Buddha in a standing posture with the position of his hands in a gesture of instruction. A typical position is with his right hand by his side and his left hand raised to his chest, or with both palms facing outward in a gesture that calms and reassures, sometimes referred to as the 'absence of fear'.

The last great episode of the Buddha's life seen in Khmer art is his death. He knows he is dying, but he continues teaching until the end. He died on his 80th birthday, and, at the moment it happened, the earth shook and trees burst into bloom. The Buddha had entered Nirvana ('extinguish'), the state of perfection. This moment is depicted on the fronton above the east door of the entry tower at Preah Palilay with the Buddha reclining on his right side with his left hand folded under his head, his right one lying along his side.

Sacred footprints of the Buddha are seen at some temples such as Phnom Bakheng and symbolise the many years he spent wandering through India teaching his doctrine. They are flat stones shaped like the sole of a foot with 11 parallel lines crossed by other lines forming compartments that contain representations of a great variety of signs, the whole grouped around a central wheel.

Following pages: the paved inner courtyard of the third level, Angkor Wat.

A Day on the Hill of the Gods

This is the most solitary place in all Angkor—and the pleasantest. If it was truly the Mount Meru of the gods, then they chose their habitation well. But if the Khmers had chanced to worship the Greek pantheon instead of that of India, they would surely have built on Phnom Bakheng a temple to Apollo; for it is at sunrise and sunset that you feel its most potent charm. To steal out of the Bungalow an hour before the dawn, and down the road that skirts the faintly glimmering moat of Angkor Wat, before it plunges into the gloom of the forest; and then turn off, feeling your way across the terrace between the guardian lions (who grin amiably at you as you turn the light of your torch upon them); then clamber up the steep buried stairway on the eastern face of the hill, across the plateau and up the five flights of steps, to emerge from the enveloping forest on to the cool high terrace with the stars above you— is a small pilgrimage whose reward is far greater than its cost in effort.

Here at the summit it is very still. The darkness has lost its intensity; and you stand in godlike isolation on the roof of a world that seems to be floating in the sky, among stars peering faintly through wisps of filmy cloud. The dawn comes so unobtrusively that you are unaware of it, until all in a moment you realize that the world is no longer dark. The sanctuaries and altars on the terrace have taken shape about you as if by enchantment; and far below, vaguely as yet, but gathering intensity with every second, the kingdom of the Khmers and the glory thereof spreads out on every side to the very confines of the earth; or so it may well have seemed to the King-God when he visited his sanctuary—how many dawns ago?

Soon, in the east, a faint pale-gold light is diffused above a grey bank of cloud, flat-topped as a cliff, that lies across the far horizon; to which, smooth and unbroken as the surface of a calm sea, stretches the dark ocean of forest, awe-inspiring in its tranquil immensity. To the south the view is the same, save where a long low hill, the shape of a couchant cat, lies in the monotonous sea of foliage like an island. Westward, the pearl-grey waters of the great Baray, over which a thin mist seems to be suspended, turn silver in the growing light, and gleam eerily in their frame of overhanging trees; but beyond them, too, the interminable forest flows on to meet the sky. It is only in the north and north-east that a range of mountains—the Dangrengs, eighty miles or so away—breaks the contour of the vast, unvarying expanse; and you see in imagination on its eastern rampart the almost inaccessible temple of Prah Vihear.

Immediately below you there is movement. The morning is windless; but one after the other, the tops of the trees growing on the steep sides of the Phnom sway violently to and fro, and a fussy chattering announces that the monkeys have awakened to a new day. Near the bottom of the hill on the south side, threadlike wisps of smoke from invisible native hamlets mingle with patches of mist. And then, as the light strengthens, to the south-east, the tremendous towers of Angkor Wat push their black mass above the grey-green monotony of foliage, and there comes a reflected gleam from a corner of the moat not yet overgrown with weeds. But of the huge city whose walls are almost at your feet, and of all the other great piles scattered far and near over the immense plains that surround you, not a vestige is to be seen. There must surely be enchantment in a forest that knows how to keep such enormous secrets from the all-seeing eye of the sun?

In the afternoon the whole scene is altered. The god-like sense of solitude is the same; but the cool, grey melancholy of early morning has been transformed into a glowing splendour painted in a thousand shades of orange and amber, henna and gold. To the west, the Baray, whose silvery waters in the morning had all the inviting freshness of a Thames backwater, seems now, by some occult process to have grown larger; and spreads, gorgeous but sinister, a sheet of burnished copper, reflecting the fiery glow of the westering sun. Beyond it, the forest, a miracle of colour, flows on to be lost in the splendid conflagration; and to the north and east, where the light is less fierce, you can see that the smooth surface of the sea of tree-tops wears here and there all the tints of an English autumn woodland: a whole gamut of glowing crimson, flaring scarlet, chestnut brown, and brilliant yellow; for even these *tropic trees must 'winter'.*

By this light you can see, too, what was hidden in the morning: that for a few miles towards the south, the sweep of forest is interrupted by occasional patches of cultivation; ricefields, dry and golden at this season of the year, where cattle and buffaloes are grazing.

...As for the Great Wat, which in the morning had showed itself an indeterminate black mass against the dawn; in this light, and from this place, it is unutterably magical. You have not quite an aerial view—the Phnom is not high enough for that; and even if it were, the ever-encroaching growth of trees on its steep sides shuts out the view of the Wat's whole immense plan. But you can see enough to realize something of the superb audacity of the architects who dared to embark upon a single plan measuring nearly a mile square. Your point of view is diagonal; across the north-west corner of the moat to the soaring lotus-tip of the central sanctuary, you can trace the perfect balance of every faultless line. Worshipful for its beauty, bewildering in its stupendous size, there is no other point from which the Wat appears so inconceivable an undertaking to have been attempted—much less achieved—by human brains and hands.

But however that may be, even while you watch it, the scene is changing under your eyes. The great warm-grey mass in its setting of foliage, turns from grey to gold; then from gold to amber, glowing with ever deeper and deeper warmth as the sun sinks lower. Purple shadows creep upwards from the moat, covering the galleries, blotting out the amber glow; chasing it higher and higher, over the piled up roofs, till it rests for a while on the tiers of carved pinnacles on the highest towers, where an odd one here and there glitters like cut topaz as the level golden rays strike it. The forest takes on colouring that is ever more autumnal; the Baray for ten seconds is a lake of fire; and then, as though the lights had been turned off the pageant is over...and the moon, close to the full, comes into her own, shining down eerily on the scene that has suddenly become so remote and mysterious; while a cool little breeze blows up from the east, and sends the stiff, dry teak-leaves from the trees on the hillside, down through the branches with a metallic rattle.

There is one more change before this nightly transformation-scene is over: a sort of anti-climax often to be seen in these regions. Soon after the sun has disappeared, an after-glow lights up the scene again so warmly as almost to create the illusion that the driver of the sun's chariot has turned his horses, and come back again. Here on Bakheng, the warm tones of sunset return for a few minutes, but faintly, mingling weirdly with the moonlight, to bring into being effects even more elusively lovely than any that have gone before. Then, they too fade; and the moon, supreme at last, shines down unchallenged on the airy temple.

It is lonelier now. After the gorgeous living pageantry of the scene that went before it, the moon's white radiance and the silence are almost unbearably deathlike: far more eerie than the deep darkness of morning with dawn not far behind. With sunset, the companionable chatter of birds and monkeys in the trees below has ceased; they have all gone punctually to bed; even the cicadas for a wonder are silent. Decidedly it is time to go. Five almost perpendicular flights of narrow-treaded steps leading down into depths of darkness are still between you and the plateau on the top of the Phnom: the kind of steps on which a moment of sudden, silly panic may easily mean a broken neck—such is the bathos of such mild adventures. And once on the plateau you can take your choice of crossing it among the crumbled ruins, and plunging down the straight precipitous trace that was once a stairway—or the easy, winding path through the forest round the south side of the hill, worn by the elephants of the explorers and excavators. Either will bring you to where the twin lions sit in the darkness—black now, for here the trees are too dense to let the moonlight through; and so home along the straight road between its high dark walls of forest, where all sorts of humble, half-seen figures flit noiselessly by on their bare feet, with only a creak now and again from the bundles of firewood they carry, to warn you of their passing. Little points of light twinkle out from unseen houses as you pass a hamlet; and, emerging from the forest to the moat-side, the figures of men fishing with immensely long bamboo rods, from the outer wall, are just dimly visible in silhouette against the moonlit water.

H W Ponder, Cambodian Glory, The Mystery of the Deserted Khmer Cities and their Vanquished Splendour, and a Description of Life in Cambodia today
(Thornton Butterworth, London, 1936)

Khmer Art and Architecture of the Angkor Period

The temples of Angkor are majestic and grand. Their beauty is astonishing and, as you walk through these centuries-old monuments, you are struck by the wonder of the art and architecture. How did the builders manoeuvre such huge blocks of stone? Where did they come from? How was the carving done? The questions that arise are endless as you stare at the wondrous temples. In this chapter we look at the materials and methods the builders used, the architectural features, the profusion of carved decoration that embellishes the walls of the temples, and the symbolism of the forms and motifs.

What is a Khmer temple? It can be one or several structures. Baksei Chamkrong, for example, is a single shrine with one enclosure wall; Preah Khan, on the other hand, is a series of buildings interconnected by passageways with four enclosure walls. The fundamental architectural element of a temple is a shrine in the form of a tower situated at the centre of the plan. The shrine housed the sacred image which embodied the power of the king and represented a symbolic relationship between ruler and divinity. An appropriate temple had to be constructed for the ceremony that consecrated this relationship. Only then was harmony with the order of the universe ensured; without it society could not prosper and proliferate.

The ruler-divinity relationship lasted as long as the king lived, but when he died another ruler started the process anew. He would initiate his own so-called state temple, bigger and grander than his predecessor's, dedicating it to the religion of his preference. It was also common for a king to build a temple dedicated to his parents and other ancestors to ensure the continuation of the royal lineage.

The temple, then, served as a link between man and the gods. It was built according to carefully ordered principles and based on a geometric plan with orientation to the cardinal points. Emphasis was on the east-west axis, which associated the temple with the rising and setting of the sun. Although the cosmological symbolism and astronomical calculations are less understood than other aspects of Khmer architecture, it is clear that the movements of the sun, moon, stars and planets had significant bearing on architectural forms of the Angkor period. Although a temple was never re-used by a succeeding ruler, some, such as Angkor Wat, continued service even after the death of the king and are thought to have functioned as mausoleums containing the ashes of the deceased ruler.

Other elements of a temple include an open area or courtyard around the main tower and a high wall with one or more entry gates on the axis enclosing the entire

Preah Khan's beauty and symmetry have held up well against the test of time.

Encadrement d'une porte du sanctuaire

(above) Line drawing of decoration on a pilaster with a female divinity; (below) cross section of a pilaster.

area. At larger temples, a moat surrounds the wall and is bisected by a raised causeway extending across the moat and up to the entry gate of the enclosure wall.

As the ground plan developed, it expanded outward in size and complexity and more elements were added to the basic ones already mentioned. Long halls appeared in the courtyard. Later, they became continuous galleries. A narrow passageway with columns or walls and windows surrounding the central buildings were common components of temples from the 11th century onwards. Pavilions in the corners on each level of a tiered base increased the complexity of the temple. Galleries, porches, halls, terraces, bathing pools, more towers and more enclosure walls were other additions. You can perceive the different layouts and components of a temple by studying the ground plans which accompany most of the descriptions in this guide.

In addition to building state and ancestor temples, a king solidified his power by constructing a *baray*, or large reservoir, and naming it after himself. A *baray* is easily recognisable because of its rectangular shape and east-west orientation. A temple positioned on an artificial island in the centre reinforced the aesthetic and symbolic significance of the *baray*.

The first one, Indratatakata, was built in the ninth century at the ancient capital of Hariharalaya (today Roluos), south of Angkor. This vast *baray* (3,200 by 750 metres; 10,500 by 2,500 feet) was constructed to store rainwater for use during the dry season and to supply water for the surrounding rice fields on the plain of Roluos. It marked the beginning of royal-sponsored irrigation works during the Angkor period.

The next king, Yasovarman I, built an even larger *baray* (7,000 by 1,800 metres; 23,000 by 5,900 feet) during the first year of his reign in the late ninth century. The Yasodharatataka, now known as the East Baray, lies east of the Siem Reap River. An estimated 6,000 workers took three years to build this *baray*.

Yet another vast reservoir, the West Baray (8,000 by 2,100 metres; 26,000 by 6,900 feet), was probably started in the 11th century by Suryavarman I and finished somewhat later by Udayadityavarman II. The only one filled with water today, it was occasionally used as a landing area for seaplanes in the middle of this century. An-

other, the Jayatataka (3,700 by 900 metres; 12,100 by 2,900 feet), lies west of Preah Khan and is about half the size of the East Baray. It was built by Jayavarman VII in the second half of the 12th century. The small temple of Neak Pean is situated on an island at the centre of this *baray*, which is often referred to as the Preah Khan or Northern Baray.

(above) Line drawing of a false door with decorative centre panel and a pattern of rosettes; (below) cross section of a door.

The function of the *barays* has recently been the subject of debate amongst modern scholars. The symbolic association between a *baray* and the king, as a divine protector of his people and provider for their welfare, is undisputed. Inscriptions commemorating the consecration of Yasodharatataka, found in the four corners, testify to the religious significance of the *baray*. The original theory as to the practical function held that *barays* and a network of canals, laid out in a rectangular grid, were part of a hydrological system on the scale of

those instituted by civilisations at Babylon, Egypt and pre-Columbian Mexico. Engineers and historians have more recently questioned, however, whether these *barays* were part of a centralised irrigation system. The absence of archaeological and historical evidence supporting a widespread, controlled irrigation system raises questions as to whether the Khmers had the knowledge of advanced irrigation techniques. It also questions whether they ever engineered this kind of system, or were even capable of flood control on a such a large scale.

The original theory presumed that the 'three or four rice harvests a year' noted by Zhou Daguan, the 13th century Chinese emissary who lived at Angkor for a year and wrote an account of his observations, meant that the Khmers engaged in irrigated rice agriculture. Curiously, though, Zhou Daguan did not mention the *barays* that dominated the surrounding areas of the city of Angkor Thom, nor is there any mention of an irrigation system in over 1,200 inscriptions. Further doubt is cast by results of aerial photography, which show that the canals at Angkor connect with the moats surrounding the walls of temples, rather than with a feeder system to carry the water from the *barays* to the rice fields for irrigation.

In light of this evidence it has been suggested that the control of water was on a small scale and just sufficient to support flood retreat rice cultivation. Another idea is that the *barays* were built only for urban use to provide water for bathing, drinking and transportation.

Despite this recent evidence, the original theory should not be discarded until further research is conducted and results are analysed. An understanding of the role of water at Angkor and the Khmers' manipulation of it is crucial to elucidation of the whole complex.

BUILDING MATERIALS USED IN THE MONUMENTS

The Khmers used limited materials to develop a style of architecture renowned for its beauty and creativity. The following is a brief description of those materials commonly found in the monuments.

TIMBER

The earliest structures were built of wood, but because of its perishable nature, most of the evidence has disappeared. Wood, as in India, was a revered material and reserved for exclusive use by kings, court officials and priests. As such, it played an important role in the decoration of temple complexes. Domestic timber structures for royalty would have included the superstructure of the king's palace and administrative buildings. A relief in a fronton at Banteay Srei depicts a palace on stilts with a tiered roof and gives a glimpse of what the wooden structures may have looked like.

Nature and man — a unique and acquired relationship at Angkor.

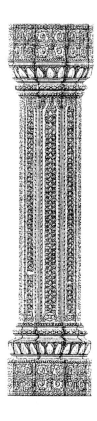

(above) Elaborately decorated pillar with a band of lotus petals at the top and bottom; (below) cross section of pillar base.

The detail of this relief is so complete that you can get an idea of the furnishings, fabrics and window treatments of the period. Besides buildings, wood was also used for temple furniture, such as altar tables and canopies for images, structural supports and decoration in Khmer architecture.

Evenly spaced, circular indentations or post-holes in the paving of the lower sanctuary at Phnom Bakheng from the east side suggest a canopy supported by wooden posts once stood there. Carved timber, double doors would have been placed in all doorways leading to towers or shrines. There are visible remains of timbers used as lintels on the third level of Angkor Wat. A wooden coffered ceiling would have covered the cavernous space created by the corbel vaults; carved and painted with lotus motives and even gilded for added highlights. A modern concrete reconstruction of a timber coffered ceiling has been installed by the EFEO as an example in the south-east gallery at Angkor Wat.

Jointing techniques used in carpentry were often transferred to sandstone constructions, leaving a long legacy that lasted throughout the Angkor period. Some common carpentry techniques, recognisable in the stone work, are the mitred joints used to frame window and door openings. Examples of designs borrowed from timber decorations are the turned balusters used in window openings and the octagonal columns on either side of door openings and the elaborately carved colonettes.

BRICK

This was the first durable material used in the construction of Khmer temples. Whereas all wooden structures have disappeared, remains of several brick structures dating to the sixth century have been found at pre-Angkor sites. The earliest from the Angkor period are the three ninth-century temples of the Roluos group, Bakong, Lolei and Preah Ko. Another fine example is the single brick shrine at Baksei Chamkrong — its near-perfect proportions and majestic base give this temple a special appeal. The towers at East Mebon and Preah Rup are also built of brick, but have suffered more than others from the effects of weathering. In the central tower of Prasat Kravan, extraordinary, imposing brick carvings of the Hindu god Vishnu and his wife (Laksmi) decorate the interior. Bricks used for Khmer temples were most likely fired in nearby kilns, as the region has abundant suitable clay. Brick structures were built using rectangular bricks which were bonded with a vegetable-base mortar for strength and solidity.

STUCCO

From the beginning of the Angkor period, stucco was used selectively for fine decoration to disguise the brickwork. The Khmers produced some exquisite and delicate undercut stucco decoration which some believe is unequalled. The composition of the stucco was a mixture of slaked lime, sand, tamarind, sugar palm and clay from termite mounds. Holes were pierced in the brick walls in horizontal and vertical rows or the stone work was roughened to provide a better bonding or key. These holes can be seen at the towers of the East Mebon. The stucco may have been embellished even further with painting or gilding. Over the centuries most of the stucco has disintegrated because of the elements. Remarkably, however, some examples have survived over ten centuries and can be seen at Preah Ko and Bakong. A painstaking programme to conserve the stucco of the former has recently been completed.

SANDSTONE

Initially introduced into Khmer architecture for decorating door and window openings, sandstone had eclipsed brick as the main building material by the late tenth century. Sandstone is generally a durable material and is ideal for carved decoration, which Khmer artisans accomplished with great skill. Later, its use extended to building façades, roofs, galleries with columns, and halls. You only need to look at the false doors of Bakong, the tympanums of Banteay Srei or the bas-reliefs of Angkor Wat to see the high quality of competency in this medium.

The main quarries for sandstone were located in the Kulen hills, or Phnom Kulen, some 30 kilometres (19 miles) north-east of Angkor. Sandstone used in temples from the late 12th century onwards is often of inferior quality and suggests that the source of superior grey/green sandstone had been depleted. The different types of sandstone used for the monuments of Angkor were probably determined by availability. The sandstone at early temples, such as the Roluos group, is fine grained and gives a sharpness of detail. The pinkish sandstone of Banteay Srei enabled a crisp chiselling effect that is reminiscent of wood carving — some say this temple even smells like sandalwood. Reliefs at the Bayon were carved from a softer volcanic sandstone, which enabled a deeper carving, but with less sharpness than other types. One of the most beautiful sculptures ever created by the Khmers, the 'Lady of Koh Krieng' in the National Museum in Phnom Penh, is carved from a rare greenish sandstone. This so-called 'waxed sandstone' has a dark patina and a high polish.

LATERITE

Laterite is a porous, aerated mudstone that is found in abundance throughout Cambodia and north-eastern Thailand. At the time of quarrying the high water content makes it soft, but when exposed to sunlight it hardens. Laterite cannot be finely carved or sculpted because of its coarse grain, but it was used to build foundations, the internal structure of thick walls and for the construction of plinths, bridges and roads. You can see laterite cores behind sandstone facades in many of the temple-mountain edifices and especially at Angkor Wat. In the 13th century, laterite was often used in place of sandstone for the construction of walls and roofs, perhaps because the source of sandstone was depleted; laterite was probably excavated from the moats surrounding the temples. It was open quarried, cut into blocks, dressed and then left in the sun to harden; any soft clay around the blocks was washed away.

METAL

Sheets of copper or bronze may have lined the walls of important central shrines where the sacred image was housed. Regular holes in the walls of the main approach and the central shrine at Preah Khan suggest this function. Although there is no trace of the metal, its use could explain the plainness of the interiors today. Metal was certainly used to embellish the temples in other areas such as spires on central shrines as noted by the 13th-century Chinese observer, Zhou Daguan. He described the 'Golden Tower (of the Bayon), a golden bridge guarded by two lions of gold, with eight golden Buddhas; and a Tower of Bronze (the Baphuon) that was even higher than the golden ones'.[25]

FIRED CLAY TILES

Zhou Daguan also noted that yellow glazed, fired clay tiles had been used on the roofs of temples. A typical tile is rectangular and curved on the upper surface with a nib that enabled it to interlock with another. Fragments of unglazed tiles of similar form have been found during restoration of several temples and still litter the ground at Banteay Samre.

Several buildings also suggest that the roofs were pitched and covered with fired clay tiles. The two-storey pavilion at Preah Khan and structures leading to the Bakong clearly show the use of timber rafters which would have supported the tiles.

METHODS OF CONSTRUCTION

As you walk through the temples you will probably wonder where the enormous blocks of stone came from and how they were transported and put into place. The accomplishment of these tasks is considered one of the great technical achievements of the Khmers.

A scene on the west side, south aisle of the inner gallery of the Bayon depicts some of the methods used in handling the stone blocks. The sandstone was cut from the quarry face, shaped into blocks of random size and floated along the Siem Reap River from Phnom Kulen to Angkor. The blocks were then transported to the building site by elephant or ox

An intricately carved floral and geometric pattern.

cart, depending on the sizes. Pairs of bamboo pegs were driven into specially pre-pared holes—two sets to a block—and linked by ropes. The blocks could then be hoisted into place using tripods, leavers and pulleys.

The basic form of construction used for stone structures, such as towers, pavil-ions and galleries, was a base or platform. In cases of temple-mountains, a high plat-form would be formed using laterite to shape the platform, which would be filled with rammed earth. In most cases the laterite would be covered by sandstone blocks. All structures would be built with blocks of dressed, but uncarved stone, which would be carefully bedded and in many cases matched with very complicated shapes to mirror the joint of the adjacent stone. The joints themselves are remarkably fine and tight, even today, as they were laboriously rubbed to form an exact match. Stones would be ground together with abrasive sand between them, and rocked back and forth until a tight joint was formed.

In the construction of the towers, it is strange that the stones were seldom keyed together. Instead, vertical joints were laid one on top of the other, creating an inher-ent weakness in the structure and a place where tree and vine roots could easily lodge and prise the structures apart. No mortar was used between the stones and only occasionally would stones be held together with metal clamps. As metal was a valuable commodity, stone joints have been cut open by looters to remove the metal clamps at many temples.

Once in place and only then, were the structures decorated. No doubt hundreds of stone carvers would have been employed to rough out and finish *in situ* the de-signs of the master carvers. There are many examples which clearly indicate that this was the process used. The joints between stones bear no relationship to the figures carved on them. For example joints will often cut through a head or face. In many instances, the actual window opening has been only partly cut with a simple archi-tectural decoration traced around the opening. In the case of the reliefs, several sections show where designs have been 'sketched' by the chisel of the master carver and are still awaiting completion.

TYPICAL ARCHITECTURAL FEATURES

One of the overriding design features of the Khmer temples is the symmetry with which they were built. Layouts of temples and monasteries are all symmetrical around a central axis. This symmetry provides mirrored images, profiles or silhou-ettes around a central dominant architectural feature such as the central tower on the grand scale or the main porticos on the axial routes.

There are several distinct architectural features common throughout Khmer architecture and typically seen at Angkor. For ease of recognition, these features are described in some detail in the following pages. As the architectural themes were largely imported from south India the original nomenclature has also been retained. A typical example of this is *gopura* meaning 'gateway' or 'entry tower'.

TEMPLE MOUNTAIN

The Khmers adapted the Indian concept of a temple-mountain so successfully and uniquely that today it is synonymous with Khmer architecture. Kings of the early Angkor period established their sovereignty by building a temple-mountain. The temple draws its symbolism from Hindu mythology. It is an earthly facsimile of Mount Meru, the sacred abode of the gods. The temple as a microcosm of a central mountain was an essential concept that had a profound influence on Khmer art.

The physical form is a square-shaped tower elevated on a tiered base. Some temple-mountains, such as Phnom Bakheng, were built on natural hills, but artificial mounds like the one constructed at Preah Rup provided the basis for others. The earliest temple-mountain of the Angkor period is Bakong, a single shrine set on a tiered base. By its height in the tenth century, however, the temple-mountain concept had expanded to a five-tower arrangement, or the quincunx, with a central tower and four smaller towers placed on the corners at the top level of a tiered base. Four axial staircases, often guarded on each tier by pairs of stone lions sculpted in the round, gave access to the top level of the temple-mountain. This formation of five towers symbolises the five peaks of Mount Meru. The central shrine was sometimes given additional height with porches and steps on each side. Preah Rup and Ta Keo are fine examples of this majestic feature.

The symbolism of Mount Meru appears in both Hindu and Buddhist mythology and, although the legends differ somewhat, the general theme remains the same. The world is a central continent divided into regions with heavens above and hells below. Mount Meru separates earth from the heavens and is situated at the exact centre of the continent. Six concentric chains of mountains surround Meru and they are separated by six oceans. The Ocean of Infinity encloses the entire mass. Symbolically, Meru marks the axis of the world and the chains of mountains represent the successive stages towards knowledge.

It is believed by Hindus that Mount Meru, which is associated with the Himalayas in Central Asia, is ruled by Indra and is the mythical dwelling place of Brahma and other gods. The mountain is surrounded by eight guardians at each cardinal and sub-cardinal point. In Buddhism, a continent shaped liked an island lies beyond the ocean in each of the four cardinal regions of space. Layers of heavens soar above Mount Meru. The four rulers of the cardinal points live at the summit of the mountain. Fantastic animals inhabit the forest at the base of the mountain, which serves as a refuge for ascetics to meditate.

MONASTIC COMPLEX

In strong contrast to the concept of the temple-mountain, the monastic complexes are an intricate but symmetrical plan laid out on a horizontal plane, as opposed to the strong vertical emphasis. However, comparisons are possible in the concentric walls representing the platforms getting smaller in plan as they rise, and an almost indiscernible difference in height between the entrance and the central shrine. The main entrance to the monastery and its principal temple follows a similar pattern from the east, is lined with guardians and is proportionally grander than other access points.

However, the monastery is like a small town and within the first enclosure wall there was space for the community to live. In Preah Khan, for example, the inscription tells of a community of 97,840 being closely associated with the monastery. The second enclosure wall envelopes the temple proper and from this point the complex gives the appearance of being on a higher level. The temple complex is further divided into a series of different sectors by cloistered arcades and courtyards, but the layout focuses on the central shrine.

It is often difficult to find ones bearings in these monastic complexes especially as many of them have become ruinous. It is worthwhile studying a plan of the complex to get an understanding of its layout. Originally doors would have enclosed each space and would only have been opened to permit worshipping monks to enter the sanctuaries. Therefore, most of the spaces would have been dark and gloomy, a fact often forgotten as you look along the 100 metre (320 feet) long axial corridors.

GOPURA

A *gopura* or gateway is the main architectural feature of the wall that surrounds a Khmer temple. The name, which is derived from Sanskrit, originated in the 7th century Pallava architecture of south India. Even in its simplest form, the *gopura* placed on the principal axes stands out in contrast to the simple laterite wall. Early *gopuras* are rectangular in plan, but later, as the form developed in complexity, they became cruciform. Over time, they were built much larger and more elaborately, with extensions such as porches and steps.

By the 12th century, the proportions were such that they took on the appearance of separate buildings. A good example of this is the *gopura* of the outer enclosure wall at the west entrance of Angkor Wat. A new form appeared in the 13th century, and contrasted dramatically with the profile of the earlier *gopura*. The new style which provided access to the Angkor Thom complex soared to a height of over 20 metres (65 feet) and is crowned with four enormous heads, possibly representing the Buddha or the profile of Jayavarman VII, one facing in each cardinal direction.

False window openings carved in stone are characteristic of Khmer artistry.

Causeway

The combination of a causeway and a moat provided a dramatic backdrop for the *naga* or serpent balustrade that made its first appearance at Bakong in the ninth century. In this example, the *naga* was not carried by gods and demons, a theme that did not become fully developed until the 13th century. Long rows of giant stone figures sculpted in the round—majestic gods on one side of the causeway and ferocious demons on the other—flank the causeway from end to end and hold the scaly body of the *naga* whose head and tail rise up at each end of the causeway. You can see splendid examples of *naga* balustrades at the entrances to Angkor Thom, although many of the heads are missing as a result of theft. Others have been replaced with copies, and the originals taken to the Conservation Office store, to prevent further loss.

Enclosure Wall

One of the most striking features following the *gopura* and the causeway are the massive enclosure walls that surround most of the temple complexes. The purpose of these walls was to provide psychological barriers between the communities — they were never intended as fortifications — and to differentiate between the sacred and the profane. In many of the monastic complexes, for example, there are as many as three or four concentric walls defining the usage of space. The walls

(left) A female divinity in a niche; (above) Garuda, the mount of the Hindu god, Vishnu.

were built of the coarse, yellow laterite stone, which contrasted well with the fine sandstone of the *gopura*. In some cases the walls were also embellished with sandstone decoration and were capped with a row of continuous carved images such as the Buddha in flaming niches. A singular example of rather grandiose embellishment are the three- metre high *garudas* that are placed every 40 metres (130 feet) around the outer enclosure wall of Preah Khan.

SIKHARA OR TOWER
The tower is the predominant architectural feature of Angkor. Its form is derived from the south Indian temple, which has an easily recognisable silhouette. The base stands firm on a platform with symmetrical doorways on each façade. These doorways either open or are false, depending on the use of the tower. Above the cornice level, the tower begins to taper slowly at the base, but more pronounced towards the top creating a rounded effect. The tower is crowned with a lotus, which possibly served as the base for a gilded metal spire — a typical feature in other Asian temples. The tower is constructed with cantilevered stones following the principles of vault corbelled construction with the exposed outer surface being elaborately carved. Often there are added embellishments to the towers such as the flamelike acroteria seen on the towers at Angkor Wat.

PAVILION OR SHRINE
Pavilions and shrines are more often isolated or paired structures that encompass the designs and details of the larger structures only much smaller in size. They are normally constructed in exactly the same way, with vaulted roofs, doors and window openings as well as similar decorative features. They are often located in pairs on either side of the axial route leading to the temple proper.

During the early period of research, the EFEO tended to refer to all single structures as *bibliothèque* or 'library' following its discovery of scenes from the legend of the 'Nine Planets of the Earth' carved on the stones of one such building. In some cases, these structures did serve as libraries where the sacred texts were kept. But more recent research suggests most of them were chapels to house *agni*, the sacred flame; or pilgrims' rest houses or family shrines.

CORBELLED VAULT
The Khmers generally used the corbelled vault to form a roof between walls and columns. This reliance on the most primitive type of arch reverts no doubt to the Indian influence on Khmer architecture. Corbelled vaults are constructed by cantilevering rectangular blocks and projecting each stone one third of its length from

each side until the span between walls can be capped by a single ridge stone. Khmer architects carried this method to remarkable heights as can be seen in the constructions of the central shrine at Ta Keo, where enormous blocks of stone were carefully cantilevered, one on top of the other, from each of the walls until they met in the centre. The construction of a corbelled vault obviously limits the spans that can be achieved and its exclusive and continuous use in buildings of the Angkor period accounts for the narrow galleries and passageways that are prominent in Khmer architecture. To experience the volume and narrowness created by corbelled vaults, walk through the long gallery on the third level of the Baphuon.

TYPICAL ARTISTIC FEATURES

As with the architectural features, much of the artistry was derived from concepts imported from south India. But because of the Khmers' remarkable artistic talents they were able to embellish these concepts in many wonderful ways. It is hard to believe that the artistry found in the decorated lintels and the kilometres of reliefs is often over nine hundred years old, centuries before the Rococo work of Europe and South America.

STATUARY

Khmer sculpture is among the finest in the world. Remarkable figures in stone and bronze reflect the skills of Khmer artists. An excellent starting point for visitors to Angkor is the National Museum in Phnom Penh, which has the finest and most extensive collection of Khmer sculpture in the world. Life-size sculptures carved in stone were an integral part of temple architecture. Guardians protecting the temple, lions guarding stairways, elephants adding grandeur to tiered platforms and sensitive renditions of the Buddha and of the gods and goddesses graced all Khmer temples, adding dimension and majesty to their overall appearance. Today, most of the free-standing sculptures have been stolen or removed for safe keeping, somewhat diminishing the significance of the temples.

At several of the sites there are still decorative pieces in the form of free-standing guardian lions, the torsos of *dvarapala* — guardians armed with clubs; the multi-headed *naga* — protective snakes; the *deva* and *asura* or gods and demons, often supporting the *naga* on either side of the causeway and the *garuda* or mythical bird which serves as protector. There are also elements of worship such as the *linga* and *yoni*, symbolic Shivaite images of the male and female, which represent destruction and rebirth, and the *stelae*, beautifully inscribed stones with information on the foundation and function of the temples, are still present in many of the complexes.

RELIEFS

Reliefs carved in stone are among the greatest artistic achievements of the Khmers. Narrative scenes inspired by the great Hindu epics, the *Ramayana* and the *Mahabarata*, sacred books and military history of the period unfold on the walls of temples conveying sublime beauty, power, majesty, humour and always consummate good taste. Rows of graceful *apsaras* or celestial nymphs line a cornice in perfect unison or dance lithely on a lotus, geometric medallions filled with an intricate floral and leaf motif cover walls like tapestry, fantastic mythical beasts bound across the walls, battle scenes spring to life — the scenarios created in the reliefs provide endless fascination and make you want to return again and again. The reliefs surpass the function of portraying events; they transform the temples into celestial dwellings.

The carved decoration at Angkor Wat is called bas or 'low'-relief, whereas the deeper carving at the Bayon is haut or 'high'-relief, depending on the degree of undercutting. Khmer artists struggled with the technique of perspective or the creation of a three-dimensional illusion. To show objects and people in the distance, the

Female divinities in niches and a lintel above a doorway, damaged by nature and looters.

Khmers used planes, placed one above the other. The higher up the wall, the further away is the scene. Sometimes even seven or eight planes were used to establish the right degree of perspective. Another convention used to show scale was to carve faces peering through gaps or behind the wheels of a chariot.

As in Egyptian art, a person's rank was indicated by size — the higher the ranking the greater the size. Khmer artists incorporated detail with finesse as a means of controlling the composition, and remarkable results were achieved using only shape and texture. Even the crowded, complex scenes which most of them are, have an underlying form. For example, the bas relief of the 'Churning of the Ocean of Milk' in the south-east gallery at Angkor Wat culminates in the centre with the divinity Vishnu, the largest and most important figure, balanced on either side by the smaller in scale divinities and demons; the top of the panel depicts an ethereal scene of floating *apsaras* offset at the bottom with the mighty ocean of milk. By deliberately placing important elements in key positions and balancing the components in the distance, middle and background, an ordered composition was achieved.

There is a sheen to be seen on the surface of some of reliefs at Angkor Wat. Some say that the position of the sheen may have resulted from visitors rubbing their hands over them. Others think it was the result of applying a lacquer in former times. There are also traces of gilding and black and red paint are visible too, which are probably the remains of an undercoat or a fixative.

Apsaras

The *apsaras* or celestial nymphs are sensuous, graceful females which adorn the temple walls and they are amongst the most beautiful examples of relief carving. French art historians differentiate between the figures depending on their stance. Those who dance or fly are referred to as *apsaras,* while the standing figures are called *devatas.* The generic term used in this guide refers to all female figures carved in relief as *apsaras* because of the wide usage and acceptance of this name.

Window Openings

Openings to windows were protected by finely-turned stone balusters. The designs drew inspiration from similar constructions in wood. This window treatment has become a hallmark of Khmer architecture and a variation often seen to simulate a symmetrical facade is a solid window depicting balusters on the lower half and a roller blind on the upper portion.

Doorways

A set of intricately sculpted collonettes flanking doorways and supporting lintels are a regular feature in a Khmer temple. The carving on the octagonal drums which reached a high artistic level varies, but it is always elaborate and divided into registers by rings and decorated with popular motifs, flowers and leaves between them. False doors are the same size and shape as a true door, but instead of being built of wood they are carved from sandstone.

A typical arrangement in a tower used as a shrine is an opening door on the principal axis, usually facing east, with false doors on the remaining three sides as design features. Sometimes a flight of stairs precedes the false door, adding height and elegance. The stone work framing the false door emulates the decoration that was carved on the surface of the timber, double-leaf door in every detail. The motifs and workmanship on the false doors represent some of the most beautiful elements in Khmer architecture. A lion's face in place of a brass door knocker is a special ninth-century feature found on the towers of Bakong.

LINTELS

Lintels in Khmer architecture are highly decorated rectangular sandstone blocks spanning a doorway, window or any opening, and often support the fronton. The Khmers carved the face of the lintel with superb decoration that filled the entire space with scenes inspired by mythology, as well as intricate floral motifs and fanciful beasts. The fine grain and hardness of the grey sandstone used on the earliest lintels enabled crisp and skilfully undercut sculpting. The decorative lintels of the East Mebon temple and those found at the Roluos group exhibit remarkably fine workmanship.

A typical decorative arrangement on an early lintel includes for example Vishnu on his mount, the garuda, surmounting the head of a monster, *kala*, spewing garlands with jewelled tassels; a pattern of foliage surrounds this central scene and fills out the lintel; small personages or fanciful animals sometimes frolic lithely among the flowers and leaves; and the scaly crocodile-like body of the mythical beast, *makara*, borders the entire scene and terminates with heads at the bottom left and right sides of the lintel.

FRONTONS OR PEDIMENTS

Fronton is more commonly used at Angkor to describe the pediment or triangular motif above a lintel normally located over a portico or door. Some of the best examples can be found in Khmer art of the tenth century at Banteay Srei. A fronton is the source of rich decoration, especially for narrative scenes for divinities set in abundant foliage. Two undulating *nagas* with multiple heads often frame the interior. At Banteay Srei three frontons have been superimposed, which is an innovation of great beauty. The head of a *kala*, spewing a five-headed serpent is a motif that also made its first appearance at Banteay Srei. This popular theme lasted throughout the Angkor

period. The frontons at Angkor Wat are mainly narrative scenes and draw inspiration from Hindu mythology, particularly the *Ramayana*.

STYLISTIC PERIODS OF KHMER ART AND ARCHITECTURE

Khmer art and architecture are divided into stylistic periods, each one designated by the name of the principal architectural monument that exhibits the most characteristic elements of the period. The chronology used in this guide follows that developed by Philippe Stern and is the one generally accepted today. General comments on sculpture are included, but the development of the dress in male and female figures has been omitted because there are so few examples of sculpture remaining at Angkor. The following paragraphs summarise the evolution of Khmer art and architecture and provide the names, dates and monuments associated with each stylistic period from the sixth to the thirteenth century.

PRE-ANGKOR PERIOD (6TH TO LATE 8TH CENTURY)

The earliest temple remains in Cambodia date from the sixth century and are to be found in the south-eastern region, 25 kilometres (15 miles) north of Kompong Thom. Indian-inspired elements in the early pre-Angkor temples such as a moulded plinth, a carved lintel and a corbelled vault set the foundation for the architectural principles of the classical Angkor period. Pre-Angkor sculpture was elegant with refined detail that, like its architecture, drew inspiration from India. The form and anatomy of the sculpture was naturalistic and, in profile, the stance is slightly curved. Garments are diaphanous and cling to the body.

ANGKOR PERIOD (802-1432)

The earliest stylistic period in this group is the **Kulen style**. Today the Kulen Mountain range, from which this style derives its name, is inaccessible. The few remaining temples there are in poor condition and, in some cases, just heaps of stones, which makes it difficult to appreciate the art form and decoration.

The most easily accessed, earliest group of temples is at Roluos, 12 kilometres (7 miles) south-east of Siem Reap, which belong to the **Preah Ko style**, dating from the last quarter of the ninth century. The simplest form of a tower can be seen at Preah Ko. It is a square brick structure built on a low plinth and faces east. The upper part of the sanctuary comprises square brick tiers each of a diminishing size. The tiers on buildings of this period are easily identifiable as each one emulates the façade of the shrine below. Miniature false doors are seen at the axis on each tier.

A natural development of the single tower was to build between three and six towers all similar in size, forming and aligning them in one or two rows at ground

A buddha image seated on a naga base.

level or on a platform. Concurrent with the expansion of more towers at ground level, the temple mountain concept increased in importance. Although it is uncertain when the first temple-mountain form appeared, it is probable that the temple of Bakong in Roluos was the earliest to be constructed at Angkor.

Sculpture of the Preah Ko style is characterised by an architectonic rigidity, and the figures are heavier and more powerful than pre-Angkor examples. Sculptures of standing gods are awesome and large-scale, sometimes over life-size. The Khmers invented a special arch around the sculpture to support these large and heavy images which grew from the base at the back of the sculpture and framed the entire standing figure. Either the hands or attributes and the back of the head were attached to the arch. Several examples of this convention can be seen in the National Museum in Phnom Penh. The form appeared in the seventh century and continued in use until the ninth century at which time sculptures became smaller and they did not require the extra support.

The great architectural innovation of the **Bakheng style** was the temple-mountain structure with five towers arranged in a quincunx. The temple that gives its name to the art style stands majestically on top of a 67-metre (220 feet) hill overlooking Angkor Wat, whose form was derived from it. Other examples of temples belonging to this style are Phnom Krom (ninth-tenth centuries) and Phnom Bok (tenth century), both built on natural hills.

The art and architecture of the **Koh Ker style** reflects the tyranny of that time. In AD 921 Jayavarman IV, a usurper, set up a rival capital about 64 kilometres (40 miles) east of Angkor at Koh Ker that lasted for about 20 years. Little remains of the mainly brick temples, but there are some remarkable examples of free-standing sculpture from this period in the National Museum. They are a departure from previous examples of sculpture as, for the first time in Khmer art, they express movement. The figures are also very large, some say because the king was a megalomaniac. Two outstanding pieces of this style in the National Museum are a pair of wrestlers and Sugriva and Valin, the monkey-headed brothers from the *Ramayana,* locked in hand-to-hand combat.

The architectural achievement of the middle of the tenth century can be found in the **Pre Rup style**. The temple of this name is a remarkable example of the temple-mountain built by Rajendravarman II. It is an impressive site with five towers which were formerly stuccoed, arranged in a quincunx on top of a very high tiered, laterite platform with steep staircases leading up to the top. A neighbouring temple, the East Mebon, is of the same period and design although its platform is not so elevated.

The **Banteay Srei style** has given one of the most endearing legacies to posterity, that is the temple of the same name. Situated 19 kilometres (12 miles) north-east of Angkor, its size and scale are diminutive in comparison to the temple-mountain structures of Angkor. A magnificent sculpture from Banteay Srei, now in the National Museum, which depicts the seated image of the Hindu divinity Shiva with Uma on his knee, typical of the sculptural skills of this period. The head of Uma was unfortunately stolen from the museum in the 1970s.

The **Kleang style** is represented by two long rectangular sandstone structures known as the North and South Kleangs. The function of these buildings is constantly being debated and, although the name means 'storehouse', it has been suggested that they served as halls or for receiving foreign dignitaries. Another key temple of this style is the majestic temple-mountain of Ta Keo with its mighty five towers with no carved decoration. The lack of adornment emphasises the massive stone blocks and the complexity of the temple's construction as well as the remarkable use of space and volume.

When the **Baphuon style** was developed in the middle of the 11th century, temples had reached gigantic proportions. Continuous vaulted and columned galleries, which were constructed off tiered platforms, were common features of this period and they formerly encircled the central tower at Baphuon. The sculpture of the Baphuon style is very distinctive as it moved towards a new form, which was even more naturalistic than previous styles. Gods and goddesses were still idealised, but with more apparent realism, and their lines and volumes flow harmoniously.

The Khmers' artistic genius culminated in the **Angkor Wat style** of the first half of the 12th century, and the temple-mountain reached its apogee at Angkor Wat. Encircling galleries, vaulted passages, elaborate porches leading to towers, grand staircases between terraces and an extensive gallery of bas-reliefs complimented the temple plan. Despite its complexity, the elements blend together with remarkable harmony and balance. Tower pinnacles in the form of a lotus are a distinctive silhouette of Angkor Wat and their profile has become synonymous with Cambodia, gracing all five of the recent variations of the national flag. The sculpture of the Angkor Wat style was inspired by forms of the first half of the tenth century. Figures are distinguised by a frontal stance, symmetrical posture and wide shoulders and hips.

The **Bayon style** is a synthesis of the previous styles which is characterised in the Buddhist temples of the late 12th and early 13th centuries. The temples are of a complex architectural layout constructed at ground level and auxiliary structures including interconnected galleries and rooms. Examples of this type of temple style are the Buddhist monastic complexes of Banteay Kdei, Preah Khan and Ta Prohm. The sculpture of the Bayon style reflects the new religious beliefs of that time and is best exemplified in the image of the Avalokiteshvara (Lokeshvara), or Lord of Infinite Compassion, which is identified by a small seated Buddha at the base of the crown. Images of the Buddha seated on the coils of the *naga* are associated with sculpture of the Bayon period.

Following pages: the Khmer army in a battle with the Chams, Outer Gallery of Reliefs, Bayon.

COSMOLOGY IN KHMER ARCHITECTURE

The layout, architecture and decoration of a Khmer temple were modelled according to a series of magical and religious beliefs. Devotees moved from the mundane world to a spiritual one by walking along one of the four axes, each of which has a different astrological value.

East, the direction of the rising sun, is auspicious, representing life and the sexual prowess of the male. Most of the Khmer temples were built with the entrance to the east, as this was the formal approach to most Hindu shrines except for Angkor Wat. For example, the main approach to Angkor Wat, which originally housed images of Vishnu, is from the west. In general, however, west is considered inauspicious and represents death, impurity and the setting sun. North is also auspicious and is associated with the elephant because of its strength. South has a neutral value.

Numbers represent universal order

A frieze of apsaras in the Hall of the Dancers, Preah Khan.

and serve as a means of effecting the interplay between man and the gods. Numerous mathematical schemes have been put forth to explain the proportional measurements of specific temples and, in particular, Angkor Wat. The Khmers adhered to the Hindu belief that a temple must be built correctly according to a mathematical system in order for it to function in harmony with the universe. Thus, if the measurements of the temple are perfect then there will be perfection in the universe also.

A study has shown that when Angkor Wat was laid out by the Khmers originally, the distances between certain architectural elements of the temple reflect numbers

related to Hindu mythology and cosmology. The positions of the bas-reliefs were regulated for example by solar movement. Scenes on the east-west reflect those related to the rising and setting of the sun.

Under the surface of the earth are numerous hells and above it are paradises or heavens. Hell in Khmer cosmology is a place of suffering where the damned expiate their sins and crimes and each hell is more horrific than the last. Afterwards they are reborn to begin a new life. In the south gallery of bas-reliefs at Angkor Wat, the sins and the punishments of its 32 hells are depicted. There are numerous paradises above the earth, and above the last one is *nirvana* or heaven. The duration of life in these paradises increases at each higher level with earth representing neutrality.

Preservation at Angkor

— John Sanday

Evidence suggests that some monuments remained in use after Angkor was abandoned by its royal sponsors as a political centre. However, most have been neglected since the 15th or 16th centuries, until the EFEO began its work at the beginning of the 20th century. During this time, most of the monuments had been engulfed by the jungle and seen little or no maintenance, and it is a wonder that so many structures are still standing. This situation has led to some unusual material and structural failures in the monuments, which will be an interesting highlight for the visitor.

The engineering concepts were very poor and are the main reason for the state of collapse of most of the principal structures. The stones were originally laid as large blocks with no mortar or metal fixings to hold them together. Inadequate bonding between stones, even though great trouble was taken to create perfect and tight joints, and crude vaulting in nearly all cases to form the roof structures, are the principle causes for failure.

Another inherent problem was the selection of sandstone taken from quarries in the Kulen Hills. The quality and strength of stone differed depending from which part of the quarry it was taken. Stones used in Angkor Wat, for example, have eroded badly, mainly because of the quality of the stone and the presence of bentonite clays in the stratification of the stone beds. Bentonite expands when it is exposed to water and causes the stratification to flake. In nearly all cases, stones have been bedded vertically. As sedimentation takes place in the quarry. The beds are naturally laid on a horizontal bed. Because length is required, the columns are cut along the horizontal bed and are upended to form monolithic columns; the stone, therefore, is laid on a vertical bed and moisture can creep, by capillary attraction, between the sedimentation layers causing the bentonite clay to expand and, subsequently, the stone to spall. Most damage to the base of columns and walls at Angkor Wat, and elsewhere, is caused by this phenomena.

Damage to the structures has been attributed also to the rise and fall of the water table causing rising damp and foundation settlement. Such generalities are built on false assumptions, as the water table has risen and fallen continuously since the time the structures were built. If you look at the stones laid at the ground level, in almost all cases you will see they run precisely parallel and maintain very tight joints. If there

Some of the temples will only be partially restored, to preserve the full history of Angkor.

was foundation settlement, the stones would have shifted drastically at this point. Much of the attributed damage has usually resulted from deformation of the structure at the upper levels, in the roofs and vaults, thus allowing monsoon weather to penetrate and weaken the bearing strength of the laterite stone used as a backing or foundation base for the sandstone.

There is no denying the very drastic damage caused by vegetation. The indigenous tropical forest grows very fast, as can be witnessed in many temples over the last 20 years, during which time much of the good work in site clearance undertaken by the EFEO has been reversed. The effects of some ficus trees and vines on the stone structure is parasitic. In the first instance, the tree is dependent on the stone structure for its moisture. After time, the roles are reversed, and the structures, torn asunder by the tree roots, become dependent on the tree for support. Today, therefore, control of young vegetation in the monuments is of great importance; but, where the roles have been reversed, preservation of the trees is also necessary, particularly as they may be part of a site's history.

Another point for great debate is the cleaning of the stonework. There has been considerable press coverage on the work the Indian government has been doing at Angkor Wat, and as to the merits and demerits of cleaning. In a tropical jungle climate it is unlikely that any application to kill or control biological growths on stone will ever be successful as monsoon rains render any treatment ineffectual. Also the physical process of cleaning stone causes unnecessary surface abrasion and removes the natural protective surface of the stone. In general, biological growths do little to harm undecorated stonework and only in exceptional circumstances should stone exposed to the natural elements be cleaned.

Conservation Projects

Some 40 temples are accessible to visitors and, today, several of them are benefitting from international assistance. Work on each of these sites is a joint effort between the Royal Cambodian Government and an international organisation providing technical assistance. The ICC monitors all projects. A prime objective of the foreign expertise is to help with the training of local, professional staff and craftsmen to enable them to care for their monuments in the future. Students from the University of Fine Arts in Phnom Penh, for example, are undergoing basic training on several of the sites. A summary of the monuments where work is currently in progress and the international organisations assisting is given below in alphabetical order by temple.

BANTEAY KDEI

This 12th-century Buddhist monastic complex is the site of a research programme directed by the Institute of Asian Cultures (IAC) of Sophia University, Toyko. Work includes the development of site inventories, archaeological and historical research, and collection of geological and botanical specimens. Ethnographic studies of two other neighbouring monuments — Srah Srang and Kutisvara — and the surrounding villages are also part of the project.

BAPHUON

The massive 11th-century temple-mountain of Baphuon is one of the sites the French were working on in the 1970s. It undoubtedly reflected the pinnacle of architecture of the period, but today little evidence of its grandeur is visible as much of the temple has collapsed including the central shrine. In February 1995, the EFEO resumed work on this temple following the closure of the site due to the conflict. Stones of the temple at the time were scattered in their thousands in the neighbouring jungle. The EFEO is now using the latest computer technology to piece together the site as the original documentation was pillaged.

PHIMEANAKAS (NORTH AND SOUTH GOPURA)

The Indonesian Government has completed the dismantling and reconstructing of the south *gopura* of the enclosure wall around the temple of Phimeanakas, an early 11th-century site. This is the second of four gopura they plan to restore.

PREAH KHAN

The World Monuments Fund (WMF), a private non-profit organisation based in New York, is undertaking work at Preah Khan, another immense Buddhist monastic complex of the late 12th century. It is set deep in its own jungle and plans include developing this aspect so visitors can enjoy these surroundings. The WMF aims to conserve and present Preah Khan as a partial ruin. By clearing paths, opening galleries and corridors, and ensuring structural stability, visitors will be able to experience a feeling for the temple's past glory and importance.

PREAH KO

Conservation work at Preah Ko, a tenth-century Hindu temple located south-east of Angkor at Roluos, is currently under the direction of the Royal Angkor Foundation (RAF), Budapest, Hungary, but is funded mainly by Germany. The site consists of six brick towers which were originally elaborately decorated with stucco. Although much of the stucco still exists, it is in an extremely fragile state. The RAF team of international consultants is consolidating the stucco, and the sandstone lintels and sculptures on the towers. Further work to stabilise the towers is also planned.

ROYAL PLAZA OF ANGKOR THOM (EASTERN PART); PRASAT SUOR PRAT; THE BAYON (NORTH-EAST LIBRARY)

A team from Waseda University in Japan has begun a scientific research and restoration programme on part of the Royal Plaza. It is also studying one of the Prasat Suor Prat structures with a view of its reconstruction. Additionally, the team is working on one of the libraries at the Bayon. These projects are funded by the International Aid Programme of the Japanese Government.

TERRACE OF THE LEPER KING

This 12th-century, so-called terrace is part of the Royal Plaza of the city of Angkor Thom, and was under re-construction in 1972-1973 when the French were forced to leave by the Khmer Rouge. Thus, it is fitting that the EFEO has returned and completed its work which involved re-building the terrace structure on re-inforced concrete retaining walls and restoring the complete terrace. An inner retaining wall behind the facade of the terrace was built earlier, but its exact purpose, date and fuction are much debated. It is now possible to walk between the walls and see the earlier carved retaining wall which was buried until the French discovered it. The EFEO at present are working on the adjacent northern section of the Elephant Terrace.

A reflection of the glory of Angkor Wat.

PART II
THE MONUMENTS

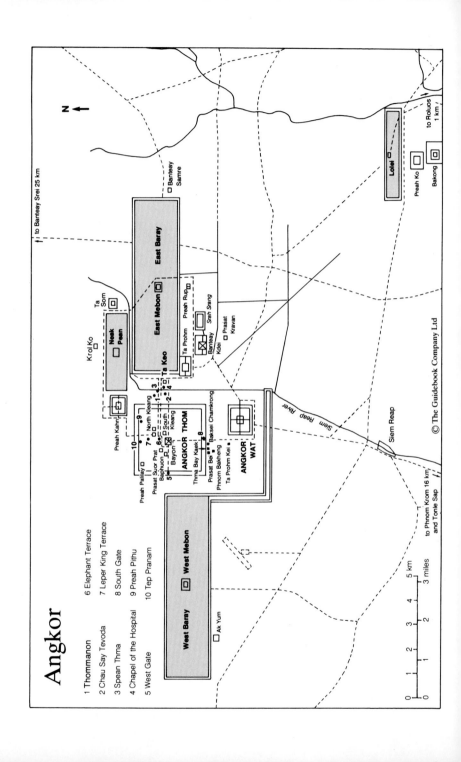

Angkor

1 Thommanon
2 Chau Say Tevoda
3 Spean Thma
4 Chapel of the Hospital
5 West Gate

6 Elephant Terrace
7 Leper King Terrace
8 South Gate
9 Preah Pithu
10 Tep Pranam

N

to Banteay Srei 25 km

to Roluos
1 km

Ta Som

Krol Ko

Neak Pean

Preah Kahn

East Baray

East Mebon

Banteay Samre

Ta Keo

Preah Rup

Srah Srang

Ta Prohm

Banteay Kdei

Prasat Kravan

North Kleang

South Kleang

ANGKOR THOM

Preah Pallilay

Prasat Suor Prat

Bayon

Baphuon

Baksei Chamkrong

Thma Bay Kaek

ANGKOR WAT

Prasat Bei

Ta Prohm Kel

Phnom Bakheng

West Baray

West Mebon

Ak Yum

Siem Reap River

Siem Reap

to Phnom Krom 16 km
and Tonle Sap

Lolei

Preah Ko

Bakong

© The Guidebook Company Ltd

0   1   2   3   4   5 km

0   1   2   3 miles

Temple Itinerary

GROUP 1
Angkor Wat 3 hours

GROUP 2
Angkor Thom (South Gate) 1/4 hour
Royal Palace 1/4 hour
Terrace of the Elephants 1/4 hour
Terrace of the Leper King 1/4 hour
Phimeanakas 1 hour
Baphuon 1 hour
Bayon 1 1/2 hours

GROUP 3
Preah Khan 2 hours
Neak Pean 1/2 hour
Krol Ko 1/4 hour
Ta Som 1/2 hour

GROUP 4
Roluos 3 hours

GROUP 5
Prasat Kravan 1/2 hour
Srah Srang 1/4 hour
Banteay Kdei 3/4 hour
Preah Rup 3/4 hour
East Mebon 3/4 hour

GROUP 6
Ta Prohm 1 1/2 hours
Ta Keo 1/2 hour
Chapel of the Hospital 1/4 hour
Spean Thma 1/4 hour
Chau Say Tevoda 1/4 hour
Thommanon 1/4 hour
Baksei Chamkrong 1/2 hour
Phnom Bakeng 1 hour

GROUP 7
Banteay Srei 2 hours
Banteay Samre 1 hour

GROUP 8
West Baray 2 1/2 hours
West Mebon 1/2 hour
Ak Yum 1/4 hour

© The Guidebook Company Ltd

Rahu, a demon with claws.

GROUP 9
Tonle Sap 2 hours
Phnom Krom 1 hour

GROUP 10
Preah Pithu 1/2 hour
The Kleangs 1/2 hour
Prasat Suor Prats 1/2 hour
Tep Pranam 1/2 hour
Preah Palilay 1/2 hour

Introduction

This section of the book is intended as a practical guide for visiting the monuments at Angkor. It is designed for use at the sites, to help you get around the temples, and to enhance your appreciation of the art and architectural features. Points of special interest are indicated and explanations of art and architectural features are given to make your visit enjoyable and memorable. This section can also be read afterwards to reinforce the experience. Historical quotes from early visitors and legends told by natives have been included to try to capture the spirit of Angkor's past glory. It is recommended that travellers visit the National Museum in Phnom Penh before proceeding to Siem Reap, as many of Angkor's most precious art has been moved there for safe keeping.

The nearest temples are about six kilometres (four miles) from Siem Reap, so before setting off you will need to decide on a means of transport and to purchase a visitor's permit for the temples. You can hire a car or van with a driver and you can also rent a bicycle or motorcycle (with or without a driver). Some motorcyle drivers even double as guides. Whatever type of transport you choose, it is preferable to hire it for the duration of your stay at Angkor. Permits to visit the temples can be purchased individually for one or several days. Carry your permit with you in case you are asked to show it at any time.

An early start is recommended to avoid being at the temples during the hottest part of the day and also so you will not miss the many photographic chances that occur before the sun is directly overhead. Try to be en route by seven or seven-thirty in the morning; return to Siem Reap for lunch around one or one-thirty; then depart for the temples again by two-thirty or three in the afternoon for more sightseeing; climb to one of several vistas for the sunset, returning to Siem Reap just before dark, which is about six-thirty all year round.

The sunsets are magnificent, and are best seen from the uppermost level of one of the several temples that affords a splendid view. As you sit on the blocks of sandstone, warm at the end of the day from the sun's rays, gaze over the vast plain of Angkor and imagine what it must have looked like a thousand years ago, think of the people who lived at Angkor, of the battles they fought and the temples they built to sustain their civilisation. The best vistas for sunset are Angkor Wat, Phnom Bakheng, Preah Rup, East Mebon and Ta Keo.

The monuments included in the suggested temple itinerary have been arranged into ten groups based on proximity. Either the groups or the temples within a given group can be taken in any order. Each one consists of between three and four hours of actual time at the monument plus approximately twenty minutes to reach the site from Siem Reap and another twenty minutes to return, except for Groups 4, 7 and 9 which are further away. For a more leisurely pace allow a half day for each of the groups. Numbers which appear in bold type and in parenthesis throughout the text refer to locations on the relevant temple diagram. Throughout the guide *gopura* is marked up on the corresponding map or plan as 'entry tower'.

Warning Visitors are advised to keep to the paths provided for access to the temples as not all areas have been cleared of landmines. 'Danger Mines' signs are placed in areas that are off-limits. The rectangular danger signs are red with the skull and cross bones drawn in white. Visitors travelling alone or in small groups should be cautious at remote sites such as Banteay Srei and Banteay Samre.

In recent years, tourists have been, if infrequently, ambushed. Some large tour operators will not take responsibility for customers who visit the more remote but,

The tranquil moat surrounding Angkor Wat.

nonetheless, popular monuments, like Banteay Srei. Independent guides, however, will take parties, and it is possible to hire armed guards. Despite this, many tourists do go under their own steam, and usually arrive back safe and sound, exhilarated by the picturesque journey and the most beautiful temples. Checking the latest security news with locals, nevertheless, is probably advisable before making any decision.

The most popular monuments with visitors are Angkor Wat, the Bayon and Ta Prohm, followed by Angkor Thom and Preah Khan. Banteay Srei and the monuments of Roluos are also among the most significant. If you have time, plan to visit Angkor Wat and the Bayon twice, once in the morning and once in the afternoon, to see these great monuments in different lighting conditions. Ta Prohm is at its best in the early morning when the dew is lifting. The jungle growth entwined around the stones glistens with drops of moisture, and as the night air fades the sun rises, casting haunting shadows in the crevices of fallen stones.

The terraces of Angkor Thom and façades of other ruins within the royal city are visible from the road and can, therefore, be seen in just a few minutes while passing by, but this neither does justice to the ancient city nor gives you any feel of what it must have been like in its heyday. The jungle behind the terraces and across the road is peaceful and serene with footpaths guiding you to the ruins; it is one of the most undisturbed and least visited parts of central Angkor. Walk around this area leisurely and enjoy the beauty of the Baphuon, the Kleangs, the Prasat Suor Prat, Phimeanakas, Preah Palilay, Tep Pranam and the terraces — all in the city of Angkor Thom.

It is not difficult to find your way around Angkor because the temples are linked by a system of roads built by the EFEO earlier in this century. Most of the roads have recently been re-surfaced and are in good condition and give convenient access to the vicinity of the ruins. Entrance to some of the actual temples, though, requires walking along a footpath for a few metres. To get to the ruins, except Groups 4, 7, 8 and 9, leave Siem Reap by the paved road at the north of the town and continue until the road comes to a T-junction, approximately six kilometres (four miles).

About halfway along this road there is a kiosk where you can purchase your permit for visiting the temples. At the junction look straight ahead and you will see the south moat and enclosure wall of Angkor Wat. Turn left and follow the road which will take you to the west or main entrance of the temple. Continue north on the main road and you will come to the south *gopura* of Angkor Thom; cross the causeway, pass through the gate, then follow the main road to the T-junction; look straight ahead and you will see the towers of the Bayon; turn either left or right and go around the temple and connect again with the main road leading north. For Group 3 continue straight passing through the north *gopura* of Angkor Thom; for Groups 5, 6, and 7 turn right on the first road (opposite the Terrace of the Elephants) and pass through the east *gopura* of Angkor Thom.

The monuments and surrounding jungle afford unlimited photographic opportunities. Photography is best either early morning or late afternoon. Clouds are common and tend to diffuse light — which is somewhat flat even though it is intense. As most of the temples face east, the best lighting conditions are in the morning, except for Angkor Wat where the best light is in the afternoon because it faces west. The temples surrounded by jungle such as Ta Prohm and Preah Khan can be photographed with good results when the sun is directly overhead and shining through the foliage.

Just as you are never prepared for the immensity and overwhelming beauty of Angkor, you are never ready to leave it. With photographs and visions etched in memory, 'one need never say good-bye to Angkor, for its magic will go with you wherever fate and the gods may take you to colour your thoughts and dreams to life's very end.'[26]

GROUP 1   Angkor Wat: 'the city which is a temple'

Angkor Wat, in its beauty and state of preservation, is unrivaled. Its mightiness and magnificence bespeak a pomp luxury surpassing that of a Pharaoh or a Shah Jahan, an impressiveness greater than that of the Pyramids, an artistic distinctiveness as fine as that of the Taj Mahal.[27]

Location: six kilometres (four miles) north of Siem Reap; one kilometre (two thirds of a mile) south of Angkor Thom
Access: enter and leave Angkor Wat from the west
Date: Angkor Wat was built in the first half of the 12th century (approximately 1113–50)
King: Suryavarman II (reigned 1113-circa 1150)
Religion: Hindu (dedicated to Vishnu)
Art style: Angkor Wat

BACKGROUND

Angkor Wat, the largest monument of the Angkor group and one of the most intact, is an architectural masterpiece. Its perfection in composition, balance, proportions, reliefs and sculpture make it one of the finest monuments in the world. This temple is an expression of Khmer art at its highest point of development.

Wat is the Thai name for temple (the French spelling is *vat*), which was probably added to Angkor when it became a Theravada Buddhist monument, most likely in the 16th century. After the capital gradually shifted to Phnom Penh, Angkor Wat was cared for by Buddhist monks.

Some believe Angkor Wat was designed by Divakarapandita, the chief adviser and minister of the king, who was a brahmin with divine honours. The Khmers attribute the building of Angkor Wat to the divine architect Visvakarman. Construction probably began early in the reign of Suryavarman II and because his name appears posthumously in the bas-reliefs and inscriptions it is believed that Angkor Wat was completed after his death. The estimated time for construction of the temple is about 30 years.

There has been considerable debate amongst scholars as to whether Angkor Wat was built as a temple or a tomb. It is generally accepted that the architecture and decoration identify it as a temple where a god was worshipped and that it was a mausoleum for the king after his death. Its orientation is different from other temples at Angkor as the main entrance is at the west, rather than the east. The bas-reliefs are arranged for viewing from left to right, a practice used in Hindu religious ceremonies for tombs. This emphasis on the west conforms with the symbolism

Following pages: a view towards the western entrance of Angkor Wat.

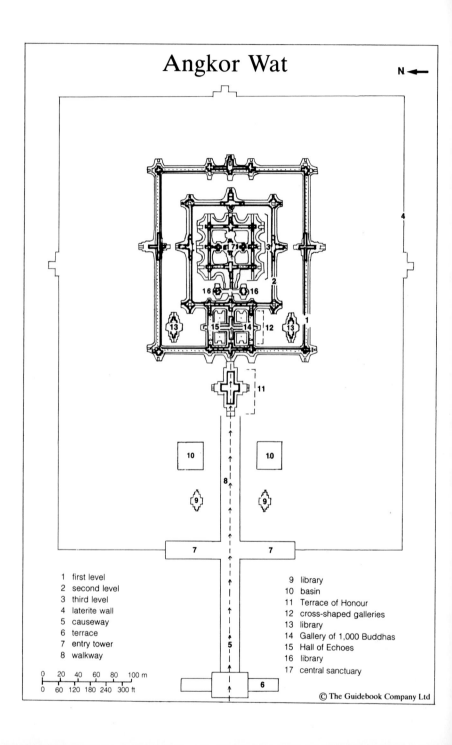

Angkor Wat

N ←

1	first level	9	library
2	second level	10	basin
3	third level	11	Terrace of Honour
4	laterite wall	12	cross-shaped galleries
5	causeway	13	library
6	terrace	14	Gallery of 1,000 Buddhas
7	entry tower	15	Hall of Echoes
8	walkway	16	library
		17	central sanctuary

0   20   40   60   80   100 m
0   60   120 180 240 300 ft

© The Guidebook Company Ltd

between the setting sun and death.

ARCHITECTURAL PLAN

The plan of Angkor Wat is difficult to grasp when walking through the monument because of its enormity. Its complexity and beauty both attract and distract one's attention. From a distance, Angkor Wat appears to be a colossal mass of stone on one level with a long causeway leading to the centre, but close up it is a series of elevated towers, covered galleries, chambers, porches and courtyards on different levels linked by stairways.

It is recommended that you read this section and study the ground plan before visiting the temple, then keep this guide close at hand while looking at the different elements, particularly the bas-reliefs.

At 65 metres (213 feet), the height of Angkor Wat from the ground to the top of the central tower is greater than it might appear, achieved by using three rectangular or square platforms (1–3). Each one is progressively smaller and higher than the one below, starting from the outer limits of the temple. Covered galleries with columns define the boundaries of the first and second platforms.

At the third level, the platform supports five towers—four of the corners and one in the middle—and these are the most prominent architectural features of Angkor Wat. Graduated layers, one rising above the other, give the towers a conical shape and, near the top, rows of lotuses taper to a point. The overall profile imitates a lotus bud.

Several architectural lines stand out in the profile of the monument. The eye is drawn left and right to the horizontal aspect of the levels and upward to the soaring height of the towers. The ingenious plan of Angkor Wat allows a view of all five towers only from certain angles. They are not visible, for example, from the main entrance. Many of the structures and courtyards are cruciform shaped. The stone vaulted roof on galleries, chambers and aisles is another characteristic of Angkor Wat. From afar, this roof looks as though tiled, but close up the vault format identifies itself.

Steps provide access to the various levels. Helen Churchill Candee, who visited Angkor in the 1920s, thought their usefulness surpassed their architectural purpose. The steps to Angkor Wat 'are made to force a halt at beauteous obstructions that the mind may be prepared for the atmosphere of sanctity', she wrote.[28]

To become familiar with the composition of Angkor Wat it is advisable to learn to recognise the repetitive elements in the architecture. Galleries with columns, towers, vaulted roofs, frontons, steps and the cruciform plan occur again and again. It was by combining two or more of these aspects that a sense of height was achieved. This system was used to link one part of the monument to another. A smaller replica of the central towers was repeated at the limits of two prominent areas — the galleries and the *gopuras*. The long causeway at the west entrance is repeated on the eastern side of the first gallery.

SYMBOLISM

Angkor Wat, according to Cœdès, is a replica of the universe in stone and represents an earthly model of the cosmic world. The central tower rises from the centre of the monument symbolising the mythical Mount Meru, situated at the centre of the universe. Its five towers correspond to the peaks of Meru; the outer wall to the mountains at the edge of the world; and the surrounding moat to the oceans beyond.[29]

A study has shown that when Angkor Wat was laid out by the Khmers originally, the distances between certain architectural elements of the temple reflected numbers which were related to Hindu mythology and cosmology. The positions of the bas-reliefs were regulated, for example, by solar movements. Scenes on the east-west sides reflect those relating to the rising and setting of the sun.

LAYOUT

Even though Angkor Wat is the most photographed Khmer monument, nothing approaches the actual experience of seeing this temple. Frank Vincent grasped this sensation over 100 years ago: 'The general appearance of the wonder of the temple is beautiful and romantic as well as impressive and grand...it must be seen to be understood and appreciated.'[30] Helen Churchill Candee experienced a similar reaction some 50 years later: 'One can never look upon the ensemble of the Vat without a thrill, a pause, a feeling of being caught up into the heavens. Perhaps it is the most impressive sight in the world of edifices.'[31]

Angkor Wat is an immense monument occupying a rectangular area of about 210 hectares (500 acres), defined by a laterite enclosure wall (4) which is surrounded by a moat that is 200 metres (660 feet) wide. The perimeter of the enclosure wall measures 5.5 kilometres (3 1/2 miles). The moat is crossed by a huge causeway built of sandstone blocks 250 metres long (820 feet) and 12 metres (39 feet) wide (5). With such impressive statistics it is easy to understand why some local inhabitants believe that Angkor Wat was built by the gods.

Start your tour at the west entrance, where you can see the first of many wonders at Angkor Wat. Climb the short flight of steps to the raised sandstone terrace (6) in the shape of a cross. You are standing at the foot of the long causeway leading to the interior. Look at the balance, the proportions and the symmetry, then the beauty of Angkor Wat begins to unfold. Giant stone lions on each side of the terrace guard the monument.

Look straight ahead to the end of the causeway at the *gopura* with three towers of varying heights, of which much of the upper sections have collapsed. The form of this *gopura* is so developed and elongated that it looks almost like a separate building. A long, covered gallery with square columns and a vaulted roof extends along the moat to the left and right of the *gopura*. This is the majestic façade of Angkor Wat and a fine example of classical Khmer architecture. It originally had another row of pillars with a roof. You can see evidence of this in a series of round holes set in square bases in front of the standing pillars.

Helen Churchill Candee must have been standing on this terrace almost 70 years ago when she wrote: 'Any architect would thrill at the harmony of the façade, an unbroken stretch of repeated pillars leading from the far angles of the structure to the central opening which is dominated by three imposing towers with broken summits.'[32] **Tip:** before proceeding along the causeway, turn right, go down the steps of the terrace and walk along the path a few metres for a view of all five towers.

Then return to the centre of the terrace and cross the causeway towards the main part of the temple taking in the grandeur that surrounds you. The water in the moat shimmers and sometimes you can see lotus in bloom, birds bathing, buffaloes wallowing and children playing. The left-hand side of the causeway has more original sandstone than the right-hand side which was restored by the EFEO. In the 1920s, when RJ Casey walked on this causeway he noted it was 'an oddity of engineering.... The slabs were cut in irregular shapes, which meant that each had to be chiselled to fit the one adjoining. The effect as seen under the noonday sun...is like that of a long strip of watered silk.'[33]

On the left side, just before the midway point in the causeway, look for two large feet carved in a block of sandstone. It is possible that they belong to a figure at one of the entrances to Angkor Thom and were brought to Angkor Wat in this century when the causeway was repaired with reused stones.

The causeway leads to the cruciform *gopura* or entry tower (7) mentioned earlier. The gateways at ground level on each end of the gallery probably served as passages for elephants, horses and carts, whereas the other entrances are accessed by steps and lead onto the central promenade. When Helen Churchill Candee saw these entrances in the 1920s, she remarked that 'architecture made to fit the passage of elephants is an idea most inspiriting'.[34] A huge standing stone figure, carrying symbols that indicate it was originally a Vishnu image, has been transformed into an image of Buddha by giving the torso a new head, is inside on the right of the centre entrance. This image is worshipped by modern Cambodians and is usually adorned with flowers, gold leaf and incense. Traces of original colour can be seen on the ceiling of the *gopura*.

From the central entrance turn right and walk along the columned gallery

coming to the end, where the quality of carving and intricacy of decoration on the false door is of exceptional beauty. Walk through the opening at the end of the gallery towards the east. Here you will see the first full view of the splendid five towers of Angkor Wat. (But there are even better views of them to come.) Take a sharp left turn at the porch and walk along the ledge of the inner side of the gallery, back towards the centre. Along the upper portion of this wall you will see an array of divinities riding fantastic animals framed with an exquisite leaflike motif. The liveliness of these figures, the variety and the crispness of carving is exceptional. As you near the centre of the temple, the female divinities, the *devatas*, on the walls of the porch are some of the most beautiful in all of Angkor Wat.

You are now back to where you entered the gallery and looking towards the main temple complex (which forms the celebrated view of Angkor Wat that appears on the Cambodian flag). Standing at this point you feel compelled to 'get to the wondrous group of the five domes, companions of the sky, sisters of the clouds, and determine whether or not one lives in a world of reality or in a fantastic dream'.[35]

Continue eastward along the raised walkway of equally imposing proportions (length 350 metres, 1,150 feet; width 9 metres, 30 feet) (8). A low balustrade formed by short columns supporting the scaly body of a *naga* borders each side. As you walk along the causeway notice the ceremonial stairs with platforms, always in pairs (to your left and right). These may have given access to the streets between dwellings. The serpent balustrade also frames the stairs. It terminates with the body of the serpent making a turn at right angles towards the sky and gracefully spreading its many heads to form the shape of a fan. This arrangement is sometimes called a landing platform.

Two buildings, so-called libraries (9), stand in the courtyard on the left and right, just past the middle of the causeway. These 'jewel-boxes of Khmer art' are perfectly formed. A large central area, four porches, columns and steps present a symmetrical plan in the shape of a cross. Some of the columns have been replaced with concrete copies for support. An original pillar lies on the ground before the library on the left.

In front of the libraries are two basins (length 65 metres, 215 feet; width 50 metres, 165 feet), ingeniously placed to capture the reflection of the towers in the water (10). The one on the left is filled with water, whereas the other one is usually dry. **Tip**: turn left at the first steps after the library, but before the basin, and follow the path for about 40 metres (131 feet) to a large tree for a superb view of the five towers of Angkor Wat, particularly at sunrise.

The architectural triumph on this walkway is the cruciform-shaped Terrace of Honour, just in front of the principal *gopura* of Angkor Wat (11). Supporting columns and horizontal, carved mouldings around the base accentuate the form of the

Sixty-five metres tall, Angkor Wat appears higher because of its three progressive platforms.

terrace. Steps flanked by lions on pedestals are on three sides of the terrace. Ritual dances were performed here, and it may also have been where the king viewed processions and received foreign dignitaries.

RJ Casey sensed such activity in the 1920s: 'One cannot but feel that only a few hours ago it was palpitating with life. The torches were burning about the altars. Companies of priests were in the galleries chanting the rituals. Dancing-girls were flitting up and down the steps....That was only an hour or two ago, monsieur...it cannot have been more.'[36]

From the top of the terrace there is a fine view of the famous Gallery of Bas-reliefs (215 by 187 metres, 705 by 614 feet) on the first platform level (1). The vaults over the gallery are supported by a row of 60 evenly-space columns providing light to the inner wall decorated with bas-reliefs. **Tip**: at this point, you have the choice of continuing straight to the central towers or turning right to see the reliefs.

The cross-shaped galleries provide the link between the first and second levels (12). This unique architectural design consists of covered cruciform-shaped galleries with square columns forming four courtyards each with paved basins and steps. The corbel vaults are exposed all along the galleries. Several decorative features stand out: windows with stone balusters turned like wood, rosettes on the vaults, a frieze of *apsaras* under the cornices and ascetics at the base of the columns. Many of the pillars in the galleries of this courtyard have inscriptions written in Sanskrit and Khmer. At both ends of the north and south galleries are two libraries of similar form, but smaller than the ones along the entrance causeway (13). There is a good view of the upper level of Angkor Wat from the northern one.

The Gallery of 1,000 Buddhas, on the right, once contained many images dating from the period when Angkor Wat was Buddhist, but only a few of these figures remain today (14). The Hall of Echoes, on the left, is so named because of its unusual acoustics (15). **Tip**: to hear the resonance in the Hall of Echoes walk to the end of the gallery and into the alcove, stand with your back to the wall, thump your chest and listen carefully.

Return to the centre of the cruciform-shaped galleries and continue walking eastward toward the central towers. Another set of stairs alerts you to the continuing ascent. The outer wall of the gallery of the second level, closest to you (100 by 115 metres, 330 by 380 feet), is solid and undecorated, probably to create an environment for meditation by the priests and the king (2).

The starkness of the exterior of the second level gallery is offset by the decoration of the interior. Over 1,500 *apsaras* ('celestial dancers') line the walls of the gallery, offering endless visual and spiritual enchantment. These graceful and beautiful females delight all visitors. They were born from the Churning of the Ocean of Milk. From their ethereal origins to their realistic appearance on the walls of Angkor

Angkor Wat: Galleries of Bas-reliefs

N
↑

NORTH GALLERY

10   9   8

GALLERY   11   7   EAST

GALLERY

6

WEST   1   5   GALLERY

2   3   4

SOUTH GALLERY

WEST GALLERY

1 Battle of Kurukshetra
11 Battle of Lanka

CORNER PAVILION

2 Scene from the *Ramayana*

SOUTH GALLERY

3 Army of King Suryavarman II
4 Judgement by Yama /
    Heaven and Hell

EAST GALLERY

5 Churning of the Ocean of Milk
6 Inscription
7 Victory of Vishnu over the Demons

NORTH GALLERY

8 Victory of Krishna over Bana
9 Battle between the Gods and the Demons

CORNER PAVILION

10 Scene from the *Ramayana*

Wat they offer timeless joy. When you first walk into the courtyard the multitude of these female figures on the walls and in the niches may seem repetitive, but as you move closer and look carefully you become aware of the variations and quickly see that each one of these celestial nymphs is different. The elaborate coiffures, head-dresses and jewellery befit, yet never overpower, these 'ethereal inhabitants of the heavens'.

Female divinities appear at Angkor Wat for the first time in twos and threes. These groups break with the traditional formality of decoration in other parts of the temple by standing with arms linked in coquettish postures and always in frontal view except for the feet, which appear in profile. Pang, a Cambodian poet, in a tribute to the Khmer ideal of female beauty wrote of the *apsaras* in the 17th century: 'These millions of gracious figures, filling you with such emotion that the eye is never wearied, the soul is renewed, and the heart never sated! They were never carved by the hands of men! They were created by the Gods — living, lovely, breathing women!'[37]

Only the king and the high priest were allowed on the upper or third level of Angkor Wat (3). This level lacks the stately covered galleries of the other two, but as the base of the five central towers, one of which contains the most sacred image of the temple, it has an equally important role in the architectural scheme.

Like all of Angkor Wat, the statistics of this level are imposing. The square base is 60 metres (197 feet) long, 13 metres (43 feet) high, and rises over 40 metres (131 feet) above the second level. Twelve sets of stairs with 40 steps each — one in the centre of each side and two at the corners — ascend at a 70-degree angle giving access to the topmost level. Standing at the bottom on the stairs, looking up, the ascent can seem formidable. But persevere and forge ahead for the effect is worth it when you reach the top. **Tip**: the stairway on the west (centre) is less steep, but those who suffer from vertigo should use the south stairway (centre), which has concrete steps and a handrail. The steps on all sides are exceptionally narrow. It is suggested you ascend and descend sideways.

All the elements of repetition that make up the architectural plan of Angkor Wat are manifested on the upper level. The space is divided into a cruciform-shaped area distinguished by covered galleries and four paved courts. A *gopura* with a porch and columns is at the top of each stairway. Passages supported on both sides with double rows of columns link the *gopura* to the central structure. The corners of the upper level are dominated by the four towers. Steps both separate and link the different parts. A narrow outer gallery with a double row of pillars, windows and balusters surrounds this third level. **Tip**: walk all the way around the outer gallery of the upper level and enjoy the view of the surrounding countryside, the western causeway.

The central sanctuary (17) soars 42 metres (137 feet) above the upper level. Its

*Covered galleries with columns define the boundaries of the first and
second platforms at Angkor Wat.*

height is enhanced by a tiered plinth. The highest of the five towers is equal in height to the cathedral of Notre Dame in Paris. This central sanctuary originally had four porches opening to the cardinal directions and sheltered a statue of Vishnu. Today it is possible to make an offering to a modern image of the Buddha and light a candle in this sacred inner sanctum.

The central core of the temple was walled up some time after the sacking of Angkor in the middle of the 15th century. Nearly 500 years later French archaeologists discovered a vertical shaft 27 metres (89 feet) deep with a hoard of gold objects at its base.

From the summit, the layout of Angkor Wat reveals itself at last. The view is a spectacle of beauty befitting the Khmer's architectural genius for creating harmonious proportions. There it is, the spectacular mass of stone that makes up Angkor Wat, the largest religious monument ever constructed.

GALLERY OF BAS-RELIEFS (SEE PLAN PAGE 135)

'By their beauty they first attract, by their strangeness they hold attention', Helen Churchill Candee wrote of the bas-reliefs in the 1920s.[38] The Gallery of Bas-reliefs, surrounding the first level of Angkor Wat, contains 1,200 square metres (12,900 square feet) of sandstone carvings. The reliefs cover most of the inner wall of all four sides of the gallery and extend for two metres (seven feet) from top to bottom. The detail, quality, composition and execution give them an unequalled status in world art. Columns along the outer wall of the gallery create an intriguing interplay of light and shadow on the reliefs. The effect is like 'the work of painters rather than sculptors'. The bas-reliefs are of 'dazzling rich decoration—always kept in check, never allowed to run unbridled over wall and ceiling; possess strength and repose, imagination and power of fantasy; wherever one looks [the] main effect is one of "supreme dignity"', wrote a visitor 50 years ago.[39]

The bas-reliefs are divided into eight sections, two panels flanking each of the four central entrances and additional scenes in each pavilion at the north and south corners of the west gallery. The scenes on the bas-reliefs run horizontally, from left to right, in a massive expanse along the walls. Sometimes decorated borders are added. The scenes are arranged in one of two ways: either without any deliberate attempt to separate the scenes; or in registers which are sometimes superimposed on one another. The latter form was probably introduced at a later date.

Each section tells a specific story inspired by one of three main sources — either Indian epics, sacred books or warfare of the Angkor period. Some scholars suggest that the placement of a relief has a relevance to its theme. The bas-reliefs on the east walls, for example, depict creation, birth and a new beginning (all associated with the rising sun), whereas those on the west walls portray war and death and aspects related to the setting sun.

Parts of some of the reliefs have a polished appearance on the surface. There are two theories as to why this occurred. The position of the sheen and its occurrence in important parts of the reliefs suggest it may have resulted from visitors rubbing their hands over them. Some art historians, though, think it was the result of lacquer applied over the reliefs. Traces of gilt and paint, particularly black and red, can also be found on some of the reliefs. They are probably the remains of an undercoat or a fixative.

Tip: as the bas-reliefs at Angkor Wat were designed for viewing from left to right, the visitor should follow this convention for maximum appreciation. Enter the Gallery of Bas-reliefs at the middle of the west side, turn right into the gallery and continue walking counter-clockwise. If you start from another point always keep the monument on your left.

If your time at Angkor is limited, the following bas-reliefs are recommended (the numbers refer to the plan):

Location	Theme
1 West Gallery	Battle of Kurukshetra
3 South Gallery	Army of King Suryavarman II
5 East Gallery	Churning of the Ocean of Milk
11 West Gallery	Battle of Lanka

In view of the vast number of bas-reliefs at Angkor Wat and recognising that only so much art can be absorbed at one time, descriptions in this guide include just the highlights in the main galleries and one or two identifiable scenes in the corner pavilions. Descriptions begin in the middle of the west gallery and continue in a counter-clockwise direction around the square.

■ WEST GALLERY: BATTLE OF KURUKSHETRA (1)
This battle scene is the main subject of the Hindu epic *Mahabharata,* and it unfolds in action-packed drama on the walls of Angkor Wat. It recalls the historic wars in Kurukshetra, a province in India, and depicts the last battle between rival enemies (the Kauravas and the Pandavas, who are cousins). In fierce, hand-to-hand combat the ferocious battle ensues. With commanders (represented on a larger scale) giving instructions from elaborately carved chariots or the backs of elephants, arrows fly in all directions, warriors fight bravely, others march in unison,

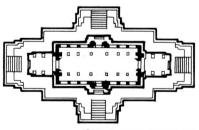

© The Guidebook Company Ltd

Plan of a library at Angkor Wat.

Early photograph of the central towers of Angkor Wat from the second causeway at the west entrance.

The south-west corner pavilion of the Gallery of Bas-reliefs, c. 1880.

horses rear in fright and slain bodies are strewn across the battlefield. The armies of the Kauravas and the Pandavas march into battle from opposite ends towards the centre of the panel where they meet in combat. Headpieces differentiate the warriors of the two armies. Musicians play a rhythmic cadence to keep the soldiers in step. The scene builds up gradually and climaxes in a mêlée in the centre of the panel. Identifiable figures in the panel include: Bisma, one of the heroes of the *Mahabharata* and commander of the Kauravas (at the top, near the centre) is pierced with arrows fired by his arch enemy Arjuna; his men surround him as he lies dying; Arjuna (near the centre holding a shield decorated with the face of the demon Rahu) shoots an arrow at Krishna, his half-brother, and kills him; after death, Krishna (four arms) becomes the charioteer of Arjuna.

■ SOUTH-WEST CORNER PAVILION: SCENE FROM THE RAMAYANA (2)
Unfortunately, many of the bas-reliefs in this pavilion have been damaged by water. The scenes are inspired by the Indian epic, the *Ramayana* and the life of Krishna. One such episode from his life is found on the north branch, east face in a well-known story of Krishna lifting Mount Govardhana. He does this after persuading the pastoral people of India to shift their allegiance from Indra to him. Enraged, Indra sends a deluge of rain and thunder to the land of the shepherds as punishment. Krishna comes forth to provide shelter for them and their flocks by 'lifting up Mount Govardhana from its base in one hand, he holds it in the air as easily as a small child holds a mushroom'. He supports the mountain for seven days before Indra admits defeat; (above the north door) Rama kills Marica, who, disguised as a golden stag, helped in the abduction of Sita; (south branch, east face) A fight between the brothers, Valin and Sugriva (king of the monkeys), who are enemies, duel for possession of Sugriva's kingdom. Rama intervenes and kills Valin by piercing him with an arrow. Below, Valin lies in the arms of his wife and on adjoining panels monkeys cry over Valin's death.

■ SOUTH GALLERY: ARMY OF KING SURYAVARMAN II (3)
This gallery also depicts a battle scene, but it differs from the previous one because it is a historical, rather than mythical, portrayal of a 'splendid triumphal procession' from a battle between the Khmers and their enemies. The reliefs show methods used in warfare, mainly hand-to-hand combat, as they had no machinery and no knowledge of firearms. The naturalistic depiction of trees and animals in the background of this panel is unusual. The central figure of this gallery is the king, Suryavarman II, the builder of Angkor Wat, who appears twice in the reliefs, once standing and again seated. An inscription on the panel identifies him by his posthumous name. It is uncertain when the rectangular holes randomly cut in this gallery were done or by

Following pages: a drawing of the western façade of Angkor Wat.

whom. They may have contained precious objects belonging to the temple.

On the upper tier, the king (seated and with traces of gilt on his body), with a brahmin standing nearby, holds an audience on a mountain while below, a procession of women from the palace carried in palanquins and accompanied by female servants descends from a mountain in the forest. The army gathers for inspection and the commanders mounted on elephants join their troops who are marching towards the enemy. The commander's rank is identified by a small inscription near the figure. King Suryavarman II stands on an elephant (conical headdress, sword with the blade across his shoulder) and servants around him hold 15 ceremonial parasols, indicating his position and rank.

The lively and loud procession of the Sacred Fire (carried in an ark) follows with standard bearers, musicians and jesters. Brahmins chant to the accompaniment of cymbals. The royal sacrificer rides in a palanquin. Towards the end of the panel: the military procession resumes with a troop of Siamese soldiers (pleated skirts with floral patterns; belts with long pendants; plaited hair; headdresses with plumes; short moustaches) led by their commander, who is mounted on an elephant. The Siamese troops were probably either mercenaries or a contingent from the province of Louvo (today called Lopburi) conscripted to the Khmer army. A number of the Khmer warriors wear helmets with horns or animal heads (deer, horse, bird) to frighten the enemy and some of their shields are embellished with monsters for the same purpose.

■ JUDGEMENT BY YAMA/ HEAVEN AND HELL (4)

This is a fierce scene, where brutality and torture abound. Three tiers recount the judgement of mankind by Yama and two tiers depict heaven and hell. Inscriptions

have identified 37 heavens, where one sees leisurely pursuits in palaces, and 32 hells, with scenes of punishment and suffering. Draperies and *apsaras* separate the two and a row of *garudas* borders the tier on the bottom. Traces of gilt can be seen on those mounted on horseback at the beginning of the panel. The lower section of the panel was badly damaged and was later repaired with cement plaster.

Lower tier: Yama, the supreme judge (with multiple arms, holding a staff and riding a buffalo), points out to his scribes the upper road representing heaven and the lower one of hell. Departed spirits await judgement. Assistants to Yama shove the wicked through a trap door to the lower regions using a pitchfork, where torturers deliver punishments such as sawing a body in half for those who overeat; law breakers have their bones broken; thieves of rice have their stomachs filled with red-hot irons and some of the punished wear iron shackles or have nails pierced through their heads. Upper tier: the virtuous are rewarded by a life of leisure in a celestial palace. A frieze of *garudas* holding up the celestial palace with *apsaras*, floating in the skies above, separates the two tiers.

■ EAST GALLERY: CHURNING OF THE OCEAN OF MILK (5)
This is the most famous panel of bas-reliefs at Angkor Wat and one of the greatest scenes ever sculpted in stone. The myth derives from the Hindu epic *Bagavata-Pourana* and centres on gods and demons who have been churning the ocean of milk for 1,000 years in an effort to produce an elixir that will render them immortal and incorruptible. The figures are carved with such consummate skill that you sense the strength of their muscles as they pull the serpent's body, you see the effort in their expressions and you rejoice at the rewards yielded from their churning that float effortlessly in the celestial heavens above.

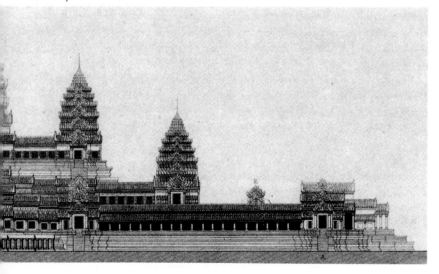

The scene is divided into three tiers. The main tier, in the middle, is bordered along its base by various real and mythical aquatic animals in a churning ocean which is framed by a serpent's body; whilst above these are flying *apsaras*. At each end of the panel, soldiers and charioteers stand by waiting to carry the participants away after the churning is completed.

The story begins with the gods, who are discouraged because they have been unsuccessful in producing the elixir and are exhausted from fighting the demons. They seek help from Vishnu, who tells them to continue churning and to work together, with, rather than against, the demons in helping to extract the *amrita* (elixir of immortality). In the middle tier of the panel, you will see, on the side of the head of the serpent Vasuki, a row of 92 demons (round bulging eyes, crested helmets) and on the side of his tail, a row of 88 gods (almond-shaped eyes, conical headdresses). They hold Vasuki's body waist-high, stretched horizontally across the whole expanse of the panel.

As Vishnu instructed, the gods and demons are working together and churning with the assistance of Hanuman, the monkey god. But as they churn difficulties develop. The pivot, Mount Mandara, begins to sink. The churning nauseates Vasuki and he vomits a mortal venom that floats on the waves and threatens to destroy the gods and demons. Brahma intervenes and requests that Shiva drink the venom, but it is so powerful that it burns his throat leaving an indelible trace, an incident that henceforth gives him the name of 'the god with the blue throat'.

In a scene that climaxes in the centre of the panel, Vishnu comes to the rescue in his reincarnation as a tortoise and offers the back of his shell as support for the mountain. The serpent Vasuki serves as the rope and curls himself around the pivot. Fortified with new support, they start again, pulling rhythmically, first in one direction and then in the other, causing the pivot to rotate, churning the water, and trying to generate the elixir. Vishu appears in this scene again, in yet another reincarnation — as a human being (four arms, holding a disc in his upper left hand) — to preside over the churning which continues for yet another thousand years.

Finally, their efforts are rewarded. The churning yields not only the elixir of immortality, but also many treasures including among others the three-headed elephant Airavata, the goddess Laksmi, a milk-white horse, Chanda, the moon god, the conch of victory, the cow of plenty, and the wonderful *apsaras*.

■ INSCRIPTION (6)
Continuing towards the north, just past the middle of the east gallery, there is an interesting inscription of the early 18th century when Angkor Wat was a Buddhist monastery. It tells of a provincial governor, who built a small tomb where he deposited the bones of his wife and children. You can see this spire-shaped tomb in its

original location (although in poor condition), directly in front of the inscription in the gallery.

■ VICTORY OF VISHNU OVER THE DEMONS (7)
The stiffness of the figures and the cursory workmanship suggest that the bas-reliefs in this section of the east gallery and the east part of the north gallery may have been carved at a later date, perhaps the 15th or 16th century. Nevertheless, there is plenty of action. The scene begins with an army of demons marching towards the centre of the panel and coming at Vishnu with a vengance. Centre: Vishnu (four arms), mounted on the shoulders of his vehicle, the *garuda*, fights bravely and successfully slaughters the enemies on both sides. The leaders of the demons (mounted on animals or riding in chariots drawn by monsters) are surrounded by marching soldiers. Another group of warriors (bows and arrows) with their chiefs (in chariots or mounted on huge peacocks) follows.

■ NORTH GALLERY: VICTORY OF KRISHNA OVER BANA THE DEMON KING (8)
At the beginning of the panel Vishnu in his incarnation as Krishna (eight arms, multi-heads, framed by two heroes) is mounted on the shoulders of a *garuda*, and is followed by Agni, the god of fire (multiple arms), riding his vehicle, the rhinoceros. This scene is repeated several times as Krishna advances with his army of gods towards Bana. However, he is stopped by a fire engulfing the wall surrounding the city. The *garuda* extinguishes the fire with water from the sacred river, Ganges. The demon Bana approaches from the opposite direction in a splendidly carved chariot drawn by a pair of fierce lions. On the extreme right, Krishna (1,000 heads, hands across his chest) kneels in front of Shiva, who sits enthroned on Mount Kailasa with his wife, Parvati, and their son, Ganesha, as they demand that Shiva spares the life of Bana.

■ BATTLE BETWEEN THE GODS AND THE DEMONS (9)
This is an epic battle scene on a grand scale engaging 21 gods of the Brahmanic pantheon, who march in procession carrying classic attributes and riding their traditional vehicles. One god battles against a demon, while warriors on both sides fight in the background. A series of adversaries follow; then Kubera, god of riches (with bow and arrow), appears on the shoulders of a *yaksha*; followed by Skanda, god of war (multiple heads and arms), mounted on a peacock; Indra stands on his mount the elephant; Vishnu (four arms) rides his vehicle, the *garuda*; a demon (tiered heads) shaking swords; Yama, god of death and justice (sword and shield), stands in a chariot drawn by oxen; Shiva draws a bow; Brahma, the creator, rides his sacred goose; Surya, god of the sun, rides in a chariot pulled by horses; and Varuna, god of the

water, stands on a five-headed *naga* harnessed like a beast of burden.

■ NORTH-WEST CORNER PAVILION: SCENE FROM THE RAMAYANA (10)
As in the south-west pavilion, the *Ramayana* is the main source of inspiration for the bas-reliefs in the north-west corner pavilion. A scene worth seeking out is found on the south branch, west face which depicts Vishnu seated (with four arms) surrounded by a bevy of *apsaras* (east branch, north face). At the top of this scene we see the *apsaras* floating with lissom grace; underneath, Vishnu reclines on the serpent Ananta, and floats on the ocean. His upper torso rests on his elbow. His wife, Laksmi, sits near his feet. A golden lotus emerges from the navel of Vishnu, signifying the beginning of a new cosmic period. The lotus opens and Brahma appears to preside over the new creation. At the bottom of the scene a procession of nine gods on their vehicles request that Vishnu undergo a new incarnation on earth. They include: Surya in a chariot pulled by horses; Kubera standing on the shoulders of a *yaksha*; Brahma riding a goose; Skanda on a peacock; Vayu on a horse; Indra on a three-headed elehant; Yama riding a buffalo; Shiva on a bull; and an unidentified god on a lion.

■ WEST GALLERY: BATTLE OF LANKA (11)
This is a popular scene from the *Ramayana* and among the finest of the bas-reliefs at Angkor Wat. It portrays a long and fierce struggle between Rama and the demon king, Ravana (10 heads and 20 arms), seen near the centre. The battle takes place in Lanka (Sri Lanka) and ends with the defeat of Ravana, captor of Sita, the beautiful wife of Rama. The central figures are the monkey warriors who fight against the *rakasas* on Rama's side. The brutality of war is juxtaposed with a graceful rendition of lithesome monkeys.

First past the centre: Rama stands on the shoulders of Sugriva, surrounded by arrows; Laksmana, his brother, and an old demon, stand by Rama. Nearby, the demon king Ravana (10 heads and 20 arms) rides in a chariot drawn by mythical lions. Further on, Nala, the monkey who built Rama's bridge to Lanka, is between them, leaning on the heads of two lions. He throws the body of one he has just beaten over his shoulder. A monkey prince tears out the tusk of an elephant, which is capped with a three-pointed headdress and throws him and the demon to the ground.

At this point you have returned to the central west *gopura* from where you started and this ends your tour of Angkor Wat. You have only to retrace your steps by crossing the two long causeways, and as you do, pause often to turn back, look at the grand temple and remember 'There is no such monument to a vanished people anywhere else in the world.'[40]

GROUP 2   # Angkor Thom

Angkor Thom is undeniably an expression of the highest genius. It is, in three dimensions and on a scale worthy of an entire nation, the materialization of Buddhist cosmology, representing ideas that only great painters would dare to portray....Angkor Thom is not an architectural "miracle"....It is in reality the world of the gods springing up from the heart of ancient Cambodia....[41]

Location: 1.7 km (1.06 miles) north of Angkor Wat
Access: from Siem Reap, enter Angkor Thom by the South gopura
Date: end of the 12th century–beginning of the 13th century
King: Jayavarman VII (reigned 1181-1220)
Religion: Buddhist
Art style: Bayon

BACKGROUND

Angkor Thom, the last capital, was indeed a 'Great City' as its name implies, and it served as the religious and administrative centre of the vast and powerful Khmer Empire. It was grander than any city in Europe at the time and must have supported a considerable population — which may have been as high as one million. Within the city walls were the residences of the king, his family and officials, military officers and priests while the rest of the people lived outside of the enclosure. The royal structures were built of wood and have all perished, but remains of stone monuments let us glimpse at the past grandeur of this once great capital. You can walk amongst the Bayon, the Terrace of the Elephants, Terrace of the Leper King, the Prasat Suor Prat and others, as well as the earlier monuments of the Baphuon and Phimeanakas — all within the walls of Angkor Thom. Looking at these ruins it is easy to imagine why foreigners referred to Angkor Thom as 'an oppulent city'.

Zhou Daguan, the Chinese emissary who provided the only first-hand account of the Khmers, described the splendour of Angkor Thom: 'At the centre of the kingdom rises a Golden Tower [Bayon] flanked by more than twenty lesser towers and several hundred stone chambers. On the eastern side is a golden bridge guarded by two lions of gold, one on each side, with eight golden Buddhas spaced along the stone chambers. North of the Golden Tower rises the Tower of Bronze [Baphuon], higher even than the Golden Tower: a truly astonishing spectacle, with more than ten chambers at its base. A quarter of a mile further north is the residence of the King. Rising above his private apartments is another tower of gold. These are the

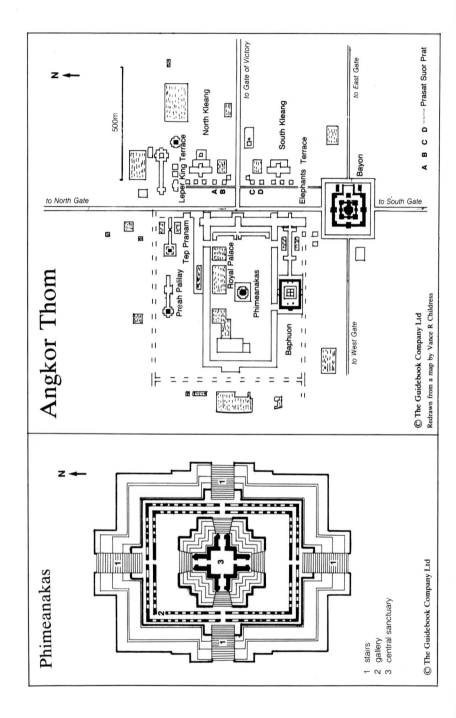

Angkor Thom

N

500m

to North Gate

North Kleang

Leper King Terrace

to Gate of Victory

South Kleang

Elephants Terrace

A
B

C
D

Bayon

to South Gate

Preah Palilay

Tep Pranam

Royal Palace

Phimeanakas

Baphuon

to West Gate

to East Gate

A   B   C   D —— Prasat Suor Prat

© The Guidebook Company Ltd
Redrawn from a map by Vance R Childress

Phimeanakas

N

1   stairs
2   gallery
3   central sanctuary

© The Guidebook Company Ltd

monuments which have caused merchants from overseas to speak so often of 'Cambodia the rich and noble'.[42]

Layout

A laterite wall eight metres high encloses the city of Angkor Thom, which is laid out on a square grid. Each side of the wall is about three kilometres (1.9 miles) long and it encloses an area of 145.8 hectares (360 acres). A moat with a width of 100 metres (328 feet) surrounds the outer wall. The city is accessed along five great causeways, one in each cardinal direction, plus an additional Gate of Victory on the east aligned with the Terraces of the Elephants and the Leper King. A tall *gopura* distinguished by a superstructure of four faces bisects the wall in the centre of each side. Four small temples, all called Prasat Chrung, stand at each corner of the wall around the city of Angkor Thom. An earth embankment 25 metres (82 feet) wide has been created along the inner side of the wall and serves as a path around the city. The five principal entrances lead to the Bayon, situated at the centre of the capital. This temple, in its present form, was the creation of Jayavarman VII and its architecture reflects the dynamism and expansiveness of his reign. Massive towers rise around a 16-sided central sanctuary, each one with four faces gazing afar, yet near.

Causeways

The stone causeways across the broad moat surrounding Angkor Thom with their unique *gopuras*, are one of the great sights at Angkor, never ceasing to fill visitors with wonder. The south gate is the one most frequently photographed, and the lighting is best in the morning. Get out at the south side, ask your transport to wait on the north, and walk across the causeway to get a sense of the size and scale of the demons and gods protecting the entrances leading to the *gopuras*.

The causeways leading to the *gopuras* are flanked by a row of 54 stone figures on each side — gods on the left and demons on the right — to make a total of 108 mythical beings guarding each of the five approaches to the city of Angkor Thom. The demons have a grimacing expression and wear a military headdress, whereas the gods look serene with their almond-shaped eyes and conical headdresses. Some of the heads on these figures are copies; the original ones have either been stolen or removed to the Conservation Office for safekeeping. The gods and demons hold the scaly body of a *naga* on their knees. This composition defines the full length of the causeway. At the beginning of the causeway, the *naga* spreads its nine heads in the shape of a fan.

Gopuras

'Through here all comers to the city had to pass, and in honour of this function it has been built in a style grandiose and elegant, forming a whole, incomparable in its strength and expression.'[43]

Following pages: the majestic entrances to Angkor Thom each have four faces — one for each cardinal direction.

Each of the five sandstone *gopuras* rise 23 metres (75 feet) to the sky and is crowned with four heads, one facing each cardinal direction. At the base of each gate are finely modelled elephants with three heads. Their trunks are plucking lotus flowers, in theory out of the moat. The Hindu god, Indra, sits at the centre of the elephant with his consorts on each side. He holds a thunderbolt in his lower left hand. Stand in the centre of the *gopura* and you will see a sentry box on each side. Also remains of wooden crossbeams are still visible in some of the *gopuras*. Beneath the *gopura* you can see the corbelled arch, a hallmark of Khmer architecture.

SYMBOLISM

Jayavarman VII's capital of Angkor Thom is a microcosm of the universe divided into four parts by the main axes. The temple of the Bayon stands as the symbolic link between heaven and earth. The wall enclosing the city of Angkor Thom represents the stone wall around the universe and the mountain ranges around Meru. The surrounding moat suggests the cosmic ocean. This symbolism is reinforced by the presence of the Hindu god Indra on his mount, the three-headed elephant.

What do the dramatic causeways that culminate in *gopuras* of such unusual form with four faces symbolise? Not everyone agrees, and the subject has been the source of considerable debate amongst scholars. The long-held and most well-known idea is that the gods and demons holding the body of the *naga* represent the myth of creation as depicted in the Churning of the Ocean of Milk, the famous relief on the east gallery (south side) at Angkor Wat. The three-headed white elephant seen at the base of each *gopura* was born of the churning of the ocean of milk.

Another idea is that they represent the rainbow uniting the worlds of man and the gods. As you walk across the causeway you are transgressing from the earthly world to a heavenly one. A more recent theory (put forth by Boisselier) draws on a historical event from Buddhist texts and Khmer inscriptions, which suggest the causeway and *gopura* theme represents Indra's miraculous victory over the demons. The stone figures, which are two families of *yaksas* (demon giants) not gods and demons, stand guard at the gates of the city to ward off any future surprise attack. The city itself represents Indra in Tavatimsa Heaven situated at the centre of the kingdom.

ROYAL PALACE

Situated at the heart of the city of Angkor Thom, the Royal Palace area is distinguished by two terraces that parallel the road. Evidence of the Royal Palace itself is illusive because only the stone substructure remains. It is difficult, therefore, to conceive its original layout or scale. An additional difficulty is that some of the parts which still remain, pre-date Jayavarman VII's rebuilding of the original site of the

Royal Palace. Like much of Angkor Thom, the residences of the king, and those who worked in the palace, were built of wood and have disintegrated, leaving no traces.

The recognisable remains of the palace complex start from the main road with two foundations now known as the Terrace of the Elephants and the Terrace of the Leper King. Projections with steps evenly spaced along the terraces lead to an open area that was a Royal Plaza used by Jayavarman VII for reviewing troops, processions, hosting festivals and ceremonies. These terraces probably supported wooden pavilions from where the king and his court sat and viewed the activities and the people assembled below. Behind the terraces, a rectangular laterite wall with *gopuras* delineates the private areas of a former palace complex. Inside the enclosure is the temple of Phimeanakas and the king's and the queen's rectangular bathing pools.

Terrace of the Elephants

An Imperial hunt in the sombre forests of the realm. There are formidable elephants....The forest in which they travel is impenetrable to all but tiny creatures, able to squeeze their smallness between the fissures of the undergrowth, and to the biggest animals, which crush chasms for their passage in the virgin vegetation. The elephants are ridden by servants and princes, and tread as quietly as if they were on an excursive promenade. Their steps of even length have no respect for any obstacle.[44]

Location: Royal Plaza of Angkor Thom
Access: from the road at the east
Date: end of the 12th century
King: Jayavarman VII (reigned 1181-1220)
Religion: Buddhist
Art style: Bayon

BACKGROUND

The Terrace of the Elephants shows evidence of having been rebuilt and added to, and it is believed that alterations took place during the reign of Jayavarman VII at the end of the 12th or the beginning of the 13th century. It is located directly in front of the east *gopura* of the Royal Palace enclosure wall.

LAYOUT

The Terrace of the Elephants extends over 300 metres (984 feet) in length from the Baphuon to the Terrace of the Leper King. It has three main platforms and two subsidiary ones. The south stairway is framed with three-headed elephants gathering

lotus flowers with their trunks (which form columns). The central stairway is decorated by lions and *garudas* in bas-reliefs in a stance of support for the stairway.
Several projections above are marked by lions and *naga* balustrades with *garudas*
flanking the dais. The terrace has two levels: one of which is square and another
which has a gaggle of sacred geese carved along its base. It is likely that these platforms originally formed the bases for wooden pavilions which were highlighted with
gold.

One of the main attractions of this terrace is the façade decorated with elephants
and their riders depicted in profile. Photograph them from the main road then walk
up close to get a sense of scale and proportion. 'All the pachyderms, almost life-size,
are magnificent...and the whole effect has an indescribable splendour.'[45] The elephants are using their trunks to hunt and fight while tigers claw at them.

HORSE WITH FIVE HEADS

At the northern end of the platform behind the outer wall, a large horse with five
heads sculpted in high relief stands on each side at the base of the inner retaining
wall. This wall must have been part of an earlier retaining wall for the terrace. The
horse is an exceptional piece of sculpture, lively and remarkably worked. It is the
horse of a king, as indicated by the tiered umbrellas over his head; it is surrounded
by *apsaras* and menacing demons armed with sticks in pursuit of several people
bearing terrified expressions. Some French savants believe this is a representation of
Avalokiteshvara in the form of the divine horse Balaha.

Terrace of the Leper King

*The stone monarch is absolutely naked, his hair is plaited and he sits in
the Javanese fashion. The legs are too short for the torso, and the forms,
much too rounded, lack the strong protruberances of manly muscles;
but, however glaring are his defects, he has many beauties, and as a
study of character he is perhaps the masterpiece of Khmer sculpture.
Whilst his body is at rest his soul boils within him....His features are full
of passion, with thick lips, energetic chin, full cheeks, aquiline nose and
clear brow...his mouth, slightly open, showing the teeth. This peculiarity
of the teeth being shown in a smile is absolutely and strangely unique in
Cambodian art.[46]*

Location: immediately north of the Terrace of the Elephants
Access: from the main road
Date: end of the 12th century

A tranquil pond reflects a regal terrace and staircase of the Angkor period.

King: Jayavarman VII (reigned 1181-1220)
Religion: Buddhist
Art style: Bayon

BACKGROUND

The Terrace of the Leper King carries on the theme of grandeur that characterises the building during Jayavarman VII's reign. It is faced with dramatic bas-reliefs, both on the interior and exterior. During clearing, the EFEO found a second wall with bas-reliefs similar in composition to those of the outer wall. Some archaeologists believe that this second wall is evidence of a later addition to extend the terrace.

The original wall was only a metre-wide of laterite faced with sandstone. It collapsed and a second wall of the same materials, two metres wide, was built right in front of it without any of the rubble being cleared. Recently, the EFEO has created a false corridor which allows visitors to inspect the reliefs on the first wall.

LEPER KING

The curious name of this terrace refers to a statue of the Leper King that is on the platform of the terrace. The one you see today is a copy. The original is in the courtyard of the National Museum in Phnom Penh. The figure is depicted in a seated position with his right knee raised, a position some art historians consider to be Javanese-style. Its nakedness is unusual in Khmer art.

Who was the Leper King? Mystery and uncertainty surround the origin of the name. The long-held theory that Jayavarman VII was a leper and that is why he built so many hospitals throughout the empire has no historical support whatsoever. Some historians think the figure represents Kubera, god of wealth, or Yasovarman I, both of whom were allegedly lepers. Another idea is based on an inscription that appears on the statue in characters of the 14th or 15th century which may be translated as the equivalent of the assessor of Yama, god of death or of judgement. Yet another theory suggests that the Leper King statue got its name because of the lichen which grows on it. The position of the hand, now missing, also suggests it was holding something.

Cœdès believes that most of the Khmer monuments were funerary temples and that the remains of kings were deposited there after cremation. He thinks, therefore, that the royal crematorium was located on the Terrace of the Leper King. The statue, then, represents the god of death and is properly situated on the terrace to serve this purpose. Yet another theory derives from a legend in a Cambodian chronicle that tells of a minister who refused to prostrate before the king, who hit him with his sword. Venomous spittle fell on the king, who then became a leper and was called the Leper King thereafter.

LAYOUT

The Terrace of the Leper King is supported by a base 25 metres (92 feet) on each side and six metres (20 feet) in height. The sides of the laterite base are faced in sandstone and decorated with bas-reliefs divided into seven horizontal registers.

RELIEFS

Exterior wall: mythical beings — serpents, *garudas* and giants with multiple arms, carriers of swords and clubs, and seated women with naked torsos and triangular coiffures with small flaming discs — adorn the walls of the terrace. Interior wall: these reliefs are in remarkable condition. Walk along the corridor and enjoy a close-up view of the deeply carved scenes arranged in registers. The themes are similar to those on the exterior and include a low frieze of fish, elephants and the vertical representation of a river.

Phimeanakas: 'aerial palace (See plan page 148)

Location: inside the enclosure walls of the Royal Palace
Access: walk over the Terrace of Elephants and through the east *gopura* of the enclosure wall encircling the Royal Palace. You are on the principal access to the temple. Alternatively, follow the pathway between the two terraces, bearing left through a breech in the enclosure wall, close to the north-east *gopura*. The temple's tiered platform will be visible from here to the west
Tip: for those who want to climb to the top, use the west stairway
Date: 10th century–early 11th century
King: Rajendravarman II (reigned 941-968)
Religion: Hindu
Art style: Kleang

BACKGROUND

Phimeanakas, located inside the Royal Palace compound, was the temple where the king worshipped. It must originally have been crowned with a golden pinnacle, as Zhou Daguan described it as the 'Tower of Gold'. It is small compared with others, but, even so, it has appeal and is situated in idyllic surroundings. Although its construction seems to have been initiated by Rajendravarman II, subsequent kings made additions, Suryavarman I in the 11th century made the most significant ones.

This temple is associated with a legend that tells of a gold tower (Phimeanakas) inside the royal palace of Angkor the Great, where a serpent-spirit with nine heads lived. The spirit appeared to the Khmer king disguised as a woman and the king had to sleep with her every night in the tower before he joined his wives and concubines in another part of the palace. If the king missed even one night it was believed he would die. In this way the royal lineage of the Khmers was perpetuated.

LAYOUT

Your prelude to Phimeanakas is through the cruciform east *gopura*. Its lintels are of Kleang style with a central motif of a *kala* head; inscriptions on the door frames detail an oath of fidelity for dignitaries of the empire. Continue walking west until you reach the temple. The general plan of Phimeanakas is rectangular with cruciform *gopuras*. The temple, built of laterite and sandstone, originally consisted of a central sanctuary on a tiered platform and an enclosure wall. The grounds around the sanctuary included several courts and ponds that were part of the Royal Palace. A second enclosure wall, surrounded by a moat (now dry) was built at a later date.

■ CENTRAL SANCTUARY (3)

The single sanctuary stands on a base with three laterite tiers and is approached by four steep stairways, one on each side (1). These stairways are framed by walls with six projections — two per step — decorated with lions. Elephants once stood on sandstone pedestals in the corners of the base, but, today, they are mostly broken.

■ UPPER TERRACE

The upper terrace affords a fine view of the neighbouring temple of the Baphuon. A narrow, covered sandstone gallery (2) with windows and balusters at the edge of the upper terrace is the first appearance of a stone gallery with a central sanctuary. There were small pavilions at the corners, but only vestiges remain.

■ ROYAL BATHS

To the north of Phimeanakas, there are two ponds that were part of the Royal Palace compound. The smaller and deeper pond, known as Srah Srei or the women's bath, which is closest to the main road, is identified by moulding and laterite steps. The other larger pond or the men's bath directly to its west, can be reached by a footpath to the right of Phimeanakas. Follow it, and until you come to a large pond paved in laterite with sandstone steps. Continue walking until you are standing on the north edge of the pond. Then turn back and look at the amazing sculpted borders, in two tiers and carved in high relief, on the opposite side. You will see *nagas* sculpted in animal and human form surrounded by *naga*-princesses; on the top there are male and female *garudas* and mythical winged figures. This entire area was probably crowned by a platform with a *naga* balustrade, and may have served as a gallery for the sovereign and dignitaries of the court.

Baphuon

North of the Golden Tower [Bayon]...rises the Tower of Bronze [Baphuon], higher even than the Golden Tower: a truly astonishing spectacle, with more than ten chambers at its base.[47]

Location: 200 metres (656 feet) north-west of the Bayon, and south of Phimeanakas
Access: enter and leave at the east
Tip: access to the temple mountain is restricted as much of the temple has collapsed and is currently under repair until 2004
Date: middle of the 11th century (1060)
King: Udayadityavarman II (reigned 1050-1066)
Religion: Hindu (dedicated to Shiva)
Art style: Baphuon

BACKGROUND

The massive size and grandeur of the Baphuon is unrecognisable today because much of the temple has either collapsed or been dismantled. The EFEO was restoring this temple when it was forced to abandon work and leave Angkor in 1972 because of war; they have now resumed their work. With a total cost estimated at US$10 million, the restoration is expected to be completed in 2004. Even though the Baphuon is situated inside the royal city of Angkor Thom it dates from the 11th century. A highlight of the temple is the bas-reliefs, which differ from most others as they are vignettes carved in small stone squares set one above the other on the temple walls, similar to tiling. Unfortunately few of these are visible because of the poor state of the temple.

LAYOUT

Baphuon is a single temple-mountain sanctuary situated on a high base symbolising Mount Meru. A rectangular sandstone wall measuring 425 by 125 metres (1,394 by 410 feet) encloses the temple (1). A special feature is the long elevated eastern approach (200 metres, 656 feet) supported by three rows of short, round columns forming a bridge to the main temple. This arrangement is unusual in Khmer art. **Tip:** before walking down the approach turn left at the east *gopura* (2) and walk to the end of the gallery for a superb view of a four-faced tower of the Bayon framed in a doorway of the Baphuon, pausing on the way back to the centre for a good view of the eastern approach and columns. The approach is intercepted by a central cruciform pavilion (4) with terraces on its left and right sides. Turn left and walk to the

Baphuon

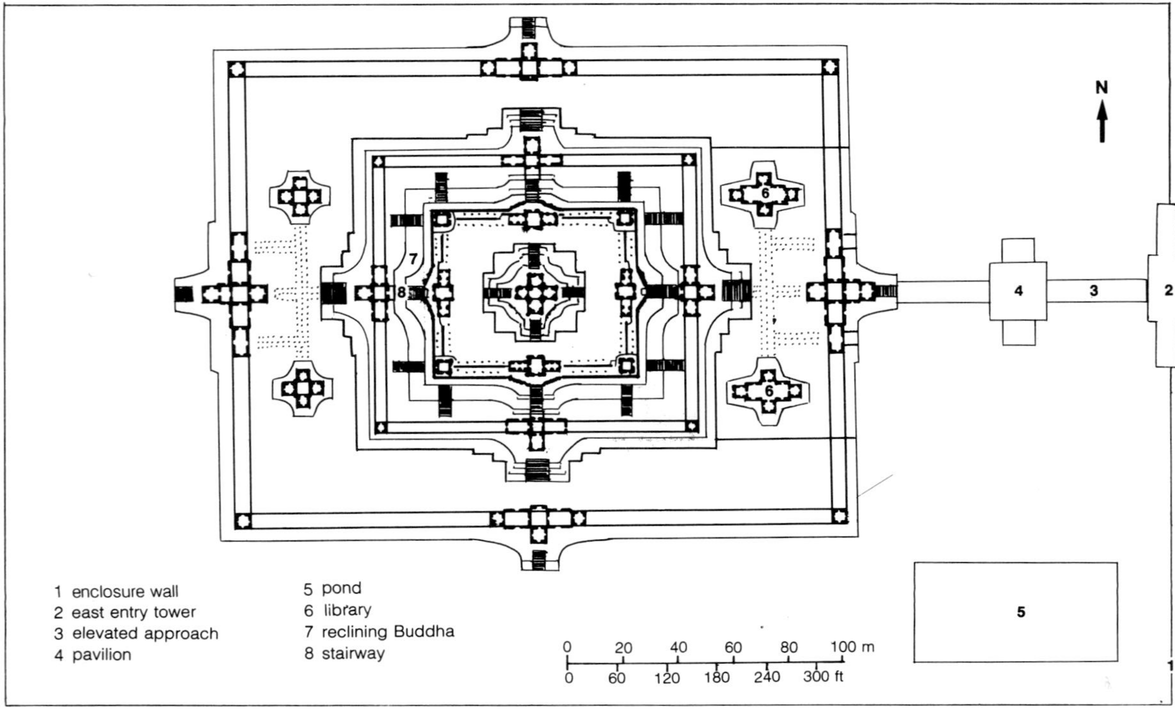

N

1 enclosure wall
2 east entry tower
3 elevated approach
4 pavilion

5 pond
6 library
7 reclining Buddha
8 stairway

0   20   40   60   80   100 m
0   60   120   180   240   300 ft

© The Guidebook Company Ltd

end of the gallery to see a rectangular paved pool (5).

Originally, a central tower shrine with four porches crowned the peak of the mountain, but it collapsed long ago. The shrine stood on a rectangular sandstone base of five diminishing platforms, rather than the more common square format. The first, second and third levels are surrounded by concentric sandstone galleries. Baphuon is the earliest example of a monument at Angkor with this feature. Two cruciform libraries (6) with four porches stand in the courtyard. They were at one time connected by an elevated walkway supported by columns.

If accessible, proceed to the temple by walking along the eastern approach, climb the steps to the first platform and enter the *gopura*. Notice the bas-reliefs on the walls and study the details and workmanship. Walk to the left and around the temple, always keeping it on your right. Continue to the west side and stand in the middle facing the temple, where you can see the outline of a colossal reclining Buddha fashioned during the 15th century with stones of collapsed sections of the temple (7). This figure spans the length of the west platform with the head of the Buddha at its northern end. It is an abstract you may find difficult to distinguish as it was never completed. A stairway (8) leading to the next level begins in the middle of the Buddha.

Climb the stairs on the west side and you will see more of the bas-relief tiles for which the Baphuon is so well-known. Themes are either scenes enacting episodes from the Hindu epics, the *Ramayana* or the *Mahabharata*, or depictions of daily life, often hunting scenes set in the jungle. They are laid out in a general plan that flows from the bottom to the top. The realism and lightness of these bas-reliefs quickly capture your attention. Look to the left and right of the entrance on both sides, where you will see lively animals, joyful musicians and mythical beasts.

After viewing the bas-reliefs return to the centre of the *gopura* and look to the south, where you will see a spectacular example of corbelling along the entire length of the gallery. Walk along the gallery to grasp a sense of the narrowness resulting from this method of construction. Then turn east and walk up a flight of stairs at the south-west corner to reach the top.

Bayon

We stand before it stunned. It is like nothing else in the land.[48]

Location: in the centre of the city of Angkor Thom, 1.5 kilometres (1 mile) from the south gate
Access: enter from the east
Date: late 12th century to early 13th century

King: Jayavarman VII (reigned 1181-1120)
Religion: Buddhist
Art style:Bayon

BACKGROUND

The Bayon vies with Angkor Wat as the favourite monument among visitors. The two temples evoke similar aesthetic responses yet are different in purpose, design, architecture and decoration. The dense jungle surrounding the temple camouflaged its position in relation to other structures at Angkor, so it was not known for some time that the Bayon stands in the exact geographical centre of the city of Angkor Thom. Even after topographical maps finally revealed its correct location, the Bayon was erroneously identified as a Hindu temple connected with the city of Yasovarman I, and, thus, dated to the ninth century.

A fronton found in 1925 depicting an Avalokiteshvara, identified the Bayon as a Buddhist temple. This discovery moved the date of the monument ahead some 300 years to the late 12th century. Although the date is firmly supported by archaeological evidence, the Bayon remains one of the most enigmatic temples of the Angkor group. Its symbolism, original form, subsequent changes and additions have not yet been understood. These aspects leave us today with a complicated, crowded plan that challenges both archaeologists and historians.

The Bayon was built nearly 100 years after Angkor Wat. While its basic structure and earliest part of the temple are unknown, it is clear that the Bayon was built on top of an earlier monument, that the temple was not built at one time, and that it underwent a series of changes. The middle portion of the temple was extended during the second phase of building. The Bayon of today with its huge central mass dates to the 13th century and belongs to the third and last phase of the art style. Jayavarman VII's goal was to rebuild the capital and to bring to the kingdom a new vibrancy, signifying a bright future for the Khmers. To accomplish this, he erected the Bayon and created a structure somewhat like a temple-mountain in its grandiose plan and scale.

The architectural composition of the Bayon exudes grandness in every aspect. Its elements juxtapose each other to create balance and harmony. Over 200 large faces carved on the 54 towers give this temple its majestic character. 'The faces with slightly curving lips, eyes placed in shadow by the lowered lids utter not a word and yet force you to guess much', wrote P Jennerat de Beerski in the 1920s. It is these faces that have such appeal to visitors and reflect the famous 'smile of Angkor'.[49]

The iconography of the four faces has been widely debated by scholars and, although some think they represent the Bodhisattva Avalokiteshvara, in keeping with

Bayon

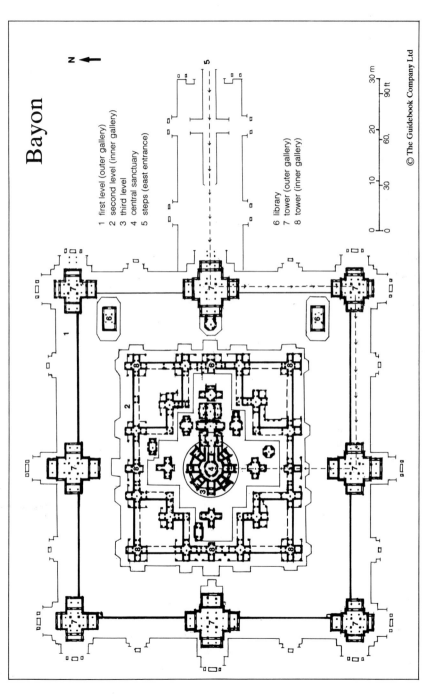

1 first level (outer gallery)
2 second level (inner gallery)
3 third level
4 central sanctuary
5 steps (east entrance)

6 library
7 tower (outer gallery)
8 tower (inner gallery)

N

30 m
90 ft

20
60.

10
30

0
0

© The Guidebook Company Ltd

Following pages: the Bayon, east entrance.

the Buddhist charcter of the temple, it is generally accepted that the four faces on each of the towers are images of King Jayarvarman VII and signify the omnipresence of the king. Besides the architecture and the smiling faces, the highlight of the Bayon is undoubtedly the bas-reliefs, presented in both the inner and outer galleries. The scenes in the outer gallery are unique as they depict many scenes from daily life.

LAYOUT

The plan of the Bayon is presented on three separate levels. The first and second levels contain galleries featuring the bas-reliefs. A 16-sided central sanctuary (4) dominates the third level, which is cruciform in plan. Despite this seemingly simple plan, the layout of the Bayon is complex due to later additions, a maze of galleries, passages and steps, connected in a way that makes the levels practically indistinguishable and creates dim lighting, narrow walkways and low ceilings.

Enter the Bayon from the east (5) at the steps leading to the raised entrance platform. The outer gallery of the Bayon, the first to be encountered, is square in plan and is interspersed with eight cruciform *gopuras* (7) — one in each corner, and four placed on the north-south and east-west axes. The gallery was originally covered.

The decoration on the pillars in front of the east *gopura* is characteristic of the Bayon style and is exceptionally beautiful. A unique motif comprising two or three *apsaras* dancing gracefully on a lotus appears on monuments of the late 12th and early 13th centuries. The depiction of this motif is especially well-executed on the columns of the outer gallery at the Bayon. The dancers are in a frontal stance, rather than in profile as seen at earlier temples such as the Roluos group. They form a triangle and are framed by an intricate and intertwined leaf pattern. The figure in the centre is larger than those on either side. **Tip:** the absence of a roof over these pillars allows sufficient light for the visitor to view and photograph this motif at all times of the day. Direct overhead sunlight at midday provides the most dramatic lighting.

The two galleries of bas-reliefs are distinguished by the degree of elevation. The outer gallery is all on one level, whereas the second or inner gallery is on different levels and access is sometimes difficult due to collapsed areas and the generally poor condition of the temple. The layout of the inner gallery can be misleading, but as long as the reliefs are in view you are still in the second gallery.

On the interior of the first level there are two libraries (6) located in the north-east and south-east courtyards. The second gallery of bas-reliefs has towers in each corner and four *gopuras* on the central axes (8). On the upper level there are a series of interlocking galleries with towers at each corner. This area is confusing and cramped due to passageways being walled up, the demolition of some parts and the filling of others.

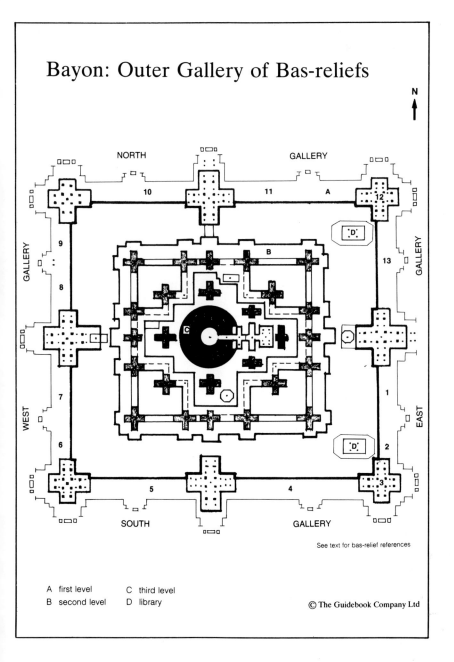

Bayon: Outer Gallery of Bas-reliefs

N

NORTH   GALLERY

10   11   A

GALLERY   GALLERY

9

8

B

12

'D'

13

WEST   C   EAST

7

6

1

'D'

2

5   4   3

SOUTH   GALLERY

See text for bas-relief references

A   first level   C   third level
B   second level   D   library

© The Guidebook Company Ltd

Following pages: nature has encroached deep into the foundations at the Bayon.

The architectural climax is at the third level (3), with the central sanctuary and the faces of Avalokiteshvara. From this level you can watch the shifting light as the sun moves about the faces producing new shadows and highlights. The multitude of faces at different levels affords endless fascination. 'Godliness in the majesty and the size; mystery in the expression', wrote de Beerski, when he looked at the faces in the 1920s.[50]

The central mass is circular, a shape that is uncommon in Khmer art. Originally, there were eight shrines which were later increased to 16. Small porches with frontons provide the bases for the monumental faces, while windows with balusters keep the diffusion of light to a minimum. The faces on the four sides of the eight towers marking the cardinal directions are exceptionally dramatic depictions. The interior of the central sanctuary is a cell surrounded by a narrow passage.

GALLERY OF BAS-RELIEFS

'They have homely human things to tell and they tell them without affectation', wrote H Churchill Candee of the bas-reliefs in the galleries of the Bayon.[51] The reliefs on the inner gallery are mainly mythical scenes, whereas those on the outer gallery are a marked departure from anything previously seen at Angkor. They contain genre scenes of everyday life —- markets, fishing, festivals with cockfights and jugglers and so on -— and historical scenes with battles and processions. The reliefs are more deeply carved than at Angkor Wat, but the representation is less stylised. The scenes are presented mostly in two or three horizontal panels. The lower one, with an unawareness of the laws of perspective, shows the foreground, whereas the upper tier presents scenes of the horizon. They both exhibit a wealth of creativity.

Descriptions of the reliefs in this guide follow the normal route for viewing the Bayon. They begin in the middle of the east gallery and continue clockwise. Always keep the monument on your right. **Tip**: do not become so absorbed in the reliefs that you forget to stop at each opening and enjoy the view of the faces on the third level.

THE OUTER OR FIRST GALLERY (See plan page 167)

This is the gallery with the wonderful scenes of daily life. It was probably open to all worshippers, whereas the other areas of the temple would have been restricted to priests and the king. The scenes may have served as a teaching vehicle to disseminate the tenets of Buddhism. Some of the scenes in this gallery are unfinished. For evidence of this, look at the extremities, such as the corners, particularly near the top of the wall.

■ EAST GALLERY

The workmanship of the reliefs in this gallery is excellent. They are divided into

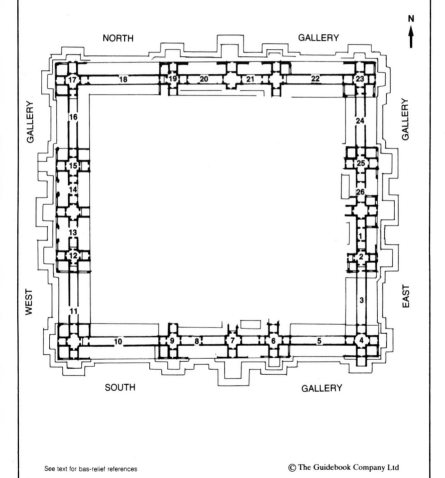

Bayon: Inner Gallery of Bas-reliefs

three panels and depict a military procession with banners and a background of tropical trees (1). On the top tier, warriors (short hair and no head covering) are armed with javelins and shields, while those on the lower tier have goatee beards and wear exotic headdresses suggesting they are Chinese. Musicians accompany the warriors. Horsemen riding bareback flank the musicians.

The commanders of the troops, including Jayavarman VII, identified by parasols with tiers and insignias, are mounted on elephants. Cavalry precede, and women of the palace follow the king. Towards the end of the procession, covered wooden carts (on the lower tier) of the same style as are used today, carry provisions of food for the military. A crouching woman blows a fire for a cooking pot. Looking through the doorway between (1) and (2) where you can see the south library.

The military procession continues (2). The reliefs follow on with genre scenes of everyday life and include a coconut tree with monkeys. A tiered wooden building may be a food shop. The headdresses, clothing and objects hanging from the ceiling suggest that the people inside the building are Chinese.

■ SOUTH-EAST CORNER PAVILION (3)

The carving in this area is unfinished. Identifiable scenes include a wooden palace with a superb *kendi* (drinking vessel) underneath the stairs of the two storeys. An ingenious depiction of a boat spans a 90-degree turn in the wall.

■ SOUTH GALLERY

The scenes in the first part of this gallery (4) contain some of the finest workmanship of all the reliefs at the Bayon. The panel begins with a historical scene depicting the naval battle of 1177 on the Tonle Sap between the Khmers (with no head covering) and the Chams, their neighbouring enemies of south-east Vietnam. They are readily identifiable by their hats, which resemble upside-down lotuses. The boats are majestically portrayed with richly ornamented prows and a galley with oarsmen and warriors armed with javelins, bows and shields. Helen Churchill Candee must have had these boats in mind when she wrote: 'One wonders if Cleopatra floated in greater elegance'.[52] Action is provided by bodies being thrown overboard, and sometimes being eaten by crocodiles.

On the bottom row, genre scenes of daily life along the shores of the Tonle Sap are depicted with spirit and candour — a woman removing lice from another woman's hair, a mother playing with her children, another woman kneeling with her arms around a figure who is writhing in pain, which may be a scene of childbirth assisted by a midwife, and a patient in a hospital. A hunter prepares his bow to shoot a large animal. A fishing scene follows: people on one of the boats play a board game; a scene of a cockfight; above, fishermen on the Tonle Sap and, below, women

The majestic Bayon temple with surrounding moat.

fishmongers. Scenes of the palace follow — princesses surrounded by their suitors, wrestlers, sword fighters, chess players and a fight between wild boars. An outline of a giant figure, perhaps the king, surmounts this entire scene.

Further along the gallery, the battle resumes. Lower tier: the Chams arrive in boats and disembark. Upper tier: the battle continues on land with the Khmers, disguised as giants (closely-cropped hair and cords around their torsos) winning. Afterwards, the king sits in his palace amidst his subjects celebrating their victory. Masons cut sandstone, blacksmiths pound iron and cooks tend fires in preparation for a celebration.

In the second part of the south gallery (5) only the lower level is finished. The scene is a military procession and the main point of interest is the weapons of war used by the Khmers such as large cross-bows mounted on the back of an elephant manned by archers and a catapult mounted on wheels.

■ WEST GALLERY
Many reliefs in this gallery (6) are unfinished. Lower tier: warriors and their chiefs, mounted on elephants, pass through mountains and forests (identified by small triangles); near the centre: an ascetic scales a tree to escape an attack by a tiger; above: scenes depict the methods used for constructing temples such as grinding and polishing sandstone. Beyond the door: a so-called civil war (7): this appears to be a street scene with crowds of men and women threatening others armed and ready for battle. The mêlée continues with hordes of warriors and elephants participating in the action.

In the second part of the west gallery (8) is a scene of hand-to-hand combat in which warriors armed with clubs harass others who protect themselves with shields. A fish swallows a deer on the lower register. An inscription, incised under a shrimp, says that 'the king follows those vanquished in hiding'. Beyond the door: (9) a peaceful procession against a background of trees depicts the king (carrying a bow) on the way to the forest where he will meditate before celebrating the consecration of the Sacred Rite of Indra.

■ NORTH GALLERY (10)
The highlights of this gallery are circus jugglers, acrobats and wrestlers, and an animated procession of various animals including a pig, rhinoceros, rabbit, deer, puffer fish and lobster. At the other end: ascetics meditate in the forest and, on the banks of a river, a group of women receive gifts. Near the door: scenes of combat between the Khmers and the Chams. The wall of the second part of the north gallery (11) is almost entirely collapsed. At each end, the battle between the Khmers and Chams continues and the Khmers flee to the mountain.

■ NORTH-EAST CORNER PAVILION

Scenes of processions of Khmer warriors and elephants (12).

■ EAST GALLERY

The battle between the Khmers and the Chams continues (13). Towards the centre of this gallery, the battle reaches a climax of action; elephants seem to be participating in the battle — one curls his trunk and tries to tear out the tusk of an opposing elephant. The Khmers appear finally to gain control of the battle.

THE INNER OR SECOND GALLERY (See plan page 171)

The galleries in this enclosure are separated by rooms and cells. They are not continuous, as are the exterior galleries. Enter the inner gallery from the east, turn left and continue in a clockwise direction with the reliefs on your right. The reliefs depict, for the most part, mythological subjects of Hindu inspiration.

■ EAST GALLERY

Between two towers; right, (1) ascetics and animals in the forest and mountains. Small room; right, (2) the king in his palace with ascetics. Above: rural and hunting scenes with lively animals and *apsaras* flying overhead. Facing, and to the left, (3) a military procession. This relief has the unusual feature of Khmer and Cham warriors intermixed; the lower tier comprises scenes of daily life.

■ SOUTH-EAST CORNER PAVILION

Warriors march in procession led by a commander mounted on an elephant (4).

■ SOUTH GALLERY

Another military procession (5) and the warriors seem to be of the same nationality. Some genre scenes of everyday life: a man climbs a coconut tree, a *garuda* and a giant fish at the base of Mount Meru with ascetics and animals. (This panel is very eroded and the scene is confused.) Small room (6): a fight between a ruler and an animal, possibly a lion, and (left) a hunter holds an elephant by the rear feet.

Between the two towers (7), on the wall; left: a procession of warriors; facing, from left to right, a scene of combat between a prince and his army; a palace and a cortège of musicians; lower tier, a fisherman in a boat throws a net into the water while a princess watches; *apsaras* fly overhead. Between the two towers (8): from the right, poor condition, (facing), Shiva standing on a lotus; from the left, Shiva deformed and carrying a trident; above, dancing *apsaras* accompanied by an orchestra. Small room; from the right at the bottom (9): a genre scene of everyday life. Above, Vishnu (four arms) descends towards Shiva carrying a trident.

In the last part of the South Gallery (10): a mountain with wild animals and a tiger devouring a man; princesses walking amidst a group of *apsaras* dancing on lotuses. Above, Shiva in his celestial palace surrounded by his followers; ascetics and animals along the banks of a pond. A tiger pursues an ascetic while other devotees converse in the palace and several worshippers prostrate before the god. Centre, Vishnu (four arms) is surrounded by flying *apsaras* and prostrating followers.

■ WEST GALLERY

Vishnu (four arms) is mounted on a *garuda* and subduing an army of demons (11).

Small room (12): a palace scene with dancing *apsaras* accompanied by an orchestra; above, dancers and, above that, a battle scene.

Between two towers; right (13): Vishnu (four arms) superimposed on scenes of the construction of a temple — workers pulling a block of stone, polishing and hoisting blocks of stone into place. A nautical scene follows, with two people playing chess in a boat, and a cockfight. From left, Shiva in a palace with Vishnu on his right; an ascetic meditating in a grotto and swimming amongst lotus flowers; a bird holds a fish in its mouth.

Beyond the centre of the west gallery: a procession of warriors on horseback with two rulers sitting in chariots pulled by horses (14). Small room (15), from the right: a palace scene with people conversing and attendants dressing young princesses.

The most interesting relief in the next area (16) depicts the Churning of the Ocean of Milk; the body of the serpent with demons on the side of the head; the monkey Hanuman assists the gods on the side of the tail. A replica of the serpent crawls along the ocean bed and is represented by a panel of fish; centre, a column resting on the back of a turtle forms the pivot; Vishnu in his human form embraces the shaft. Other items are disks symbolising the sun and the moon and a flask which is destined to contain the elixir of immortality. Left, a god mounted on a bird seems to want to pacify a group of demons who are engaged in a battle; their chief stands in a cart drawn by superb lions.

■ NORTH-WEST CORNER PAVILION

Another procession of warriors is depicted on these reliefs (17).

■ NORTH GALLERY

Palace scenes (18): a procession of servants with offerings; a mountain inhabited by wild animals (elephants, rhinoceros, serpents). One boat carries men with short cropped hair and a chief with a trident and another one bears men wearing the headdress of an inverted flower. Small room (19) facing: Shiva (ten arms) dances, with *apsaras* flying above. Vishnu (right) and Brahma (four faces) (left), with Ganesha;

(below), Rahu. Side of the wall: Shiva sits between Vishnu and Brahma; a charging boar.

Between two towers (20): (right), Shiva is surrounded by ascetics and women, with his mount the bull, Nandi, nearby; (facing), ascetics meditating in the mountains. Kama, the god of love, shoots an arrow at Shiva, who is meditating at the top of a mountain with his wife Parvati at his side. Between two towers (21): from the right, Shiva mounted on the bull, Nandi, with his wife Parvati sitting on his thigh. A palace, multiple-headed serpents and, below, dancing *apsaras*. An episode from the *Mahabharata* follows, depicting 'Shiva granting a favour to Arjuna'.

On the left of the door: another scene from the *Mahabharata* of 'Ravana shaking Mount Kailasa'. Two scenes of the palace are superimposed on each other. Servants with offerings (22): above, ascetics meditating; Shiva blesses his worshippers, with flying *apsaras* above. A king leads a procession followed by his army (short-cropped hair), musicians, elephants and horses, princesses in palanquins and a cart pulled by oxen.

■ NORTH-EAST CORNER PAVILION
Fragments of a procession (23).

■ EAST GALLERY
A military procession with musicians, foot soldiers framed by horsemen and a chariot drawn by horses, a chariot (six wheels) mounted on sacred geese, the ark of the sacred fire, an empty throne and the king carrying a bow mounted on an elephant (24). After the door: someone of rank prostrating at the feet of Shiva before going to battle. Small room (25): two large boats surrounded by fish in a pond. *Apsaras* and birds fly above.

Between two towers (26): the Legend of the Leper King. From left to right: the king fights against a serpent and a crowd watches. The serpent spews his venom on the king and he contracts leprosy. The king sits in his palace and gives orders to his servants, who descend a staircase to consult with healing ascetics in the forest. Women surround the sick king and examine his hands. The king lies on the ground while an ascetic stands at his side.

Following pages: Preah Khan, east entrance.

GROUP 3 Preah Khan: the 'sacred sword'

Preah Khan, the Beguiler, the Romancer, and the artist...it is an entrancing mystery deep in the jungle, soft and alluring in the twilight made by heavy verdure, accessible only to the ardent lover of past days who is gifted with agility....They may have been courtyards where high priests gathered and guardians slept, but now they are walled bowers over which the trees extend to heaven's blue....It all seems a wondrous mass of beauty tossed together in superb confusion.[53]

Location: north-east of Angkor Thom and west of Neak Pean
Access: most enter and leave the temple from the west entrance
Tip: the best way to access Preah Khan is from the east. Arrange for your transport to take you along the levee to the east processional way between Preah Khan's moat and the North Baray. Your transport then drives to the west entrance to collect you. Entering from the west is acceptable, but the experience has less impact as you are seeing the temple in reverse.
Date: second half of the 12th century (1191)
King: Jayavarman VII (reigned 1181-1220)
Religion: Buddhist (dedicated to the father of the king)
Art style: Bayon

BACKGROUND

Preah Khan, which served as a monastery and teaching centre, is the nucleus of a group that includes the temples of Neak Pean and Ta Som, all situated on the Jayata-taka Baray, which retains water during and, for a short period, after the rains. Ceremonial causeways with figures forming a balustrade identify Preah Khan as a royal city. It is possible that the temple was constructed early in the reign of Jayavarman VII. It probably served as his temporary residence while he was rebuilding the city of Angkor Thom after the Chams sacked it in 1177.

A stone stela inscribed on four sides, recently removed to the Conservation Office for safekeeping, gives a wealth of information about the temple and its function. The inscription, found in 1939, and subsequently translated into French, indicates that Preah Khan was the ancient city of Nagarajayacri. The second part of the name, *jayacri,* is the Siamese word for sacred sword, the meaning of Preah Khan. The sacred sword has a long history in Khmer tradition as in the late ninth century Jayavarman II left his successor a sacred sword, the 'Preah Khan', which descendants still guard. The legend, though, may have originated with the Siamese.

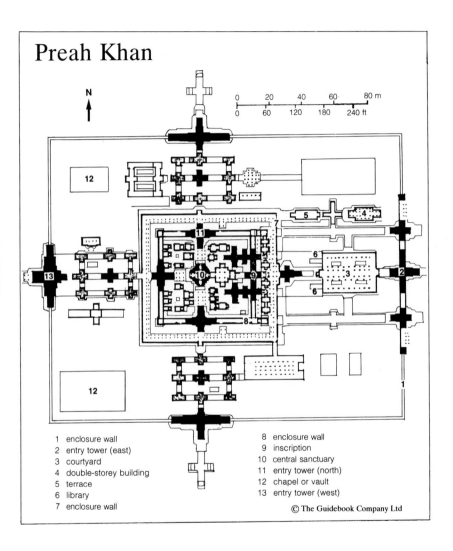

Preah Khan

1 enclosure wall
2 entry tower (east)
3 courtyard
4 double-storey building
5 terrace
6 library
7 enclosure wall
8 enclosure wall
9 inscription
10 central sanctuary
11 entry tower (north)
12 chapel or vault
13 entry tower (west)

© The Guidebook Company Ltd

Following pages: Preah Khan is a Buddhist monument, but also has several Hindu shrines.

The central sanctuary was dedicated in 1191 and then modified over the next three centuries. The Hinduisation of this Buddhist temple is an interesting aspect that is visible in several areas. The core religion was Buddhist in keeping with the king's devotion to the Mahayanist sect, but small temples and shrines in the complex dedicated to Hindu deities are also found. These were added in the 13th century after the death of Jayavarman VII during a period when Hinduism was the prevailing religion. Other evidence of efforts to change Preah Khan from a Buddhist to a Hindu temple can be seen on the lanterns lining the processional way, where images of the Buddha have been hacked out, and on the interior of the shrines, where there are several examples on the reliefs of Buddhas that have been transformed into holy men (look for cross-legged figures with beards).

The jungle surrounding Preah Khan provides a special feature. Everywhere you look you can see trees, wildly untamed and free. This natural setting enhances the feeling of serenity at the temple and frames it in a picturesque way. The jungle enclosed between the third and fourth enclosure walls, of course, is a much later phenomena. When the temple was originally built it was a large monastic complex and the living quarters for monks, students and caretakers. Although some parts of the temple may have been used throughout the 17th century, Preah Khan has not been maintained in its entirety since the middle of the 15th century, so nature appears to have settled in permanently: gigantic trees and twisted roots cling to the stones.

LAYOUT

Preah Khan comprises a vast area of 140 acres (56.7 hectares) and four enclosure walls. The outer one is a rectangular laterite wall 700 by 800 metres (2,296 by 2,624 feet) surrounded by a moat (not shown on the plan). The living quarters of those who worked and served at the temple were located inside this enclosure. A labyrinth of pavilions, halls and chapels comprising the principal religious area are enclosed by a second enclosure wall.

The main feature that signifies you have reached Preah Khan is a spectacular and unique processional way set off by a row of stone lanterns along the east and west entrances. The lantern is in the form of a pedestal with a mythical monster on the lower part and a niche, which originally contained a seated Buddha image, surrounded by a flame motif above. This ensemble precedes a paved causeway bordered by gods (on the left) and demons (on the right) holding the body of a serpent, as is found at the entrances to the city of Angkor Thom. This leads to a three-metre high laterite enclosure wall with giant *garudas* sculpted in sandstone, a motif that is reproduced every 45 metres (147 feet) around the three-kilometre (1.9-mile) long wall.

Four impressive cruciform *gopuras* provide access to the compound through the outer enclosure wall. Walk through the cruciform *gopura* and continue until you come to two enclosure walls that are quite close together. These delineate the central Buddhist complex which includes the main sanctuary. Soon you will see an intersection. Stand at this central axis and look in all directions. It is a good vantage point from which to see the perspective of rooms and galleries and the interplay of light and shade. Stroll to the south where the stone door frames the surrounding jungle. Then walk to the north for an equally rewarding view.

■ CENTRAL SANCTUARY
The central sanctuary (10) is cruciform with four porches. The centre of the interior is marked by a dome-shaped stone mound that tapers to a point (stupa). This was added in the 16th century replacing the original Avalokiteshvara carved in the likeness of Jayavarman VII's image. The walls of the central sanctuary are scored with holes, from top to bottom. These were presumably used to affix metal (perhaps bronze) panels, which may then have been engraved and gilded. It is probable the central tower was covered with intricate stucco work and gilded.

Walk through the central *gopura* and you will see to your right a series of smaller *gopura* and shrines linked by covered galleries. Directly in front of you is the stately Hall of Dancers, so-called because of the rows of *apsaras* on the lintels above eight doorways. Be sure to look at the impressive size of the doorways, especially the width. This hall is a delightful place with several good vantage points to simply sit and enjoy the surroundings. Ritual dances are occasionally performed on this terrace, proving the structure as timely today as it was eight centuries ago.

Across the terrace and, to the north, you will see an open space with a series of large thick pillars set close together on two levels.

The function of this structure (4) is unknown, although some archaeologists suggest it may have been a pavilion or a library; no trace of a stairway between the two floors has been found, as these were probably wooden and have decayed. Ascend the platform in front of you. You are now standing at the main, majestic east entrance to Preah Khan. Behind you, a footpath through dense jungle leads to the main entrance. [On the north side there is a rest house, *dharmasala*, (or possibly the Temple of the Sacred Flame) used for pilgrims, identified by the inscription of the temple (not shown on the plan). This rest house was cleared of jungle in 1993.]

Directly in front of you is a large and impressive raised platform that leads to the imposing east *gopura* (2). It connects to galleries with columns on the exterior and a wall with false windows and balusters on the interior (toward the courtyard). The walls of the *gopura* are decorated with a tapestry pattern with a base of scrolls, small female divinities and false windows with lowered blinds. The *gopura* has three porches and the centre one forms a passage to the temple. It is easily recognised because of the huge ficus tree growing amongst the stones on the south side.

Neak Pean: the 'coiled serpents'

Neak Pean is one of the temples that makes one dream of the olden days of luxury and beauty. It was worth while to live then and to be a woman among a race which has ever adored its women. It is to the overpowering temples of Civa that men and armies repaired; but it was at the tiny temple of Neak Pean that eager princesses laid their lovely offerings of wrought gold and pungent perfumes.[54]

Location: east of Preah Khan; 300 metres (984 feet) from the road
Access: enter and leave from the north entrance
Date: second half of the 12th century
King: Jayavarman VII (reigned 1181-1220)
Religion: Buddhist
Art style: Bayon

BACKGROUND

Neak Pean is located in the centre of the Jayatataka or Northern Baray and placed on the same axis as Preah Khan. A levee was built across the *baray* from the Grand Circuit by the French to provide access, and cuts directly through the north jetty and embankment of the island. Originally, it could only be reached by boat. It is a small, somewhat out-of-the-way temple with a unique layout, decoration and symbolism. The temple seems to have served as a place where pilgrims could go and take the waters, both physically and symbolically — the Khmer equivalent of a spa.

The central pond is a replica of Lake Anavatapta in the Himalayas, situated at the top of the universe, which gives birth to the four great rivers of the earth. These rivers are represented at Neak Pean by sculpted gargoyles corresponding to the four cardinal points. Lake Anavatapta was fed by hot springs and venerated in India for the curative powers of its waters. Neak Pean was probably consecrated to the Buddha coming to the glory of enlightenment. The shrine in the middle of the central pond was engulfed by a tree until 1935, when it was destroyed by a storm.

LAYOUT

The temple of Neak Pean is set in a large, square, man-made pond (70 metres, 230 feet each side), bordered by steps and surrounded by four smaller square ponds. A small circular island, with a stepped base of seven laterite tiers, is in the centre of the large square pond, and forms the base for the shrine dedicated to Avalokiteshvara. Small elephants sculpted in the round originally stood on the four corners of the pond.

The Khmers came to Neak Pean to take the waters, symbolically those of the lake at the top of the universe.

Neak Pean

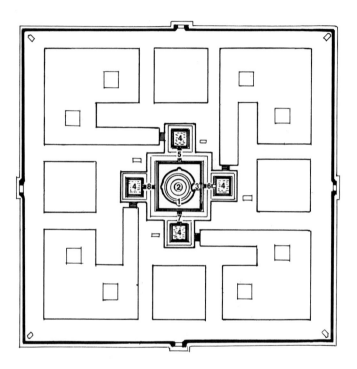

N

0   50   100   150 m

© The Guidebook Company Ltd

1 central island
2 central sanctuary
3 horse (Balaha)
4 pond
5 elephant
6 human head
7 lion
8 horse

■ CENTRAL ISLAND (1)

The bodies of two serpents encircle the base of the island and their tails entwine on the west side. It is this configuration that gave the name of 'coiled serpents' to the temple. The heads of the serpents are separated to allow passage on the east. A blooming lotus surrounds the top of the platform, while lotus petals decorate the base.

■ CENTRAL SANCTUARY (2)

It is cruciform shaped, stands on two recessed levels, opens to the east and is crowned with a lotus. The three other false doors are decorated with large images of Avalokiteshvara. The frontons depict episodes of the life of the Buddha: (east), the Cutting of the Hair; (north), the Great Departure; (west), Buddha in Meditation Protected by a Serpent.

The principal feature in the pond of the central sanctuary is a three-dimensional sculpted horse (3) swimming towards the east with figures clinging to its sides. The horse, Balaha, is a manifestation of the bodhisattva Avalokiteshvara, who has transformed himself into a horse to rescue Simhala, a merchant, and his companions of misfortune. They were shipwrecked on an island off Sri Lanka and snatched by female ogresses. The victims are holding on to the horse's tail in the hope of being carried ashore safely. This figure was found in fragments and partially reassembled by the EFEO in the 1920s. The sculpture has been badly vandalised, and most of the heads and limbs of the figures are missing.

■ FOUR SMALL CHAMBERS

These chambers have vaulted roofs and back onto the main pond, then open onto four small ponds with steps leading to the water. The interior of the vault is decorated with panels of lotus and a central waterspout in the form of an animal or human in the centre. The four buildings served a ceremonial function, where pilgrims could absolve themselves of their sins. They anointed themselves with lustral water, which flowed from the spout connected to the central pond. Each water spout is different: (north), elephant head (5); (east), human head (6); (south), lion (7); (west), horse (8). The underside of the vaults of these buildings are decorated with a lotus motif. The human head is of exceptionally fine quality workmanship and was coined the 'Lord of Men' by French archaeologists. Be sure to visit the east chamber to see it.

Zhou Daguan wrote that Neak Pean was: '...like a rich mirror, coloured by the stones, the gold and the garlands. This pool, of which the water is lit by the light of the golden prasat coloured by the red of the lotuses, shimmers in evoking the image of the sea of blood spilled by the Bhargara: on the interior there was an island taking its charm from the ponds which surround it, cleaning the mud of sin of those who came in contact with it, and serving as a boat to cross the ocean of existence.'[55]

Krol Ko: 'park of the oxen'

Location: north of Neak Pean, 100 metres (330 feet) from the road
Access: enter and leave from the east
Date: late 12th century - early 13th century
King: Jayavarman VII (reigned 1181-1220)
Religion: Buddhist
Art style: Bayon

BACKGROUND

The main point of interest at Krol Ko is the frontons on the ground. Two outstanding examples depict a bodhisattva Avalokiteshvara standing on a lotus, flanked by devotees, and a strongly modelled scene of Krishna lifting Mount Govardhana to shelter the shepherds.

LAYOUT

Krol Ko is a single tower surrounded by two laterite enclosure walls with a *gopura* at the east and a moat enclosing it with steps leading down to the water. A library built of laterite and sandstone opening to the south is on the left of the interior courtyard. The central sanctuary stands on a cruciform terrace.

Ta Som: the 'ancestor Som'

Location: east of Neak Pean
Access: enter and leave by the west entrance
Date: end of the 12th century
King: Jayavarman VII (reigned 1181-1220)
Religion: Buddhist (dedicated to the father of the king)
Art style: Bayon

BACKGROUND

Ta Som has not been restored. It is a small, quiet temple and affords a delightful undisturbed visit. A significant feature of Ta Som is the growth of a huge ficus tree on the east *gopura*, which provides a dramatic example of nature and art entwined.

LAYOUT

Ta Som is a single shrine on one level surrounded by three laterite enclosure walls. There are *gopuras* on the east and west sides, which are cruciform in shape with a small room on each side and windows with balusters. The superstructures are carved with four faces. The one on the right of the west *gopura* (south) has a beautiful smile. Walk through the west *gopura* and around the main building in a clockwise direction. At the east side, follow the footpath to the *gopura* bisecting the wall, go through it and turn back to see the tree roots entwined in the fronton. The main tower (6) is cruciform shaped with four porches. To see the inner courtyard climb through the opening in the middle of the south side.

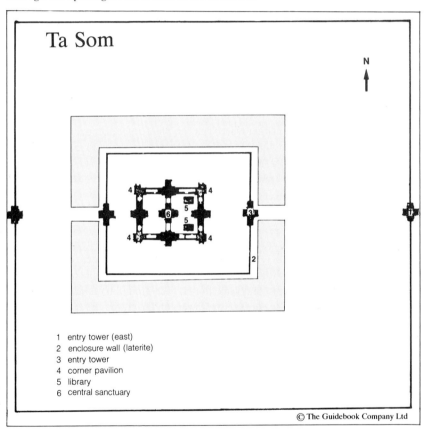

Ta Som

N

1 entry tower (east)
2 enclosure wall (laterite)
3 entry tower
4 corner pavilion
5 library
6 central sanctuary

© The Guidebook Company Ltd

GROUP 4 # Roluos

The three temples of Preah Ko, Bakong and Lolei are clustered together near the modern village of Roluos, and extend over an area of three kilometres (almost two miles) east of the Tonle Sap. The Roluos group, dating from the late ninth century, is the earliest extant site of the Angkor period that is open to visitors. The three temples belonging to this important group have similar characteristics of architecture, decoration, materials and construction methods, which combine to reveal the beginning of the classic period of Khmer art. The brick structures are decorated with magnificent sandstone deities in niches and lintels, all of which are in remarkably good condition.

To reach Roluos take the road to the Old Market in Siem Reap and continue for about 12 kilometres (7 1/2 miles). If you plan to visit the Roluos group in the morning make a short stop at the market where you can buy Cambodian textiles, cotton and silk (the market closes at 5 pm). Continue eastward for about 35 minutes — the temples are signposted down a small road on the right, which will take you to the ancestral temple of Preah Ko (on your right). This small group of six towers is exceptional in its setting, architecture and decoration.

Return to the road, turn right and continue until you come to the temple-mountain of Bakong — the temple is directly in front of you. Follow the road in a clockwise direction to the east entrance. Have your transport wait for you on the west side. You will be able to locate it from the top of the temple. Walk across the causeway which spans a moat, admiring the earliest example of a *naga* balustrade at Angkor. Enter the temple at the east and walk around it on ground level before climbing to the top. The lintels and false doors of the towers on the ground level are exceptionally beautiful.

Leave the temple at the west and continue round the temple back to the access road. Once you reach the main road turn right and look for a small road on the left; follow it to Lolei (on your left). Like the East Mebon, Lolei is situated in the middle of the Indratataka baray, which fills during the rainy season. Today, it is part of a modern temple complex. Some consider the decoration of Lolei the finest of the Roluos group. Return to the main road, turn right and follow the main road back to Siem Reap.

BACKGROUND

Roluos is the site of an ancient centre of Khmer civilisation known as Hariharalaya (the 'abode of Hari-Hara'). Some 70 years after Jayavarman II established his capital on Mount Kulen in 802 AD inaugurating the Angkor Period, he moved the capital to

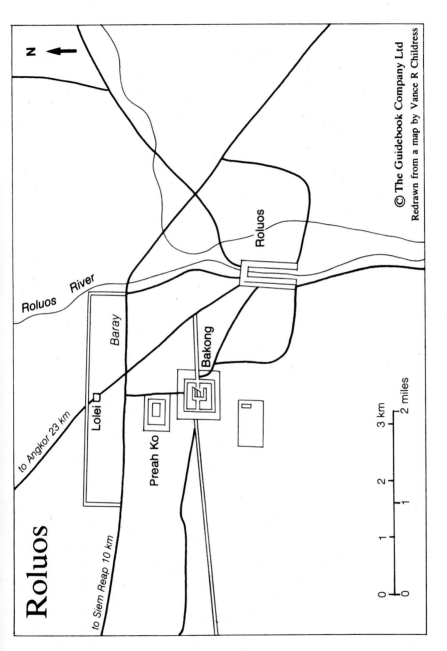

Following pages: three of the six towers at Preah Ko, dedicated to ancestors of the king.

Hariharalaya, perhaps for a better source of food or for defence purposes. Jayavarman II died at Roluos in 850 AD. It is generally believed that his successors remained there until the capital was moved to Bakheng in 905 AD.

ARCHITECTURE

The buildings of the Roluos group are distinguished by tall, square-shaped, brick towers on low pedestals. They open to the east, with false doors on the other three sides. As is typical of this period, the towers were built of brick with stucco facing; columns, lintels and decorative niches were of carved sandstone as were the sculptures set in them.

An enclosure wall originally enclosed the temples although only traces remain today. It was intersected on two or more sides by a *gopura*, an innovation of about this period (or perhaps slightly earlier). The early examples were square in plan with a tiered upper portion. The library also made its appearance at Roluos. It is a rectangular building with a vaulted roof and frontons. A temple often has two libraries, one on each side of the *gopura* preceding the central sanctuary.

DECORATION

The characteristic decorative features of the Roluos group are: a *kala* (monster head), the Hindu god Vishnu on his mount, *garuda*, female figures with abundant jewellery; and a preponderance of guardians and *apsaras*. Columns are generally octagonal and intricately adorned with delicate leaves. Decoration on the lintels at Roluos is, according to some art historians, 'the most beautiful of all Khmer art'.

Preah Ko: the 'sacred bull'

Location: between Bakong and Lolei; on the western side of the road to Bakong
Access: enter and leave the temple from the east
Date: late 9th century (879)
King: Indravarman I (reigned 877-889)
Religion: Hindu (dedicated to Shiva); funerary temple built for the king's parents, maternal grandparents, and a previous king, Jayavarman II and his wife
Art style: Preah Ko

LAYOUT

The tranquil setting and exquisite decoration of the Preah Ko towers warrant an unhurried visit. Originally square in plan and surrounded by three enclosure walls with *gopuras*, the complex seems small today because of the dilapidated state of the

Preah Ko

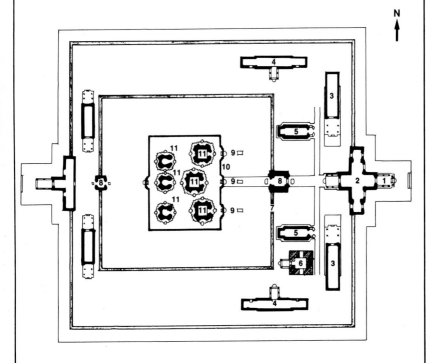

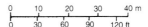

1 terrace	7 enclosure wall (brick)
2 entry tower	8 entry tower
3 base of gallery	9 crouching bulls
4 hall	10 central sanctuary base
5 gallery	11 tower
6 square brick building	

© The Guidebook Company Ltd

enclosures. The outer enclosure is 400 by 500 metres (1,312 by 1,640 feet) square with *gopuras* on the east and west sides. A small terrace (largely destroyed) (1) precedes the laterite *gopura* at the east. The sandstone pillars and windows of this *gopura* with thick balusters carved with rings, which give the appearance of being turned like wood, are still in place. The east and west wings lead to a laterite causeway that once stood at the axis of a moat.

Pass through the remains of the *gopura* and continue walking westward. Long halls or galleries parallel the middle enclosure wall, two each at the east and west, and one each at the north-east and south-east. Bases of these galleries are visible at the east. Straight ahead on the north and south sides of the walkway there are galleries with a porch opening to the east (mostly ruined) (5). An unusual, square, brick building stands between the long hall and the gallery at the south (6). It has a tiered upper portion and a porch opening to the west and is readily distinguished by rows of holes (perhaps for ventilation) and a row of figures of ascetics in niches above the holes on the upper portion of the building. The function of this building is unknown.

Continuing along the walkway in an eastward direction and you come to a brick enclosure wall (7), which has two *gopuras* at the east and directly opposite on the west (8). They are simple in design with columns and fine lintels depicting Vishnu on a *garuda*. A step at the entrance in the shape of a moonstone is noteworthy for its graceful form. An important inscription describing the temple foundations was found in the east *gopura*, which is in a dilapidated state leading through the inner enclosure wall. Beyond it are the two rectangular galleries parallel to the west enclosure wall mentioned above.

As you approach the central area at the east you see the remains of three images of *nandi*, the 'happy one', (a white bull and the mount of Shiva)(9). (Ko is the Khmer word for sacred bull). Although only portions of the bulls remain you can discern their original position facing the temple, their crouching stance and study details of these sculpted figures.

■ CENTRAL AREA

The central area consists of brick towers set towards the east in two rows on a low platform. The shrines of Preah Ko are built near ground level — a typical feature of Khmer temples that are dedicated to ancestors. A curious aspect of these is that they are unevenly spaced. In the back row, the north tower is closer to the central tower than the south one. One theory for this unusual arrangement suggests the love two ancestors had for each other in their earthly lives.

Another deviation from symmetry is that the three towers at the east are larger than those on the west; the central one in the east is the largest and set slightly back from the other two. The central tower dominates the eastern row and the north-west tower stands out in the western row. All six towers have four recessed levels at the base. Each tower contained an image of a Hindu god with whom the deceased was united. The three at the east honoured paternal ancestors of King Indravarman I and are identified by male guardians flanking the doorways, whereas the three at the west honoured his maternal ancestors and have female divinities on each side of the doorways. Three stairways leading onto the raised temple platform are guarded by pairs of sandstone lions. The only other access to the central level is a single stairway on the west side.

The central towers are square in plan with a porch in each of the cardinal directions (11). Each of the six towers of the central group was covered with elaborate stucco. Large areas of the original material are still to be found on the towers. Each door frame is of a simple design and cut in four parts with mitred corners, similar to a typical carpentry joint. The decoration on the western towers is of inferior quality to those in the front row. A curious feature of the centre tower in the back row is that the false door is brick and coated with stucco, whereas the other false doors are of sandstone.

The carved decoration on the false, sandstone doors, lintels and columns of these towers is superb. As you approach the central area, pause to study the overall façades of the three shrines at the east, so beautifully united in design, yet different in decoration. The carving on the eastern towers is of better quality than that on the western ones.

The beautiful swags of hanging garlands, seen on the lower register of many lintels, are characteristic of the Preah Ko art style. Mythical monsters, such as the kala spewing garlands, are also typical. The *kala* is a recurring theme in the decoration at Preah Ko. Identified by a monster-like head without a lower jaw, the *kala* spews foliage from its mouth which extends to the north and south sides of the lintel, where it is held by a *makara,* another mythical monster. Some outstanding carving includes: the *garuda,* surmounted by a row of small heads, on the lintels of the central tower at the west; small horsemen and figures mounted on serpents above the doors of the north-east tower.

The columns are intricately decorated with designs combining leaf, floral and geometric elements and divided into registers by carved rings. The male guardians and female divinities are finely carved and the colour of the grey sandstone contrasts dramatically with the surrounding coloured plaster and red brick background. The male figures of the eastern towers are superb examples of Khmer sculpture. The female divinities in the south-west tower hold a long-stemmed lotus.

Bakong

Location: south of Preah Ko
Access: enter and leave the temple through the east entrance. A modern, Buddhist temple occupies the north-east section of the complex
Date: late 9th century (881)
King: Indravarman I (reigned 877-889)
Religion: Hindu (dedicated to Shiva)
Art style: Preah Ko

BACKGROUND

Bakong was the centre of the town of Hariharalaya, a name derived from the god Hari-Hara, a synthesis of Shiva and Vishnu. It is a temple-mountain symbolising the cosmic Mount Meru. Four levels leading to the central sanctuary extend the symbolism, and correspond to the worlds of mythical beings (*nagas, garudas, rakasas* and *yakshas*). The fifth and topmost level is reserved for the gods — the levels represent the five cosmic levels of Mount Meru. Bakong was probably the state temple of Indravarman I.

LAYOUT

The temple of Bakong is built as a temple mountain on an artificial mound and is enclosed within two separate enclosure walls. The outer enclosure wall (not on the plan) measures 900 by 700 metres (2,953 by 2,297 feet). It surrounds a moat, and there are causeways on four sides, which are bordered by low *naga* balustrades. The inner and smaller enclosure wall (1) has a *gopura* (2) of sandstone and laterite in the centre of each side of the wall. After passing through the *gopura* at the east, follow the processional way (3) decorated with large seven-headed serpents.

Long halls (4) on each side lie parallel to the eastern wall. They were probably rest houses for visitors. Pairs of square-shaped, brick buildings at the north-east and south-east (5) corners are identified by rows of circular holes and an opening to the west. The vents in the chimneys suggest these buildings served as crematoriums. Originally, there were also buildings of this type, at the north-west and south-west corners, but today they are completely ruined. On each side of the processional way, just beyond the halls, there are two square structures with four doors (6). The inscription of the temple was found in the northern building.

Further along the processional way, there are two long sandstone buildings (7) standing parallel on each side and opening on to the causeway. These may have been storehouses or libraries. Set around the base of the tiered platform are pairs of

Bakong was at the centre of the ancient settlement of Hariharalaya.

large, brick towers which are square in plan, and which dominate the lower level. Each tower is accessible from the east only — the other three doors are false. However, stairways on each side, guarded by crouching lions, lead to the doorways. The two eastern towers have a double sandstone base. The decoration on the false doors is exceptionally fine, especially that on the north-east tower, the false door of which has remarkable handles. Niches at the corners of the towers are sheltering female and male guardians. **Tip**: the lintels of the west towers are in the best condition. A long, galleried building with a porch opening to the north (9) is situated close to the eastern enclosure wall, but it is in an advanced stage of collapse.

■ CENTRAL AREA

The diminishing platforms are square in plan with stairways on all four sides. Note the beautiful moonstones at the base of each stairway. Remains of a small structure can be seen at the base of the stairway, flanked by two sandstone blocks, which may have held sculpted figures. Elephants of diminishing size stand at the corners of the first three tiers of the base. The fourth tier is identified by 12 small sandstone towers, each of which originally contained a linga. The fifth tier is framed by a moulding, decorated with a frieze of figures (barely visible). The ones on the south side are in the best condition.

■ CENTRAL SANCTUARY

The central sanctuary (11) is visible from each of the five levels because of the unusual width of the tiers. The sanctuary is square with four tiers and a lotus-shaped finial. Only the base of the original central sanctuary remains. The upper portion was constructed at a later date, perhaps during the 12th century, which explains the lotus spire that is characteristic of that period.

Bakong

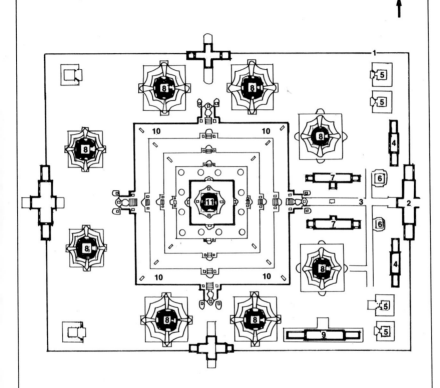

N

1 enclosure wall
2 entry tower (east)
3 causeway
4 hall
5 square building
6 square structure
7 building (sandstone)
8 sanctuary tower
9 building (gallery, porch)
10 central sanctuary base
11 central sanctuary

0   10   20   30   40   50 m
0   30   60   90   120 150 ft

© The Guidebook Company Ltd

Lolei

Location: north of the main road in the centre of the *baray*, close to a modern Buddhist temple

Access: a levee cuts across the now disused *baray* to the eastern landing platform. Enter and leave the temple by the stairs at the east

Date: end of the 9th century (893)

King: Yasovarman I (reigned 889-910)

Religion: Hindu (dedicated to Shiva); in memory of the king's father

Art style: transitional between Preah Ko and Bakheng

BACKGROUND

Lolei is worth a visit just for its exquisite carvings and inscriptions which some consider to be the finest of the Roluos group. To appreciate the setting of this temple you must imagine that the temple was originally located in the centre of a great *baray*, the Indratataka. According to an inscription found at the temple, the water in this pond was for use at the capital of Hariharalaya and for irrigating the plains in the area.

LAYOUT

The layout consists of a double platform rising originally from the *baray* surrounded by a laterite enclosure wall on all four sides. Lions on the landings of the stairways guard the temple. The four towers are set on a smaller brick platform. A sandstone channel in the shape of a cross situated in the centre of the four towers is an unusual feature. The channels extend to the cardinal directions from a square pedestal for a *linga*. It is speculated that holy water poured over the *linga* flowed in the channels.

■ CENTRAL TOWERS

The four brick towers appear randomly placed on a raised brick platform. As the two north towers are aligned on the east–west axis, it is possible that the original plan was for six towers which probably shared a common base like that at Preah Ko. Niches in the corners of the towers on the east shelter male guardians holding tridents and those of the west with female divinities holding fly whisks. They are sculpted in sandstone. The panels of the false doors have multiple figures. The inscriptions on the door frames of these towers are exceptionally fine.

The tiered upper portion of a brick tower at Lolei.

GROUP 5 Prasat Kravan: the 'cardamon sanctuary'

Location: east of Angkor Wat and south of Banteay Kdei
Access: drive off the road to the east and follow round to the east side. Enter and depart from the temple on the east
Date: first half of the 10th century (921)
King: completed during the reign of Harshavarman I (c910-923). It may have been built by high court officials.
Religion: Hindu
Art style: transitional from Bakheng to Koh Ker

BACKGROUND

Although this temple looks small and somewhat undistinguished from the outside, it contains some remarkable brick sculptures on its interior walls which stand alone as unique examples in Khmer art. The interiors of two of the five towers have sculptures depicting Vishnu and his consort, Lakshmi; the scene in the central tower is the most impressive one, but both are exceptional in stature and quality of workmanship. This temple was reconstructed by the French and given a new foundation, interior walls and drains. Much of the external brickwork was replaced with carefully made reproductions which are marked with the letters CA (Conservation d'Angkor).

LAYOUT

Prasat Kravan consists of five brick towers in a row on one platform, which are decorated with carved, sandstone lintels and columns. All of the towers open to the east.

■ CENTRAL TOWER

This is the only tower with intact recessed tiers, which are visible on the interior. The columns are octagonal, with four bare sides and sandstone rings. This tower encloses a *linga* on a pedestal. An inscription on the door frame gives the date 921 for the erection of the statue of Vishnu on the interior. The east decoration of the central tower is sculpted with male guardians in shallow niches and chevrons and framed figures on the pilasters. A frieze of small heads adorns the lintel.

The interior decoration of this tower depicts, on the left, Vishnu taking three steps to span the universe and to assure the gods of the possession of the world. It comprises a standing image of Vishnu (with four arms) carrying his attributes — a disc, a ball, a conch and a club. One of his feet rests on a pedestal. Nearby a person is meditating and another one is walking on a lotus held by his wife on a background of undulating lines, representing the waves of the ocean. On the right, Vishnu on the shoulders of *garuda* stands between two worshippers. Facing, Vishnu (with eight arms) is framed with six registers of people meditating and a giant lizard across the top (difficult to distinguish). This sculpture on brick was formerly coated with stucco and was probably highlighted with colours.

■ **NORTH TOWER**
This tower was dedicated to Lakshmi, consort of Vishnu. Her four hands hold her symbols of power and she is flanked by kneeling admirers; the niche is decorated with tassels and floral swags.

■ **SOUTH TOWER**
The walls on the interior have no decoration. A skilfully modelled lintel on the exterior depicts with Vishnu on his mount, a *garuda*.

Srah Srang: the 'royal bath'

It was, perhaps, a chapel to Kama, god of love. The spot would suit the temper of the strange power, terribly strong and yet terribly tender, of that passion which carries away kingdoms, empires, whole worlds, and inhabits also the humblest dwellings....Love could occupy this quiet nest embedded in water...gave the impression that love had come one day and had left there, when he went away, a part of his spirit.[56]

Location: across the road from the east entrance of Banteay Kdei
Access: visit Srah Srang east of the road
Date: end of the 12th century
King: Jayavarman VII (reigned 1181-1220)
Religion: Buddhist
Art style: Bayon

BACKGROUND
Srah Srang is a large lake (700 by 300 metres, 2,297 by 984 feet) with an elegant landing terrace of superb proportion and scale. It is a pleasant spot to sit and look out over the surrounding plain. Facing east, straight ahead, you can see the towers of Preah Rup. Srah Srang always has water and is surrounded by greenery. According to one French archaeologist, it 'offers at the last rays of the day one of the most beautiful points to view the Park of Angkor'.

LAYOUT

A majestic platform ('landing stage') with stairs leads to the pond. It is built of laterite with sandstone mouldings. The platform is of cruciform shape with serpent balustrades flanked by two lions. At the front there is an enormous garuda riding a three-headed serpent. At the back there is a mythical creature comprising a

The elegant terrace with stairs at Srah Srang (the royal bath).

three-headed serpent, the lower portion of a *garuda* and a stylised tail decorated with small serpent heads. The body of the serpent rests on a dais supported by mythical monsters.

Banteay Kdei: the 'citadel of the cells'

In the ruin and confusion of Banteay Kdei the carvings take one's interest. They are piquant, exquisite, not too frequent...they seem meant...to make adorable a human habitation.[57]

Location: south-east of Ta Prohm
Access: enter and leave from the east
Date: middle of the 12th century to the beginning of the 13th century
King: Jayavarman VII (reigned 1181-1220)
Religion: Buddhist
Art style: at least two different art periods — Angkor Wat and Bayon — are discernible

BACKGROUND

Banteay Kdei was built as a Buddhist monastic complex by Jayavarman VII and was undoubtedly an important temple. Today, however, it is difficult to perceive what Banteay Kdei might have looked like because of its dilapidated condition, due largely to faulty construction and the use of poor quality sandstone which has a tendency to crumble. Changes and additions carried out after the initial construction of the temple also account for its confused and unbalanced present-day layout.

Nevertheless, it is worth a visit as it has some good carving and is less crowded than other monuments of the same period. The temple is similar in art and architecture to Ta Prohm, but it is smaller and less complex. It is also not as overtaken by nature as Ta Prohm because it was occupied by monks over the centuries, except in the 1960s when it was inaccessible because it was inhabited by a herd of dangerous wild deer. It is unknown to whom this temple was dedicated as the inscription stone has never been found.

LAYOUT

According to archaeologists, the original basic plan of Banteay Kdei included a central sanctuary (5), a surrounding gallery (6) and a passageway connected to another gallery. A moat enclosed the temple, another enclosure (700 by 500 metres, 2,297 by 1,640) is made of laterite (1) and has four *gopuras* in the Bayon style, each with four faces looking in the cardinal directions, and *garudas* placed at the corners of each *gopura*, a favourite design of Jayavarman VII. These *gopuras* are of the same style as those at Ta Prohm.

A path leads from the east *gopura* to a grand rectangular terrace that is known as the Hall of the Dancing Girls, a name derived from the decoration, which includes a frieze of dancers (2). From this terrace you can see the moat that enclosed the temple. Walk across the terrace and continue westward. On the north side of the walkway you will see remains of large, thick pillars, which probably supported a building of wood. The pillars are similar although not round like those at Preah Khan.

The *gopura* of the second enclosure (3) is cruciform with three passages; the two on either end are connected to the laterite wall of the enclosure (4). The inner walls of the enclosure are decorated with scrolls of figures and female divinities in niches. In the interior court there is a frieze of Buddhas.

Continuing westward you reach the central area, which appears confused because many parts have collapsed and some of the halls and galleries are later additions. The central area is approached through a large entrance that was originally a tower, but has now collapsed. The tower was connected to a gallery with rows of pillars on each side. This arrangement of a tower with a gallery enclosed yet another gallery with four towers, one in each corner, the central sanctuary and a courtyard in a cruciform-shaped plan. Traces of carving are still visible in the central shrine.

The walls of the central sanctuary were probably covered, perhaps with metal. Two small sanctuaries, sometimes called libraries (7), open to the west in the courtyards on the left and right of the causeway.

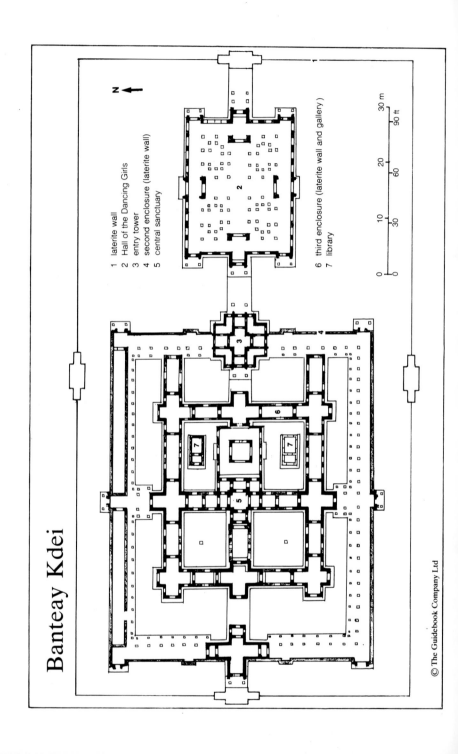

Banteay Kdei

1 laterite wall
2 Hall of the Dancing Girls
3 entry tower
4 second enclosure (laterite wall)
5 central sanctuary

6 third enclosure (laterite wall and gallery)
7 library

0   10   20   30 m
0   30   60   90 ft

© The Guidebook Company Ltd

Preah Rup: 'turn, or change, the body'

A work of great style and impeccable proportions, Maurice Glaize wrote in his guidebook of 1963

Location: north-east of Srah Srang and 500 metres (1,640 feet) south of the East Baray

Access: enter and leave the monument from the east entrance. To climb to the upper terrace use the east stairway; it is slightly less steep than the others

Tip: because the temple is built entirely of brick and laterite, the warm tones of these materials are best seen early in the morning or when the sun is setting. Two views from the top terrace are outstanding: first looking east towards Phnom Bok and the Kulen Hills; and second looking west, where the towers of Angkor Wat can be distinguished on the far horizon

Date: second half of the 10th century (961)

King: Rajendravarman II (reigned 944-968)

Religion: Hindu (dedicated to the god Shiva)

Art style: Preah Rup

BACKGROUND

Preah Rup was called the 'City of the East' by Philippe Stern, the Assistant Curator of the Musee Guimet in Paris. The boldness of the architectural design is superb and gives the temple fine balance, scale and proportion. The temple is close in style to the East Mebon, although it was built several years later. It is a temple-mountain symbolising Mount Meru.

The Cambodians have always regarded this temple as having funerary associations, but its true function is uncertain. Nevertheless, the name Preah Rup recalls one of the rituals of cremation, in which the silhouette of the body of the deceased, outlined with its ashes, is successively represented according to different orientations. Some archaeologists believe that the large vat located at the base of the east stairway to the central area (**9**) was used at cremations.

LAYOUT

Preah Rup dominates the vast plain which the East Baray irrigated. Constructed on an artificial mountain in laterite with brick towers, the plan is square and comprises two enclosure walls (**1** and **2**) with *gopuras* placed centrally in each wall. A platform of three narrow tiers (**3**) serves as a pedestal for five towers, which are set out in

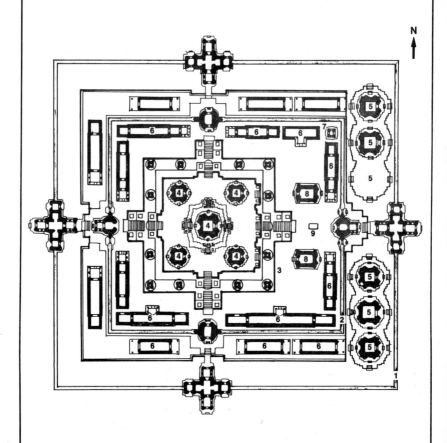

Preah Rup

0	10	20	30	40 m
0	30	60	90	120 ft

N

1 enclosure wall (laterite)
2 enclosure wall (laterite)
3 base with 3 tiers
4 tower on upper platform
5 group of three towers

6 hall
7 small square building
8 library
9 vat

© The Guidebook Company Ltd

quincunx — one in each corner and one in the centre (4). The outer enclosure wall is 127 by 116 metres (417 by 380 feet).

Within the outer laterite enclosure wall there are two groups of three towers on each side of the entrance (5); the groups share a common base. The middle tower in each of the two groups dominates and is more developed than the others. It appears that the first tower on the right of the entrance was never built or, if it was, its bricks were reused elsewhere. The most complete lintel is on the tower at the east face of the southernmost tower, and it depicts Vishnu in his *avatara* as a man-lion.

The second enclosure wall (2), also built of laterite, has four small *gopuras*, one on each side. Long halls are placed between the two enclosure walls (6). The walls of these halls, which have sandstone porches, are built of laterite. In the courtyard, there are vestiges of long halls probably for use by pilgrims. They have sandstone pillars in the east and laterite walls and windows with balusters in the west. In the north-east corner there is a curious small square building (7) built of large blocks of laterite and open on all four sides. The inscription describing the foundation of the temple was found near this building.

■ LIBRARIES

On the left and right sides of the east *gopura* of the second enclosure there are libraries (8) with high towers. They sheltered carved stones with motifs of the nine planets and the seven ascetics. In the centre there is a vat (9) between two rows of sandstone pillars. Glaize suggested, as the temple was dedicated to Shiva, that rather than being a dias for a coffin this platform was more likely to have a been a base for a wooden structure or a platform for Shiva's mount nandi.

■ CENTRAL AREA (3, 4)

The three tiered platform can be approached by a stairway on all four sides. Pedestals flanking the stairways are adorned with seated lions of which those on the lower diminish the higher they go. The first two tiers are built of laterite and have simple supporting walls with moulded bases and cornices. The third tier is built of sandstone, and there are two additional stairways on the east side guarded by lions. At the first level, 12 small shrines containing linga and opening to the east are evenly spaced around the platform.

The five central towers on the top platform are open to the east. All remaining doors are false and exquisitely carved in sandstone with figures and plant motifs. Large sections of the original stucco work are still to be seen especially on the south-west tower. There is also a depiction of Brahmi, the feminine aspect of Brahma with four faces and arms. On the west elevation of this tower there is another divinity with four arms and heads. It is Vishnu in his *avatara* as a boar. Figures in the niches are surrounded by flying *apsaras*. The figures in the two west towers are female while those at the east and central towers are male.

East Mebon

The lovely temple of Mebon, a pyramid of receding terraces on which are placed many detached edifices, the most effective being the five towers which crown the top. Could any conception be lovelier, a vast expanse of sky-tinted water as wetting for a perfectly ordered temple.[58]

Location: 500 metres (1,640 feet) north-east of Preah Rup
Access: enter and leave the temple from the east entrance
Date: second half of the 10th century (952)
King: Rajendravarman II (reigned 944-968)
Religion: Hindu (dedicated to Shiva); an ancestor temple in memory of the parents of the king
Art style: Preah Rup

Background

The East Mebon and its neighbour Preah Rup were built by the same king, just nine years apart, and are similar in plan, construction and decoration. A major difference, however, is that the East Mebon once stood on a small island in the middle of the Eastern Baray, which was a large body of water (2 by 7 kilometres, 1.2 by 4.3 miles) fed by the Siem Reap River. The only access was by boat to one of the four landing-platforms, situated at the mid-points on each of the four sides of the temple.

Today, the *baray*, once a source of water for irrigation, is a plain of rice fields and the visitor is left to imagine the original majesty of this temple in the middle of a large lake. You can get some idea of what the view must have been like from walking around the top level. Archaeologists have estimated that the original *baray* was three metres deep with a volume of 40 million cubic metres of water. The decoration on the lintels at the Mebon is superior in quality of workmanship and composition to that of Preah Rup. The motifs on the false doors, with small mythical figures frolicking amongst foliage, are particularly fine.

Layout

The East Mebon is a temple-mountain symbolising Mount Meru with five towers in quincunx atop a platform of three diminishing tiers. The whole is surrounded by three enclosure walls. Construction work in this temple complex utilises all the durable building materials known to the Khmers — laterite, brick, stucco and sandstone.

East Mebon

N

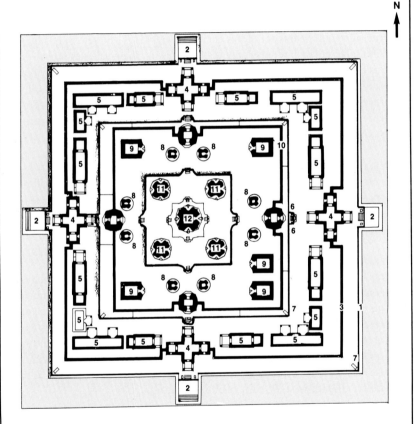

1 outer enclosure wall
2 terraced landing
3 enclosure wall
4 entry tower
5 gallery
6 lions
7 elephants

8 tower (brick)
9 rectangular building (laterite)
10 wall (sandstone)
11 tower (upper terrace)
12 central sanctuary

© The Guidebook Company Ltd

The outer enclosure wall (1) is identified by a terraced landing built of laterite with pairs of lions on each of the four sides (2). The interior of this wall is marked by a footpath. The middle enclosure wall has centrally placed cruciform *gopuras* , that provide access through the middle enclosure wall on all four sides (4). The *gopuras* containing three doors with porches are constructed of laterite and sandstone.

An inscription was found to the right of the east tower. A series of galleries built in laterite surround the interior of this enclosure wall (5). They were originally roofed in timber rafters but today only vestiges remain. These galleries probably served as halls for meditation. The stairways of the tiered base are flanked by lions (6). Beautifully sculpted two-metre high, monolithic elephants stand majestically at the corners of the first and second tiers (7). They are very realistic with details of their harnesses and other decoration. **Tip:** the elephant in the north-west corner is in the best condition.

■ GOPURAS

Lintels on the west *gopura* (4) depict Vishnu in his *avatara* of Narasingha, half-man, half-lion, where he is disposing of the king of the demons by renting him apart (east face). The lintels of the north-east *gopura* show Lakshmi standing between two elephants which, with raised trunks, are sprinkling her with lustral water.

■ INNER COURTYARD

The large inner courtyard contains eight small brick towers (8) — two on each side — opening to the east. Each one has octagonal columns and finely worked lintels with figures amongst leaf decorations. On the east side of the courtyard there are three windowless, rectangular, laterite buildings (9) opening to the west. Vestiges of bricks above the cornices suggest they were vaulted. The two on the left of the entrance are decorated either with scenes of the stories of the nine planets or with the seven ascetics. Two more buildings, without windows, of similar form stand at the north-west and south-west (9) corners of the courtyard.

■ UPPER TERRACE

The terrace with the five towers was enclosed by a sandstone wall with moulding and decorated bases (10). Lions guard the four steep flights of stairways to the top platform.

■ CENTRAL TOWERS

The five towers on the upper terrace were built of brick and open to the east; the remaining false doors on each of the towers are made of sandstone (11 and 12). Male guardians on the corners are finely modelled. Circular holes pierced in the brick, for the attachment of stucco, are visible. The false doors of the towers have fine decoration with an overall background pattern of interlacing small figures on a plant motif.

■ CENTRAL SANCTUARY: LINTELS ON THE TOWERS OF THE UPPER LEVEL
East side: Indra on his mount, a three-headed elephant, with small horsemen on a branch; scrolls with mythical beasts spewing figures under a small frieze of worshippers; west side: Skanda, god of war, rides his peacock; south side: Shiva rides his sacred bull, nandi.

■ NORTH-WEST CORNER TOWER
(East side): Ganesha is curiously riding his trunk, which is transformed into a mount.

■ SOUTH-EAST CORNER TOWER
(North side): the head of a monster is eating an elephant.

GROUP 6 Ta Prohm: the 'ancestor Brahma'

Ta Prohm's state of ruin is a state of beauty which is investigated with delight and left with regret. But one can always come again. And one always does.[59]

Location: Ta Prohm is located south-east of Ta Keo and east of Angkor Thom. Its outer enclosure wall is close to the north-west corner of Banteay Kdei

Access: arrange for your transport to take you to the east entrance of Ta Prohm and walk through the complex in sequence. Have your transport wait for you at the west entrance. As you leave the temple, you will pass the more popular west entrance, where refreshment stalls are located, as well as scores of children selling handicrafts — a barrage of shouting mostly avoided by entering from the east

Date: mid-12th century to early 13th century (1186)

King: Jayavarman VII (reigned 1181-1220)

Religion: Buddhist (dedicated to the mother of the king)

Art style: Bayon

Tip: a torch and a compass are useful for visiting this temple at all times of day

BACKGROUND

Ta Prohm was left untouched by archaeologists, except for the clearing of a path for visitors and structural strengthening to stave off further deterioration. Because of its natural state, it is possible to experience at this temple some of the wonder of the early explorers, when they came upon these monuments in the middle of the 19th century. Shrouded in jungle, the temple of Ta Prohm is ethereal in aspect and conjures up a romantic aura. Trunks of trees twist amongst stone pillars. Fig, banyan and *kapok* trees spread their gigantic roots over, under and in between the stones, probing walls and terraces apart, as their branches and leaves intertwine to form a roof above the structures.

'Everywhere around you, you see Nature in its dual role of destroyer and consoler; strangling on the one hand, and healing on the other; no sooner splitting the carved stones asunder than she dresses their wounds with cool, velvety mosses, and binds them with her most delicate tendrils; a conflict of moods so contradictory and feminine as to prove once more—if proof were needed—how well 'Dame' Nature merits her feminine title!'[60]

The monastic complex of Ta Prohm is one of the largest sites at Angkor. A

Ta Prohm remains much as it was when it was 'discovered' by the Europeans.

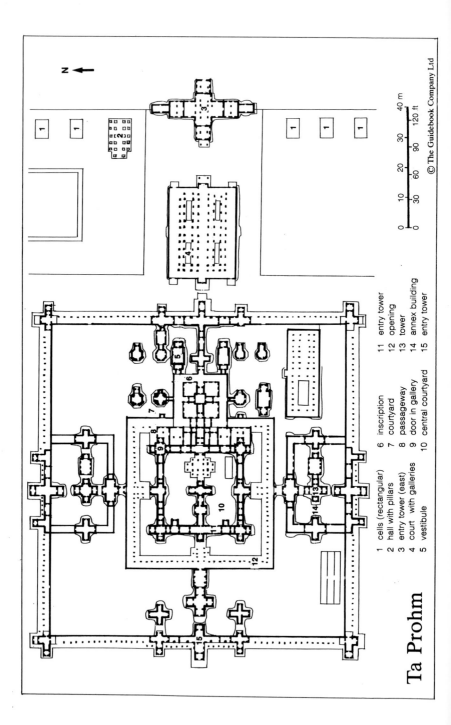

Ta Prohm

1 cells (rectangular)	6 inscription	11 entry tower
2 hall with pillars	7 courtyard	12 opening
3 entry tower (east)	8 passageway	13 tower
4 court with galleries	9 door in gallery	14 annex building
5 vestibule	10 central courtyard	15 entry tower

0 10 20 30 40 m
0 30 60 90 120 ft

© The Guidebook Company Ltd

Sanskrit inscription on stone, now removed to the Conservation d'Angkor, tells us something about its size and function. Ta Prohm owned 3,140 villages. It took 79,365 people to maintain the temple, including 18 high priests, 2,740 officials, 2,202 assistants and 615 dancers. Among the property belonging to the temple was a set of golden dishes weighing more than 500 kilograms (1,100 pounds), 35 diamonds, 40,620 pearls, 4,540 precious stones, 876 veils from China, 512 silk beds and 523 parasols.[61] Even considering that these numbers were probably exaggerated to glorify the king, Ta Prohm must have been an important and impressive monument.

LAYOUT

The monastic complex of Ta Prohm is a series of long, low buildings standing on one level connected with passages and concentric galleries framing the main sanctuary. A rectangular, laterite wall (700 by 1,000 metres, 2,297 by 3,281 feet) encloses the entire complex. While this is the layout determined by archaeologists it is not seen clearly today because of the poor condition of the temple and the invasion of the jungle. While this temple was originally built according to the symmetrical, repetitive plan that is a hallmark of Khmer architecture, Ta Prohm seems haphazard and some areas of the temple are impassable; others are accessible only by narrow covered passages and, of course, much of the temple's fascination for the visitor lies in this disarray.

The east entrance is signalled by a *gopura* in the outer enclosure wall of the temple. Pass through it and follow the path from the east entrance walking westward. You come to a grand terrace paved in sandstone and slightly elevated, which precedes the east *gopura* of the enclosure wall which surrounds the temple proper. Walk past the *gopura* and inside are rectangular cells parallelling the enclosure wall; and just north of the *gopura* is a sandstone hall, known as the Hall of the Dancers, distinguished by large, square pillars. Enclosed with high walls and connected to galleries, this impressive area is richly decorated and was probably used for the performance of ritual dances as suggested by rows of lively apsaras dancing gracefully across the walls. It cannot be entered due to the state of the ruins.

Continue walking towards the west. In the central area you see a series of galleries and shrines, some of which are very close together. Female divinities stand gracefully in niches, often entwined with roots; and Buddhist scenes, sometimes hastily and other times finely carved, decorate the facades and frontons. A fine example of the *apsara* motif is on the library in the north and south of the central galleries. A memorable aspect of this central courtyard is the many openings filled with foliage and framed by stone doorways or windows.

The central sanctuary itself is easy to miss and stands out because of its absence of decoration. The stone has been hammered, possibly to prepare it for covering with

Following pages: little has been done to restore Ta Prohm, except structural strengthening to stave off further deterioration.

stucco and gilding, which has since fallen off. This accounts for the plainness of the walls of this important shrine. Evenly spaced holes on the inner walls of the central sanctuary suggest they were originally covered with metal sheets.

From this point, visiting Ta Prohm is really going wherever your instincts lead you, to enjoy the wonder of making new discoveries, of finding hidden passages or obstructed reliefs, of climbing over fallen stones, and of experiencing the harmony between man and nature. There are many pleasant spots to simply sit and enjoy the tranquil surroundings.

Continue walking westward and pass through a central cruciform-shaped *gopura* in the first enclosure wall. Next is a terrace with remains of stone sculpture scattered in the area, which must have been imposing figures when they were in place. A walkway flanked by a serpent balustrade leads to the west *gopura* providing access through the first enclosure wall surrounding the temple. The walk westward towards your transport is along a delightful shaded path through the jungle. The large cruciform-shaped east *gopura*, recognisable by a tower with four faces, looking towards each of the cardinal points marks the west entrance to Ta Prohm and leads you through the outer enclosure wall.

'So the temple is held in a stranglehold of trees. Stone and wood clasp each other in grim hostility; yet all is silent and still, without any visible movement to indicate their struggle—as if they were wrestlers suddenly petrifed, struck motionless in the middle of a fight. The rounds in this battle were not measured by minutes, but by centuries'.[62]

Ta Keo: the 'ancestor Keo or the tower of crystal or glass'

The majestic ziggurat of Ta Keo, most enigmatic of the minor fanes, stepping up toward the sun with a dignity and power suggestive of Angkor Vat. It is dripping with green and crowned with trees, but is still supreme over the forest. Its rocky masses, rising above the tops of the coconut palms, convey the impression that it only recently emerged from some cavern underground, carrying the forest with it in its rocketing ascent. Ta Keo's lack of ornament makes it distinctive among the works of the Khmers, who were so prodigal of decoration. But its very simplicity gives it architectural importance. Its plan shows the development of a new spirit in the people, the growth of good taste.[63]

Location: east of Thommanon and Chau Say Tevoda on the east bank of the Siem Reap River

Ta Keo

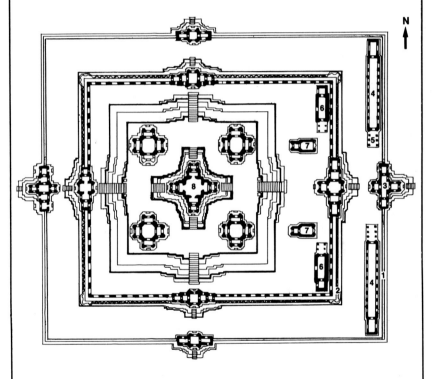

1 enclosure wall
2 enclosure wall
3 entry tower (east)
4 long hall

5 porch with pillars
6 hall (rectangular)
7 library
8 central sanctuary

© The Guidebook Company Ltd

Access: enter and leave by the east entrance
Date: end of the 10th century to early eleventh century
King: Jayavarman V (reigned 968-1001) to Suryavarman I
(reigned 1002-1050)
Religion: Hindu (dedicated to Shiva)
Art style: Kleang

BACKGROUND

Ta Keo is one of the great temple-mountains at Angkor. It was never completed and the reason is unknown, although the death of the king may well have had something to do with it. One theory also suggests that work was halted because the temple was struck by lightning. Had it been finished, Ta Keo, undoubtedly, would have been one of the finest temples at Angkor. The temple rises to a height of 22 metres (72 feet) to the sky, giving an impression of strength and power. An innovation at Ta Keo is a porch at each cardinal point on the five towers of the top level. A gallery was situated on a second base and had a roof of brick (now destroyed), also for the first time. Enormous blocks of feldspathic wacke — a very hard to carve, greenish-grey sandstone — were cut to a regular size and placed in position. The absence of decoration at Ta Keo gives it a simplicity of design that separates it from the other monuments.

LAYOUT

Ta Keo is a replica of Mount Meru with a rectangular plan and five square towers arranged in a quincunx, standing majestically on a finely moulded three-tiered pedestal that is 12 metres (39 feet) high. Two enclosure walls (1 and 2) with sandstone *gopuras* on four sides enclose the temple. Inscriptions on the pilasters of the east *gopura* describe the temple's foundation (3). The first two platforms are enclosed by a wall (lower platform) and by a narrow gallery (upper platform).

The east entrance to Ta Keo is marked by a causeway over a moat that is preceded by a pair of lions and a row of small lanterns defining the east processional way. The east *gopura* has a central opening with a tower that is flanked by two smaller gates. Long rectangular halls (4 and 6) on both levels probably sheltered pilgrims. Access to the halls was under a second terrace. It is enclosed completely by a sandstone gallery with inward facing windows. Two libraries on the east side of the platform open to the west.

■ CENTRAL AREA

The upper platform is square and stands on three diminishing tiers with stairways on each side. Most of the space on the upper level is occupied by the five towers, all unfinished, opening to the four cardinal points. The central sanctuary (8) dominates the layout. It is raised above the other towers and is given further importance by the development of porches. The interior of the central tower is undecorated, but this draws your attention to the size of the sandstone blocks raised to such a height. It overwhelms you as you wonder how the Khmers managed to manoeuvre these enormous stones into position.

Chapel of the Hospital

Location: west of Ta Keo and Spean Thma; on the west side of the road
just over the bridge across the Siem Reap River
Access: enter and leave the monument from the east
Date: end of the 12th century
King: Jayavarman VII (reigned 1181-1220)
Religion: Buddhist
Art style: Bayon

BACKGROUND
An inscription found in the area confirms the identity of this site as one of the chapels of the 102 hospitals built by the king.

LAYOUT
Traces of a cruciform-shaped gopura of sandstone and laterite situated at the east remain. A short walkway precedes the single tower of this site. The central sanctuary is cruciform-shaped opening to the east with false door on the other three sides. Female divinities adorn the exterior and a scroll surrounds the base of the tower. The pediments are decorated with images of the Buddha.

Spean Thma: the 'bridge of stone'

Location: 100 metres (330 feet) west of Ta Keo
Access: located in a bend of the Siem Reap River on the west side of the
new bridge on the road between Ta Keo and Thommanon. Walk
from the side of the road and down the path to the bank of the
Siem Reap River.

BACKGROUND
Spean Thma is a bridge constructed of reused blocks of sandstone of varying shapes and sizes, which suggests it was built to replace an earlier bridge. The orientation of

the bridge seems odd today because the course of the river has changed, probably due to the erosion of the river bed. The river has meandered to the east (parallel to the old bridge) and, then, turns sharply to the south again. Notice the great difference in the former and present levels of the river bed. This is probably one of the reasons for the dry barays, as the Siem Reap River was one of several to provide water to the irrigation system. The river now flows along the right side of the bridge instead of under its arches.

LAYOUT
The bridge is supported on massive pillars, the openings between them spanned by narrow corbelled arches. Reportedly, there are traces of 14 arches.

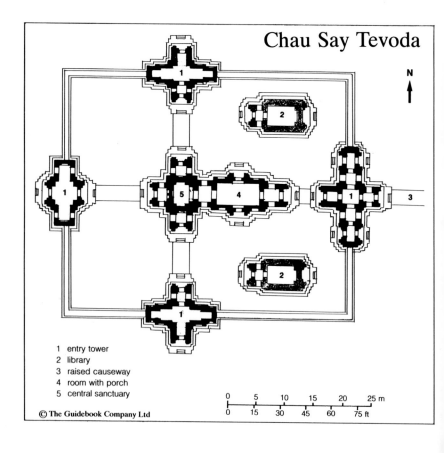

Chau Say Tevoda

N

1 entry tower
2 library
3 raised causeway
4 room with porch
5 central sanctuary

© The Guidebook Company Ltd

```
0    5    10   15   20   25 m
0    15   30   45   60   75 ft
```

Chau Say Tevoda

Two symmetrical shrines, Thom Manon and Chau Say — alike in design and structure and twins also in ruin.[64]

Location: east of the Gate of Victory of Angkor Thom, a short distance across the road south from Thommanon
Access: enter and leave by the north
Date: end of the 11th century–first half of the 12th century
King: Suryavarman II (reigned 1113-1150)
Religion: Hindu
Art style: Angkor Wat

BACKGROUND

Chau Say Tevoda and Thommanon are two small monuments framed by the jungle, that stand across the road from each other. Because of similarities in plan and form they are often referred to as the brother-sister temples. Although the exact dates of these monuments are unknown, they belong stylistically to the period of classic art and represent two variations of a single theme of composition. Chau Say Tevoda has deteriorated more than Thommanon, which has undergone a complete reconstruction.

LAYOUT

Chau Say Tevoda is rectangular in plan, with a central sanctuary opening to the east and an enclosure wall with *gopuras*, originally providing central access points through the walls. Two libraries open to the west occupy spaces in the north-east and south-east corners.

Walking towards the temple you can see traces of a moat and vestiges of laterite determining the line of the single enclosure wall.

■ GOPURAS

The *gopuras* are in a state of total collapse except for traces of their platforms and stairways. A raised causeway (3) on three rows of octagonal supports (added at a later date) and a terrace, link the east *gopura* to the nearby Siem Reap River.

■ CENTRAL SANCTUARY

Walk around the central sanctuary and notice the detailed carving on the exterior and the finely carved female divinities in the corner niches. Those on the west facade are especially beautiful. A rectangular room with a porch (4) precedes the central sanctuary (5) and connects it with the east *gopura* by a passage raised on three rows of columns of which only traces remain. The exterior wall of this long room is covered with a floral pattern inscribed in squares and sculpted with stone flowers similar to those at Banteay Srei and the Baphuon. The three false doors of the central sanctuary are decorated with foliage, while the columns have floral diamond-shaped patterns; human figures accentuate some of the bands of foliage on the columns.

Thommanon

Location: east of the Gate of Victory of Angkor Thom, a short distance (north) across the road from Chau Say Tevoda
Access: enter and leave Thommanon from the south.
Date: end of the 11th century–first half of the 12th century
King: Suryavarman II (reigned 1113 -1150)
Religion: Hindu
Art style: Angkor Wat

BACKGROUND
Thommanon is one of a pair of temples strategically placed outside the east gate (Victory) leading into Angkor Thom. In the 1960s, an extensive programme of anastylosis was undertaken at Thommanon by the EFEO, hence its sound condition today. It contrasts well with its counterpart Chau Say Tevoda.

LAYOUT
Thommanon is rectangular in plan with a sanctuary (1) opening to the east, a moat and an enclosure wall with two *gopuras*, one on the east and another on the west (2), and one library (3) near the south-east side of the wall. Only traces of a laterite base of the wall remain.

■ CENTRAL SANCTUARY
The base of the tower is finely modelled and decorated; the foliage of the middle band has raised figures. There are four porches, one on each side of the central tower. The decoration on the three false doors of these porches is exceptionally delicate. Also notice the highly stylised, yet exquisite, female divinities. The east lintel depicts Vishnu on a *garuda*. A porch with tiers on the east *gopura* connects with a long hall. The fronton above the south door is in poor condition, but it depicts Ravana (with multiple heads and arms) trying to shake the mountain where Shiva is enthroned. Over the doorway towards the adjoining vestibule, a fronton depicts the death of Vali after his battle against Sugriva.

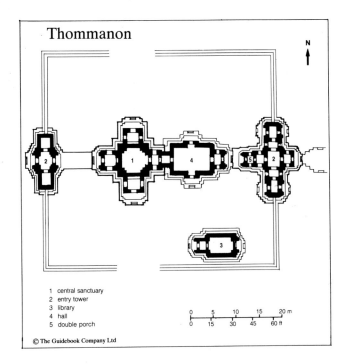

Thommanon

N

1 central sanctuary
2 entry tower
3 library
4 hall
5 double porch

0   5   10   15   20 m
0   15   30   45   60 ft

© The Guidebook Company Ltd

■ EAST GOPURA

This *gopura* is linked by a common platform to the long hall. The entrance has three openings and bays that have been walled up. The centre has four porches, and at the west is a portico in front of a porch. Cylindrical vaulting can be seen on one recessed level. The north fronton depicts Vishnu felling two of his enemies, one of whom he holds by the hair.

■ LIBRARY

The library has elongated windows with balusters that have been walled up. The interior is paved with laterite. The library opens to the west with a small porch and two windows; there is a false door on the east side.

■ GOPURA (WEST)

The *gopura* has a central gate and is flanked by two wings with windows. The building shows absolute purity of lines in its architecture, and great care has been taken with the decoration. The west fronton depicts Vishnu on a *garuda* battling against the demons. The columns and the base are ornamented with human figures; the false tiles on the end of the vaults represent lions.

Baksei Chamkrong: the 'bird who shelters under its wings'

This little temple with its four square tiers of laterite, crowned by a brick sanctuary, might serve for a model in miniature of some of its giant neighbours, and is almost as perfect as the day it was built....[65]

Location: north of Phnom Bakheng, and on the west of the road leading to the south gate of Angkor Thom

Access: a visit to Baksei Chamkrong can be combined with a stop at the south gate of Angkor Thom. Enter and leave the temple from the east entrance

Tip: the architecture and decoration of this temple can be viewed by walking around it (in a clockwise direction). The stairs are in poor condition; if you want to climb to the top use either the north or south stairway.

Date: middle of the 10th century (947)

King: perhaps begun by Harshavarman I (reigned 910-944) and completed by Rajendravarman II (reigned 944-968)

Religion: Hindu (dedicated to Shiva); may have been a funerary temple for the parents of the king

Art style: transitional between Bakheng and Koh Ker

BACKGROUND

The name of the temple derives from a legend in which the king fled during an attack on Angkor and was saved from being caught by the enemy when a large bird swooped down and spread its wings to shelter him. Baksei Chamkrong was the first temple-mountain at Angkor built entirely of durable materials — brick and laterite with sandstone decoration. It is situated near the foot of Phnom Bakheng, but it need not be overshadowed by that great temple-mountain because, even though it is small, the balanced proportions and scale of this monument are noteworthy and elevate it to masterpiece status. Inscriptions on the door reveal the date of the temple and mention a golden image of Shiva and the mythical founders of the Khmer civilisation.

LAYOUT

Baksei Chamkrong is a simple plan with a single tower on top of a square, four-tiered laterite platform of diminishing sizes (27 metres, 89 feet, a side at the base,

d 12 metres, 39 feet, high)
(1–4). Three levels of the
ase are undecorated, but the
top platform has horizontal
mouldings around it that sets
off the sanctuary. Steep stair-
ases on each side lead to the
anctuary. Originally, a brick
nclosure wall (5) with a
gopura to the east enclosed
he temple. Some vestiges are
still visible on the east side of
the temple.

■ CENTRAL SANCTUARY (7)
The square, central brick
tower stands on a sandstone
base. The fine jointing of the
brickwork is noteworthy. It
has one door opening to the
east with three false doors on
the other sides, which are in
remarkably good condition.

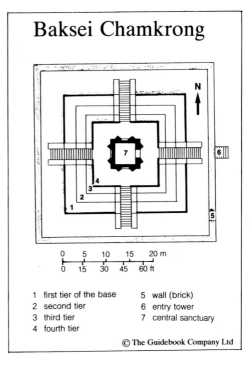

Baksei Chamkrong

| 0 | 5 | 10 | 15 | 20 m |
| 0 | 15 | 30 | 45 | 60 ft |

1 first tier of the base
2 second tier
3 third tier
4 fourth tier

5 wall (brick)
6 entry tower
7 central sanctuary

© The Guidebook Company Ltd

A vertical panel in the centre of each false door contains motifs of foliage on stems.
As is typical of tenth-century Khmer architecture, the columns and lintels are made
of sandstone and decorated in a motif that imitates wood carving. An outline of female divinities can be seen in the bricks at the corners of the tower.

Unfortunately, the stucco that once adorned this temple has disappeared, although the holes where it would have been attached are visible. Most of the lintels
are in poor condition, but, on the east, Indra riding a three-headed elephant is still
recognisable and is finely carved. The interior of the tower has a sunken floor and a
corbelled vault.

Phnom Bakheng

It is a testimony to the love of symmetry and balance which evolved its style...in pure simplicity of rectangles its beauty is achieved. It is a pyramid mounting in terraces, five of them....Below Bak-Keng lies all the world of mystery, the world of the Khmer, more mysterious than ever under its cover of impenetrable verdure.[66]

Location: 1,300 metres (4,265 feet) north-west of Angkor Wat and 400 metres (1,312 feet) south of Angkor Thom

Access: in the 1960s this summit was approached by elephant and, according to one French visitor, the ascent was 'a classic promenade and very agreeable '. This route has recently been cleared and it is the easiest way to the top taking 15 to 20 minutes. Alternatively, you can climb the hill by a steep path with some steps on the east side of the monument (height 67 metres, 220 feet)

Tip: the best times to visit are in the morning or at sunset. On a clear day from the upper platform of Bakheng it is possible to see: the five towers of Angkor Wat, Phnom Krom to the south-west near the Grand Lake, Phnom Bok in the north-east, Phnom Kulen in the east, and the West Baray. This view should not be missed.

Date: late 9th to early 10th century

King: Yasovarman I (reigned 889-910)

Religion: Hindu (dedicated to Shiva)

Art style: Bakheng

BACKGROUND

Soon after Yasovarman became king in 889 AD, he decided to move the capital north-west from Roluos, where his predecessor reigned, to the area known today as Angkor. He named his new capital Yasodharapura, and built Bakheng as his state temple. Thus, Bakheng is sometimes called the 'first Angkor'. The original city, which is barely distinguishable to visitors today, was vast, even larger than Angkor Thom. A square wall, each side of which is 4 kilometres (2.5 miles) long, surrounded the city, enclosing an area of some 16 square kilometres (6 square miles). A natural hill in the centre distinguished the site.

'It is difficult to believe, at first, that the steep stone cliff ahead of you is, for once, a natural feature of the landscape, and not one of those mountains of masonry to which Angkor so soon accustoms you...the feat of building a flight of wide stone steps up each of its four sides, and a huge temple on the top, is a feat superhuman enough to tax the credulity of the ordinary mortal.'[67]

Phnom Bakheng

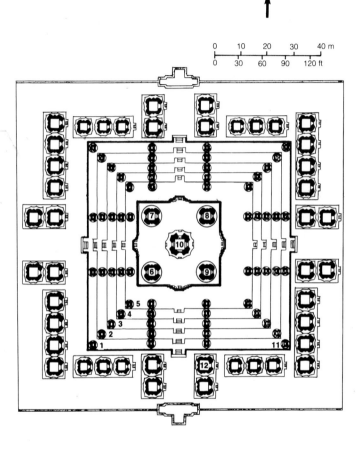

1 first tier of the base	6-9 towers on the top level
2 second tier	10 central sanctuary
3 third tier	11 tower (brick)
4 fourth tier	12 tower around base
5 fifth tier	

The temple of Bakheng was cut from the rock that formed the natural hill and faced with sandstone. Traces of this method are visible in the north-east and south-east corners. It reflects improved techniques of construction and the use of more durable materials. This temple is the earliest example of the quincunx plan with five sandstone sanctuaries built on the top level of a tiered base, which became popular later. It is also the first appearance of secondary shrines on different levels of the platform.

Symbolism

Bakheng was a replica of Mount Meru and the number of towers suggests a cosmic symbolism. The seven levels (ground, five tiers, upper terrace) of the monument represent the seven heavens of Indra in Hindu mythology. The temple must have been a spectacular site in its entirety because originally 108 towers were evenly spaced around the tiers with yet another one, the central sanctuary, at the apex of them all. Today, however, most of these towers have collapsed. Besides the central sanctuary, there were 4 towers on the upper terrace, 12 on each of the 5 levels of the platform, and another 44 towers around the base (11). The brick towers on the different levels represent the 12-year cycle of the animal zodiac. It is also possible that the numerology of the 108 towers symbolises the 4 lunar phases with 27 days in each phase. The arrangement allows for only 33 of the towers to be seen from each side, a figure that corresponds with the number of Hindu deities.

Layout

'Every haunted corner of Angkor shares in the general mystery of the Khmers. And here the shadows seem to lie a little deeper, for this hill is like nothing else in the district.'[68] At the top of the hill, Phnom Bakheng is set on a tiered platform of five levels. The temple consisting of five towers in quincunx is located on the top most platform. The platform is square and each side measures 76 metres (249 feet) long and its total height is 13 metres (43 feet). There are stairways of a very steep gradient on all four sides. Seated lions flank the steps at each of the five levels.

There are vestiges of a laterite enclosure wall with *gopuras* surrounding the complex. Beyond there is a small building to the north with sandstone pillars in which there are two *lingas*. Continuing towards the top, you come to a modern footprint of the Buddha in the centre of the path. This is enclosed in a cement basin and covered with a wooden roof. Closer to the top, remains of a *gopura* in the enclosure wall around the temple complex are visible. Two libraries opening only to the west on either side of the path are identified by rows of diamond-shaped holes in the walls; the doors on the east are modern additions.

TOP LEVEL

When Henri Mouhot stood at this point in 1859, he wrote in his diary: 'Steps...lead to the top of the mountain, whence is to be enjoyed a view so beautiful and extensive, that it is not surprising that these people, who have shown so much taste in their buildings, should have chosen it for a site.'[69] Five towers are arranged in quincunx. The central tower once contained the *linga* to which the temple was dedicated. There are openings to all four cardinal points. The remaining four sanctuaries also sheltered lingas on pedestals and are open on two sides.

The central sanctuary (**10**) is decorated with female divinities set in niches at the corners of the temple which have delicately carved bands of foliage above; the pilasters are finely worked and have raised interlacings of figurines. The *makaras* on the tympanums are lively and strongly executed. The decoration above the doors is well-preserved showing a panel of foliated cusps with the heads of 33 gods. An inscription is visible on the west side of the north door of the central sanctuary. The evenly spaced holes in the paving near the east side of the central sanctuary probably held wooden posts which supported a roof.

The view of Angkor Wat from Phnom Bakheng.

Espying the Ethereal City of Nakhon Wat

'I had already been in Siam several months before I could carry out the project which had originally taken me to that country. My plan was to cross overland into Cambodia, and there photograph the ruined temples and examine the antiquities which have been left behind by the monarchs of a once powerful empire. Mr. H. G. Kennedy, of H.B.M.'s consular service, consented to accompany me on this expedition, and we got away together on January 27, 1866.

. . . The Chow Muang of Nakhon Siamrap received us with great courtesy, placing a house at our disposal for two or three days, until a Laos chief, who had come with a considerable escort on a pilgrimage to Nakhon Wat, should have started on his homeward journey, and left room for our accommodation. The old town of Siamrap is in a very ruinous state—the result, as was explained to us, of the last invasion of Cambodia—but the high stone walls which encircle it are still in excellent condition. Outside these fortifications a clear stream flows downwards into the great lake some fifteen miles away, and this stream, during the rainy season, contains a navigable channel. On the third morning of our stay we mounted our ponies, and passed out of the city gates on the road for Nakhon Wat, and the ancient capital of the Cambodian empire. One hour's gentle canter through a grand old forest brought us to the vicinity of the temple, and here we found our progress materially arrested by huge blocks of freestone, which were now half buried in the soil. A few minutes more, and we came upon a broad flight of stone steps, guarded by colossal stone lions, one of which had been overthrown, and lay among the débris. My pony cleared this obstacle, and then with a series of scrambling leaps brought me to the long cruciform terrace which is carried on arches across the moat. This moat is a wide one, and has been banked with strong retaining walls of iron-conglomerate. The view from the stone platform far surpassed my expectations. The vast proportions of the temple filled me with a feeling of profound awe, such as I experienced some years afterwards when sailing beneath the shade of the gigantic precipices of the Upper Yang-tsze.

. . . I believe that a richer field for research has never been laid open to those who take an interest in the great building races of the East than that revealed by the discovery of the magnificent remains which the ancient Cambodians have left behind them. Their stone cities lie buried in malarious forests and jungles, and though many of them have been examined, not a few are still wholly unexplored; and indeed it is impossible for anyone who has not visited the spot to form a true estimate of the wealth and resources of the ancient Cambodians, or of the howling wilderness to which their country has been reduced by the ravages of war, the destructive encroachments of tropical jungle, . . . The disappearance of this once splendid civilisation, and the relapse of the people into a primitiveness bordering, in some quarters, on the condition of the lower animals, seems to prove that man is a retrogressive as well as a progressive being, and that he may probably relapse into the simple forms of organic life from which he is supposed by some to have originally sprung.

. . . We spent several days at the ruined city of Nakhon, on the verge of the native jungle, and amidst a forest of magnificent trees. Here we were surrounded on every side by ruins as multitudinous as they were gigantic; one building alone covered an area of vast extent, and was crowned with fifty-one stone towers. Each tower was sculptured to represent a four-faced Buddha, or Brahma, and thus 204 colossal sphinx-like countenances gazed benignly towards the cardinal points— all full of that expression of purity and repose which Buddhists so love to portray, and all wearing diadems of the most chaste design above their unruffled stony brows. At the outer gate of this city, I experienced a sort of modern 'battle of the apes'. Reared high above the gateway stood a series of subordinate towers, having a single larger one in their centre, whose apex again displayed to us the four benign faces of the ancient god. The image was partly concealed beneath parasitic plants, which twined their clustering fibres in a rude garland around the now neglected head. When I attempted to photograph this object, a tribe of black apes, wearing white beards, came hooting along the branches of the overhanging tree, swinging and shaking the boughs, so as to render my success impossible. A party of French sailors, who were assisting the late Captain de Lagrée in his researches into the Cambodian ruins, came up opportunely, and sent a volley among my mischievous opponents; whereupon they disappeared with what haste they might, and fled away till their monkey jargon was lost in the recesses of the forest.'

John Thomson, The Straits of Malacca, Indo-China, and China; or, Ten Years' Travels, Adventures, and Residence Abroad, 1875

GROUP 7 Banteay Srei: the 'citadel of the women'

The tenth century temple of Banteay Srei is renowned for its intricate decoration carved in pinkish sandstone that covers the walls like tapestry. This site warrants as much time as your schedule allows. The roads have been recently repaired and it takes about 30 minutes from Siem Reap to get to the temple. To reach Banteay Srei, follow the main road north out of Siem Reap, turn right at Angkor Wat and follow the road to Srah Srang where you turn right past Preah Rup. At the East Mebon there is a check post where you need to obtain clearance. Turn right again at the road before the East Mebon; pass through the village of Phoum Pradak, where there is a junction (if you continue straight, after about 5 minutes, you will reach Banteay Samre). At this point, you come to a fork; take the road on the left and follow it to Banteay Srei which you will reach shortly after crossing two rivers — on your left-hand side.

> *Banteai Srei...is an exquisite miniature; a fairy palace in the heart of an immense and mysterious forest; the very thing that Grimm delighted to imagine, and that every child's heart has yearned after, but which maturer years has sadly proved too lovely to be true. And here it is, in the Cambodian forest at Banteai Srei, carved not out of the stuff that dreams are made of, but of solid sandstone.*[70]

Location: 25 kilometres (15.5 miles) north-east of East Mebon
Access: enter and leave the temple by the east entrance
Date: second half of the 10th century (967)
King: Rajendravarman II (reigned 944-968) and Jayavarman V (reigned 968-1001)
Religion: Hindu (dedicated to Shiva)
Art style: Banteay Srei

BACKGROUND

The enchanting temple of Banteay Srei is nearly everyone's favourite site. The special charm of this temple lies in its remarkable state of preservation, small size and excellence of decoration. The unanimous opinion amongst French archaeologists who worked at Angkor is that Banteay Srei is a 'precious gem' and a 'jewel in Khmer art'. Banteay Srei, as it is known by locals, was originally called Isvarapura, according to inscriptions. It was built by a Brahmin of royal descent who was spiritual teacher to

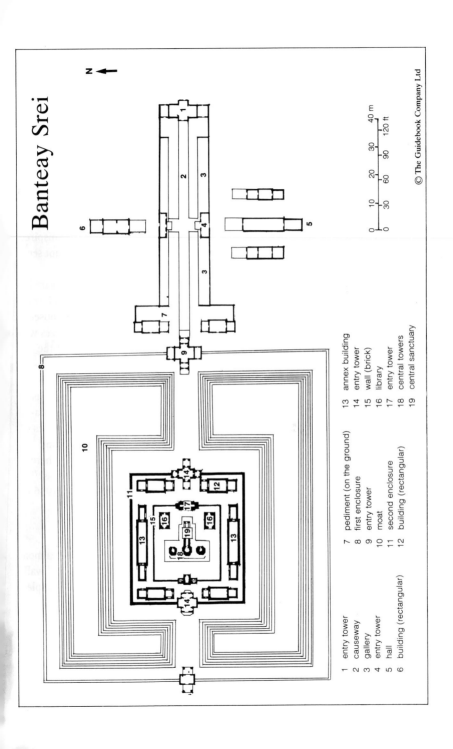

Banteay Srei

N ←

1 entry tower
2 causeway
3 gallery
4 entry tower
5 hall
6 building (rectangular)

7 pediment (on the ground)
8 first enclosure
9 entry tower
10 moat
11 second enclosure
12 building (rectangular)

13 annex building
14 entry tower
15 wall (brick)
16 library
17 entry tower
18 central towers
19 central sanctuary

0   10   20   30   40 m
0   30   60   90   120 ft

© The Guidebook Company Ltd

Jayavarman V. Some describe it as being closer in architecture and decoration to Indian models than any other temple at Angkor. A special feature of the exquisite decoration was the use of a hard pink sandstone (quartz arenite) which enabled the 'technique of sandalwood carving with even an Indian scent to it'.

Architectural and decorative features of Banteay Srei are unique and exceptionally fine. A tapestry-like background of foliage covers the walls of the structures in the central group as if a deliberate attempt had been made to leave no space undecorated. The architecture is distinguished by triple superimposed frontons with relief narrative scenes carved in the tympanums, terminal motifs on the frames of the arches, and standing figures in the niches. Panels are decorated with scenes inspired by Indian epics, especially the *Ramayana* and its execution has a liveliness not seen in the more formal decoration of earlier temples.

The temple was discovered by the French in 1914, but the site was not cleared until 1924. The theft of several important pieces of sculpture and lintels by a European expedition, meticulously planned by the young Frenchman, Malraux, caused a great public scandal in 1923, but hastened the archaeological work. The thieves were held under house arrest in Phnom Penh and only released after the return of the stolen pieces.

Banteay Srei is the first temple at Angkor to have been completely restored by the process of anastylosis, after the EFEO studied this method at Borobudur on the island of Java in Indonesia. Compared to the rest of Angkor this temple is in miniature. The doors of the central towers are narrow and barely one and a half metres (five feet) in height. The quality of architecture and decoration make up for any shortcomings in size. As M Glaize wrote, Banteay Srei is 'a sort of "caprice" where the detail, of an abundance and incomparable prettiness, sweeps away the mass'.[71] The inscription relating to the foundation of Banteay Srei was discovered in 1936 in the easternmost *gopura* of the outer enclosure wall.

LAYOUT

Banteay Srei is rectangular in plan and enclosed by three enclosure walls and a moat. Only two of the enclosure walls are visible. Enter the temple from the east and walk through the cruciform laterite *gopura* on the principle east-west axis of the temple at the axis of the enclosure wall (1). The sandstone pillars and a fronton depicting Indra on a three-headed elephant on the east porch of the *gopura* give a hint of the warm colour of the stone and the exquisite decoration to come.

After walking through the east *gopura* you will be on the processional way (2) with decorative sandstone markers. Long pillared galleries overlook the processional way. They are built with laterite walls and sandstone pillars, in the middle of which are small *gopuras* (4). Behind the galleries to the south are three long, parallel halls,

Banteay Srei's pink sandstone was carved with some of the finest decorative work at Angkor.

which are oriented north to south (5). On the north side there is a single building (6) with a superb fronton of Vishnu in his *avatara* as man-lion. Be sure to walk through the *gopura* to see this fronton.

Continue walking westward and at the end of the causeway to the south is a fronton set at the ground level (7), depicting the abduction by Viradha of Sita, wife of Rama. Take the opportunity to study the carving close up and at eye level, as it is a fine example of the workmanship to be found at Banteay Srei.

Walk through the east *gopura* (9) leading you to the middle enclosure, and you will be looking towards the central enclosure across a moat lined with laterite. Walking westwards you will pass through and enter the temple complex encircled by a laterite, enclosure wall. The *gopura* has two porches and triangular-shaped frontons reminiscent of wooden architecture, which are framed with large terminal scrolls. Inscriptions can be seen on the door frames of this tower. Inside the central complex area are six annex buildings built of laterite (12, 13), which may have served as rest houses for meditation.

■ CENTRAL GROUP

You have now reached the central area of the temple, which is the most important and the most beautiful. It is surrounded by a brick enclosure wall that has almost entirely collapsed (15). However, there are remnants on either side of the east *gopura*. Walk through the *gopura* (17) and in the central courtyard you will see two libraries on each side of the walkway (16). They both open to the west and have laterite and sandstone walls with an unusual corbelled vault in brick.

Look straight ahead, and you will see three shrines arranged side by side in a north to south line standing on a common, low platform and opening to the east (18). The principal shrine in the centre contained the *linga* of Shiva; the shrine on the south was also dedicated to Shiva, whereas the one on the north honours Vishnu. All three central shrines are of a simple form with a superstructure comprising four tiers, decorated with miniature replicas of the main shrine which symbolise the dwelling of the gods. The shrines are guarded by sculptures of mythical figures with human torsos and animal heads kneeling at the base of the stairs leading to the entrances. Most of these figures are copies; the originals have been removed for safekeeping.

Take time to study the overall appearance of the central complex before looking at the details. The buildings are a veritable assemblage of architectural, sculptural and decorative triumph. Hardly any space is left uncarved and the whole is covered with intricate and delicate motifs. Foliage designs abound, but so do geometric patterns and they are intertwined to produce work of extraordinary beauty.

Now begin to explore the elements of this total composition. It is suggested that you start by walking around the entire central area to get a perspective of the size and an understanding of the orientation of the buildings, then look at the elements in more detail following the order of this guide. There are many more discoveries to be made at this temple besides the highlights mentioned below. Allow time to see the lintels, the false doors and to probe the nooks and crannies to find new and unexpected surprises that will delight you.

Divinities on the central towers: the figures of male and female divinities standing in recessed niches at the corners are perfect in proportion, balance and artistic style. The females have plaited hair or a bun tied at the side, in a style characteristic of Banteay Srei, and simply dressed with loosely draped skirts. They wear exquisite jewellery, including heavy earrings that weigh down their elongated ear lobes, garlands of pearls hanging from their belts, bracelets, arm and ankle bands and elaborate necklaces.

The males are equally as appealing and stand guard holding a lance, a lotus or other emblem. Their dress is even more simple that the female, and consists of a loin cloth that imitates a pocket fold on the thigh. The face is sublimely noble and the hair intricately plaited and pulled up into a cylindrical chignon. The niche around the figures emulates decorated pillars on each side and a beautiful lobed arch with a flame-like design. The whole is supported by monkey-faced mythical figures.

Library on the left (south): on the east fronton is a scene from the *Ramayana*. Ravana, king of the the demons of Lanka (Sri Lanka) and the enemy of Rama, goes to Mount Kailasa, home of Shiva and his wife, Parvati, where he tries to enter, but is forbidden access. He is furious and shouts at the monkey-headed guardian, who yells back saying that Ravana's power will be destroyed by the monkeys. Ravana (multiple heads and arms) is so angry he raises the base of Mount Kailasa (represented by a pyramid on a background of stylised forest) and shakes it with all his might trying to lift up the mountain.

Shiva sits on his throne at the summit of the mountain while his terrified wife, Parvati, hovers near his left knee, clinging to his shoulder. Shiva retaliates and prepares to bring the whole weight of the mountain upon Ravana with his toe. The mountain falls on Ravana and crushes him under its mass. Ravana acknowledges Shiva's power and sings his praises for 1,000 years. As a reward, Shiva sets him free and gives him a sword. Other figures in the scene include creatures, hermits and animals living on the mountain who express their terror and flee to the jungle. On the first step the monkey-faced guardian of the mountain raises his hand, perhaps to warn Ravana that one day he will be destroyed by the monkeys.

On the west fronton: Shiva is in the Himalayas meditating and living the life of an ascetic. Parvati tries to attract his attention, but fails and is disappointed that he does not notice her. The gods ask Kama, god of love, to assist Parvati and help her

distract Shiva from his meditation. Kama shoots one of his flowery arrows into Shiva's heart. The latter is angry and shoots a fiery ray from his frontal eye, reducing Kama to ashes. Shiva casts his eyes on Parvati and is enamoured by her beauty. He marries her and Shiva brings Kama back to life. A group of ascetics below Shiva, as well as figures with human bodies and animal heads, complete the scene.

North library: on the east fronton (from the top), Indra, god of the sky, is depicted scattering celestial rain (parallel rows of oblique lines) on a stylised forest inhabited by animals. Indra rides in a chariot drawn by a three-headed elephant and is surrounded by winds and clouds (wavy lines). The rain falls on the wings of birds flying by. A *naga* (serpent), god of the waters, rises in the midst of the rain. Below, a pastoral scene is depicted with charm and skill. Krishna, as a baby, and his brother, Balarama, (holding the shaft of a plough) are surrounded by animals in the forest and seem to be enjoying the freshness brought by the rain.

On the west fronton the scene takes place in a palace and the theme concerns Krishna, who murders his cruel uncle, King Kamsa, because he tried to kill him when he was a child. Krishna approaches the dais, clutches Kamsa by the hair, and throws him off his throne. The two-storied palace is supported by columns, and is a fine example of the architecture of the period. Garlands decorate the first floor and the profile of the palace is a series of recessed stages. The two main figures in the scene are indicated by their size. The women wear expressions of shock and confusion over the murder. Below, Krishna and his brother kill wrestlers. On each side, helpers stand in chariots drawn by animals.

Central Sanctuary (19): the male guardians in the corners of the central tower are magnificent specimens of Khmer sculpture. Their hair is swept up in a cylindrical chignon and they hold a lotus in one hand and a lance in the other. The lintels on the central sanctuary are finely carved. The themes are: (north) a battle between the monkeys, Vali and Sugriva; (west) the abduction of Sita; (south) a wild boar.

Cosmic symbolism and mythology cover almost the whole of Banteay Srei.

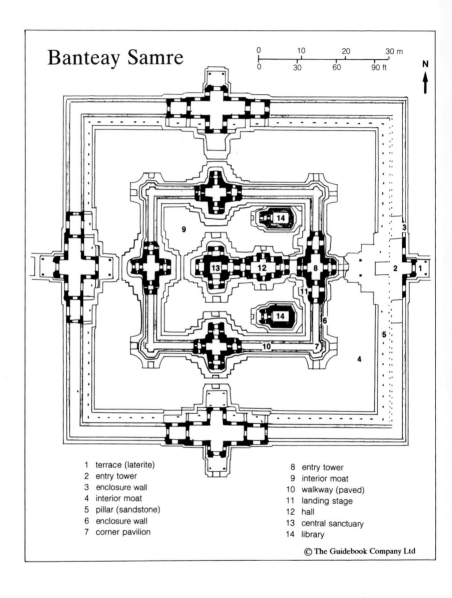

Banteay Samre

1 terrace (laterite)
2 entry tower
3 enclosure wall
4 interior moat
5 pillar (sandstone)
6 enclosure wall
7 corner pavilion

8 entry tower
9 interior moat
10 walkway (paved)
11 landing stage
12 hall
13 central sanctuary
14 library

© The Guidebook Company Ltd

Banteay Samre: the 'citadel of the Samre'

Location:400 metres (1,312 feet) east of the East Baray
Access: enter and leave Banteay Samre from the east
Date: middle of the 12th century
King: Suryavarman II (reigned 1113-1150)
Religion: Hindu (dedicated to Vishnu)
Art style:Angkor Wat

Warning This temple is somewhat isolated, and you should be vigilant of your possessions and travel with a local guide. The temple is worth the extra effort to experience the elaborate architecture, and fine carvings, although theft has mutilated many of the temple's treasures.

BACKGROUND

Banteay Samre is one of the most complete complexes at Angkor due to restoration using the method of anastylosis. Unfortunately, the absence of maintenance over the past 20 years is evident. The name Samre refers to an ethnic group of mountain people, who inhabited the region at the base of Phnom Kulen and were probably related to the Khmers. No inscription has been found for this temple, but the style of most of the architecture is of the classic art of the middle period similar to Angkor Wat. The monument most likely dates from the same period, or, perhaps, slightly later, although there are additions attributed to the Bayon style. The proportions of Banteay Samre are splendid. A unique feature is an interior moat with laterite paving, which when filled with water must have given an ethereal atmosphere to the temple. All of the buildings around the moat are on a raised base with horizontal mouldings, decorated in some areas with figures framed by lotus buds.

LAYOUT

The plan of Banteay Samre is roughly square and consists of a laterite enclosure wall with four *gopuras*. Behind the wall, overlooking the enclosed moat, are *gopuras* on each side. The central courtyard contains the main sanctuary, which has four wings and is approached by a long hall with libraries on each side. Begin your visit to this temple from the east, and walk along the laterite, paved causeway (length 200 metres, 656 feet), which leads to the east *gopura* providing access through the outer enclosure wall of the monument.

The causeway, on two levels (not shown on the plan), is bordered on each side by serpent balustrades in the style of Angkor Wat, of which only vestiges remain. The end of the causeway leads to a stairway flanked by crouching lions on short columns. This long and dramatic causeway was probably covered with a wooden roof.

A laterite terrace (1), probably built later, leads to and forms the base of the cruciform east *gopura* (2) of the outer enclosure wall (3) shown on the plan (83 by 77 metres, 272 by 253 feet). Walk through the *gopura* and you will notice the courtyard (4) is surrounded by a gallery supported with sandstone pillars (5). Vestiges of the framework are still visible. The gallery is lit by windows decorated with five to seven balusters. The remains of three *gopuras* are of similar design to that at the east.

Continue walking westward and pass through the *gopura* leading to the sanctuary. The interior moat (in front of you, now dry with mature papaya trees growing in it) is a unique feature (9).

A seated deity flanked by elephants on a fronton at Banteay Srei.

The enclosure wall (44 by 38 metres, 144 by 125 feet) around the central temple complex is raised above floor level and consists of a low, narrow, laterite gallery with pavilions (7) at each corner and *gopuras* with ridged crests central to the wall. These structures, which were probably added at a later date, have simple entrances that overlook the moat (9), and windows with balusters that have been walled up. There are stone finials across the centre ridge of the roof of the galleries and shards of which are scattered on the grounds around the temple.

A paved, sandstone cloister surrounds the interior moat (10). A walk around this path gives you the chance to view the central sanctuary from all angles. Notice especially the stairs leading to the moat, which are bordered by serpent balustrades terminating with a remarkably finely carved fan of multiple heads. These so-called 'landing stages' (11) intercept the walkway around the courtyard. My favourite of these stages is the one at the east, to the left of the *gopura*. It is best seen from the southeast side. The *gopura* on the east of the enclosure to the central area leads to an open-air platform and a long hall (12) in front of the central sanctuary (13).

■ CENTRAL SANCTUARY (13)
The central tower is square in plan and built of sandstone. Its upper portion has recessed stages in a lotus-shaped profile that typifies 12th century architecture. The tower has porches and double frontons on each side opening to the cardinal points. There are three false doors on the remaining elevations. The reliefs on the upper levels of this Hindu sanctuary depict Buddhist scenes. **Tip:** to see the decoration on the highest part of the central tower continue westward through to the end; then, either go to the left or the right on the paved, sandstone cloisters and look back at the central sanctuary.

■ LIBRARIES
The cramped placement of the libraries (14) in the north-east and south-east sections of the central sanctuary suggests a change in the original plan. The libraries have slender proportions with exposed corbelled vaulting, false aisles, pierced with long windows and frontons. The decoration on the false doors is remarkably fine. The door on the south library is the best preserved.

A particularly fine depiction of the birth of Brahma is depicted on the fronton of the north-east library, west face. In this cosmic myth, Vishnu reclines on his side on the serpent, Ananta, and floats on the ocean. His upper torso rests on his elbow. A golden lotus emerges from the navel of Vishnu signifying the beginning of a new cosmic period. The lotus opens and Brahma appears to preside over the new creation.

GROUP 8   West Baray

This half-day tour provides a break from looking at ruins of temples and enables you to take a pleasant boat trip on the West Baray, the largest man-made body of water at Angkor. You can hire a boat to take you to the island in the middle where the temple of the West Mebon once stood. Today, only traces of it remain. But the island is a pleasant spot for a picnic or just walking around when the water level is low. Alternatively, you can go for a refreshing swim.

To reach the West Baray, leave Siem Reap on the airport road to the north-west. Continue past the turning off to the airport and just prior to crossing a large canal turn to the right (north) down a bumpy road running parallel to the canal and follow it until you reach the levee around the south bank of the *baray*.

The West Baray is a vast man-made lake, surrounded by an earthen levee which forms a dyke. According to legend, the young daughter of a ruler of Angkor was grabbed by an enormous crocodile, which made a large opening in the south dyke of the West Baray that can still be seen today. The crocodile was captured and killed. The princess, still living in its stomach, was rescued.

As the temple in the middle is in the same style as the Baphuon, the *baray* was probably constructed in the 11th century. The east dyke leads to the temple of Bakheng. Some historians believe the West Baray could have been a mooring place for the royal barges as well as a reservoir and a place for breeding fish. **Tip**: it is a special experience to bathe in what must be one of the world's oldest and largest man-made swimming pools. It is also quite safe.

West Mebon

Location: access to the south levee is 11 kilometres north-west of Siem Reap
Access: the south dyke of the West Baray; take a boat to the island in the centre of the *baray*; walk to the east entrance of the temple
Date: second half of the 11th century
King: Suryavarman I (reigned 1002-1050)
Religion: Hindu (dedicated to Vishnu)
Art style: Baphuon

BACKGROUND

The West Mebon is situated at the centre of the West Baray on an island. Inscriptions relating to this baray have not been found, so it cannot be dated exactly. But based on the architecture and decoration of the temple it probably dates to the second half of the 11th century. It was from here that the magnificent, over-lifesize bronze of Vishnu was found, now on display in the National Museum in Phnom Penh.

LAYOUT

The West Mebon was originally surrounded by a square enclosure wall with three square, sandstone *gopuras* and a sanctuary on one level crowned with a lotus. Most towers have collapsed, but the three on the east side are reasonably intact. A sandstone platform at the centre is linked to a causeway of laterite and sandstone that leads to the east dyke. The sides of the towers are carved with lively animals set in small squares, a type of decoration found also at the Baphuon. **Tip**: at certain times of the year when the water level is low enough, it is possible to walk along the shore line and look back at the island to see heaps of stones from the collapsed areas.

Ak Yum

Location: southern end of the West Baray
Date: 7th to 9th century
Religion: Hindu

BACKGROUND

Ak Yum is a recently cleared site and is of great historical importance because it is the earliest site in the area. Dating from the seventh century it belongs to the pre-Angkor period. Inscriptions found on pillars give the dates of AD 609, 704 and 1001 for Prasat Ak Yum. Evidence of a *linga* and some sacred depository has also been found. During the construction of the West Baray around the 11th century this site was partially buried by the south levee of the *baray*.

LAYOUT

Ak Yum was built on three levels standing on a platform and enclosed by a brick wall. The monument was built of brick with sandstone bays. Four shrines occupied the corners of the second tier and two others stood on each side, making a total of twelve shrines. The central sanctuary was on the uppermost tier and opened to the east with false doors on the other three sides. Post holes are still visible and were probably used to support a wooden framework for the monument.

GROUP 9   Tonle Sap

A boat trip on the Tonle Sap is a pleasant break from temple roving and gives you a chance to see a fishing village. It is recommended you make this tour in the morning, so you can combine it with a trip to the hilltop temple of Phnom Krom, which is best to visit before the mid-day heat. Leave Siem Reap on the main road leading south, and continue across open land until you come to a village and a slight turn on the road angling to the left. You are at the base of the hill on which stands the early tenth century sandstone temple of Phnom Krom. The setting is magnificent and the view of the lake from the top is unsurpassable. At the top of the hill, walk through the grounds of the modern temple, veering left and up a short flight of wooden steps to the temple itself.

Phnom Krom

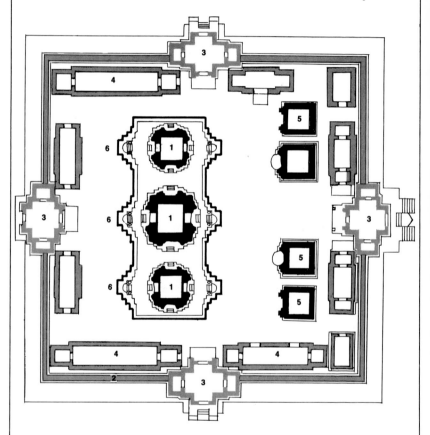

1 tower
2 wall (laterite)
3 entry tower
4 hall
5 small building
6 laterite base

© The Guidebook Company Ltd

Return to your transport at the bottom of the hill and continue along the road in a southerly direction until you come to a fishing village. Here you can hire a boat to take you to the edge of the lake. Along the way you will see the fishermen and their families who live on the water and form the so-called 'floating villages'.

The Tonle Sap is the largest permanent freshwater lake in south-east Asia. As the main source of fishing and agriculture to people living on the surrounding plain, it has played an important role in Angkor throughout history. The lake which is connected to the Mekong River by the Tonle Sap River, joins the Mekong River at Phnom Penh. From this point, the Mekong flows south into the South China Sea, and provides the means of external waterway communication for Angkor. The hydrological process that causes the lake to increase in size during the monsoon rains, and then recede, is believed to be of importance in maintaining the ecological system of the lake, which includes various species of fish and birds.

Phnom Krom: the 'mountain below'

Location: approximately 12 kilometres (7.4 miles) south-west of Siem Reap at the northern end of the Tonle Sap Lake. It is located on a mountain 137 metres (449 feet) high

Access: climb the steep stairs and curved path up the rocky slope to a modern temple complex at the top of the hill. Walk through the courtyard to the left and up a short flight of steps to the entrance. The walk affords a fine view of the lake and surrounding area. Because of the climb and the heat, it is best to visit this temple early in the morning or late in the afternoon

Date: end of the 9th century–beginning of the 10th century

King: Yasovarman I (reigned 889-910)

Religion: Hindu (dedicated to the Hindu trinity — Shiva, Vishnu and Brahma)

Art style: Bakheng

BACKGROUND

This temple is worth a visit for its dramatic setting, early architecture and spectacular views. It is one of three monuments built by Yasovarman I on hills dominating the plain of Angkor — Bakheng, Phnom Krom and Phnom Bok. The temple of Phnom Krom is visible from the aeroplane as one flies into Siem Reap from Phnom Penh. It is an imposing location perched on top of the hill and stands as a remarkable example of the early architecture of the Angkor Period. Although the façades of the three towers are intact, the decoration has been largely eroded by the elements and the friable sandstone used for construction.

LAYOUT

Phnom Krom is square in plan and consists of three towers in a row (1) situated on a hilltop. The central shrine is dedicated to Shiva, the northern shrine to Vishnu and the southern shrine to Brahma. The upper portions of the towers have collapsed and the façades are delapidated. The towers are surrounded by a laterite, enclosure wall (2) intersected on each side by cruciform *gopuras* (3). Originally, three long halls built of laterite, probably resthouses, were located two on the south; one on the north. Only the bases of these remain. Four small, square buildings (the two on the ends are built of brick and the two in the middle are sandstone) stand in the courtyard in front of the central towers (5). All four buildings open to the west and have a series of holes in the walls, features that suggest they may have been used as crematoriums.

■ CENTRAL TOWERS

The three central towers stand on a low rectangular platform and are oriented in a north-south direction (6). Even though the temples are of an early date they are built of sandstone rather than brick. Two sides of the base are intercepted by three stairways with lions on the landings. The towers are square and originally had four recessed stages on the upper portion. They open to the east and west with false doors on the north and south. Traces of decoration remain around the base of the platform near the stairs, on the pilasters, the panels of the false doors, the cornices and on niches in the corners.

GROUP 10 Preah Pithu

Location: north-east of the Terrace of the Leper King
Access: enter and leave east of the main road
Date: first half of the 12th century (parts of the 13th century)
King: Suryavarman II (reigned 1113-1150)
Religion: Hindu (dedicated to Shiva)
Art style: Angkor Wat

BACKGROUND

The complex of Preah Pithu has only recently been cleared and thus open to visitors. It is a delightful area to wander in and experience the pleasure of finding hidden stones, unseen carvings and obscure alcoves. And the proportions and decoration of the terraces are amongst the finest in Khmer art. Most of the structures are in poor condition, but their bases remain and, from the evidence, the buildings of Preah Pithu were of excellent quality in design, workmanship and decoration.

LAYOUT

The Preah Pithu group consists of two cruciform terraces and five sanctuaries situated in seemingly random order amongst enclosure walls, moats and basins. All of the shrines are square with false doors, stand on a raised platform and are oriented to the east. Starting from the main road, the first temple is approached by a cruciform terrace with columns and a *naga* balustrade. Beyond is an enclosure wall with *gopuras* on the east and west sides. The sanctuary with four staircases stands on a plinth. Female divinities in niches are seen in the corners. Notice the floral motif on their skirts. A second shrine lies on the same axis and is similar in plan and decoration to the previous one.

A third temple is situated behind the other two and to the north. The sanctuary stands on a square terrace 4 meters (13 feet) high and 40 meters (131 feet) long on each side. Four axial stairways guarded by lions give access to the sanctuary. Although the shrine has windows with balustrades it is undecorated. Fragments of frontons and lintels provide evidence that it was later used as a Buddhist sanctuary.

Continuing towards the east there is a pond where two sculpted elephants stand on each side of a staircase. This is a particularly serene and pleasant spot. Retrace your steps and you will find remains of a fourth shrine on your left (south). The decoration on the pilasters of this shrine clearly belong to the Angkor Wat period. The fifth shrine of the Preah Pithu group is further north and comprises two buildings decorated with scenes from the *Ramayana*.

The Kleangs: 'storehouse'

Location:	behind the 12 towers of Prasat Suor Prats and facing the Terraces of the Elephants and the Leper King
Access:	enter and leave from the west; walk past the Suor Prat towers towards the east
Date:	end of the 10th century–beginning of the 11th century
King:	Jayavarman V (reigned 968-1001) or Suryavarman I (1002- 1050)
Religion:	Hindu
Art style:	Kleang

BACKGROUND

Like Preah Pithu, the North and South Kleangs have been recently cleared of jungle growth and the surroundings make this a pleasant area for exploring. The Kleangs consist of a pair of large sandstone façades that look quite grand against a jungle background. They are similar in time, layout, style and decoration, although

Following pages: the Kleang ('storehouse').

inscriptions suggest that the South Kleang was built slightly later than the north one. Some scholars believe the name 'storehouse' is inappropriate for these buildings and suggest they may have been reception halls for receiving foreign dignitaries.

LAYOUT

Both buildings are long rectangular structures with cruciform porches placed centrally on the west and east facades. Windows with balusters are evenly spaced across the elevation on either side of the porches. The decoration is restrained, but thoughtful in its design and execution. The faceted columns of the doorways support lintels decorated with foliate scrolls.

North Kleang: the workmanship of the architecture and decoration is more carefully executed than that of the South Kleang. To the rear of the North Kleang there is a laterite wall with high level horizontal windows which encloses smaller halls in a courtyard.

South Kleang: the long rectangular building is unfinished, but it stands on a moulded platform. The interior decoration is limited to a frieze under the cornice.

Prasat Suor Prat: the 'towers of the cord dancers'

Location: at the beginning of the road leading to the Gate of Victory of Angkor Thom; 1,200 metres (3,937 feet) in front of Phimeanakas
Access: enter and leave the towers from the road
Date: end of the 12th century
King: Jayavarman VII (reigned 1181-1220)
Religion: Buddhist
Art style: Bayon

BACKGROUND

Since the Japanese government has been excavating around the plinths of the towers, you can walk around these towers and view them from all angles. Their purpose is a source of some controversy. According to a Cambodian legend, the towers served as anchoring places for ropes which stretched from one to another for acrobats performing at festivals, while the king observed the performances from one of the terraces. This activity is reflected in the name of the towers.

Zhou Daguan wrote about an entirely different purpose of the towers in describing a method of settling disputes between men. 'Twelve little stone towers stand in front of the royal palace. Each of the contestants is forced to be seated in one of the towers, with his relatives standing guard over him. They remain imprisoned two, three, or four days. When allowed to emerge, one of them will be found to be suffering some illness — ulcers, or catarrh or malignant fever. The other man will be in perfect health. Thus is right or wrong determined by what is called "celestial judgement" '.[72]

Henri Mouhot wrote that the towers were 'said to have been the royal treasure.....It served, they say, as a depository for the crown jewels'.[73] Another theory is that they may have served as an altar for each province on the occasion of taking the oath of loyalty to the king.

LAYOUT

Prasat Suor Prat is a row of 12 square laterite and sandstone towers, six on either side of the road leading to Angkor Thom, parallel to the front of the terraces. The two towers closest to the road are set back slightly from the others. The towers have an unusual feature of windows with balusters on three sides. Entrance porches open toward the west onto the parade ground. These features support the theory that these towers were used as some sort of viewing area, reserved for princes or dignitaries, opening on to the large parade ground in front of the Royal Palace. The interior of each tower has two levels and on the upper one there is a cylindrical vault with two frontons. The frames, bays and lintels were made of sandstone.

Tep Pranam: the 'worshipping god'

Location: 100 metres (328 feet) north-west of the Terrace of the Leper King
King: Yasorvarman I
Access: a path to the west from the main road leads to Tep Pranam
Date: parts of the temple were built at different times ranging from the end of the 9th century to the 13th century
Religion: Buddhist

BACKGROUND AND LAYOUT

The presence of Buddhist monks and nuns at this temple give it a feeling of an active place of worship. The site was originally a Buddhist monastery associated with Yasovarman at the end of the ninth centry. The entrance to Tep Pranam is marked by a laterite causeway bordered by double boundary stones at the corners and a cruciform terrace. The sandstone walls of the base of the terrace have a moulded edging. Two lions precede the walls and are in 13th century art style. The naga balustrades are probably 12th century, whereas the two lions preceding the terrace at the east are Bayon style.

Following pages: (left) a sandstone tower stands majestically on a tiered base; (right) a brick tower at Bakong with sandstone figures standing in niches surrounded by intricate stucco work.

Lotus Inspiration

...Néak Pean—the last word being pronounced 'Ponn', and the whole name signifies curved Nagas. Néak Pean is one of the temples that makes one dream of the olden days of luxury and beauty. It was worth while to live then and to be a woman among a race which has ever adored its women. It is to the overpowering temples of Civa that men and armies repaired; but it was at the tiny temple of Néak Pean that eager princesses laid their lovely offerings of wrought gold and pungent perfumes...Fancy it as it was in the old days. To begin with there was the artificial lake, a wide extent of water in the shallows of which floated the flowering lotus. In its exact centre—the surveyors of Angkor were expert—stood the exquisite miniature temple of one small chamber, the sanctuary, a temple as finely ornate and as well-proportioned as an alabaster vase. With art delicious this wonder was made to appear like a vision in the land of faerie. It floated upon a full-opened flower of the lotus, the petal tips curling back to touch the water. On the corolla of the flower, curved around the temple's base, were two Nagas whose tails were twisted together at the back and who raised their fan of heads on either side of the steps in front which mounted to the sanctuary. Thus they guarded the gem and gave gracious welcome to whosoever directed her light barque to draw close to this lovely heaven...On this circular pedestal of poetic imagination rested a square temple with four carved doors, one open occupying all the faßade except for the square columns which flank it. Above rose the tower with pointed over-door groups of carvings, symbolic, graceful, inspiring. Each closed door bore the figure of the humane god Vishnu standing at full height, but lest he impress too strongly his grandeur in this dainty spot, the space about him is filled with minor carvings which vary on each door.

Within this lovely casket was a seated stone figure. The door was ever open, suppliants might at any time lay before Buddha their offerings and their prayers.

The chamber was too small to admit them and they stood without in a bending group, swaying toward the Naga-heads for support or salaaming gracious salutations to the god of peaceful meditation. The

*golden boat floating beside the approach again...Rowers moved the
shallop so slowly that the Naga-prow seemed to progress of its own
volition. And so, the gods appeased, the spirits rose, and soft music
spread over the waters in which the rich notes of male voices blended,
and life went happily in the lovely twilight hour...one must know its
former state to love it...Néak Pean stands hidden, but it stands in
greater perfection than if it had not had the enveloping.*

H Churchill Candee, Angkor: The Magnificent, The Wonder City
of Ancient Cambodia (H F & G Witherby, London, 1925)

*Central Island at Neak Pean. This tree was destroyed by lightning in the
1950s.*

BUDDHA

The large Buddha seated on a lotus pedestal with a moulded base and coated in sandstone. He is in the position of 'calling the earth to witness'. The body of the Buddha has been reassembled from numerous reused stones. Follow the footpath to the west and you will come to Preah Palilay.

Preah Palilay

Location: north of Phimeanakas
Access: enter and leave the monument from the east. To reach Preah Palilay follow the footpath through the jungle to the north of Phimeanakas or from the main road just north of the Terrace of the Leper King
Tip: this is one of the most serene areas of Angkor. Take time to enjoy it
Date: first half of the 12th century (central sanctuary)-late 12th-early 13th century (*gopura*)
Religion: Buddhist
Art style: Angkor Wat and Bayon

BACKGROUND

Lintels and pediments lying on the ground afford a rare opportunity to see reliefs at eye level. Many depict Buddhist scenes with Hindu divinities.

LAYOUT

A large seated Buddha in front of the temple of Preah Palilay is of a recent date. A cruciform terrace precedes the temple and stands as an elegant example of the classic period of Khmer art. Serpent balustrades terminating with a crest of seven heads frame the terrace. A causeway joins the terrace to the east *gopura*, which is set in the laterite enclosure wall of which only parts remain. Enter through the cruciform east *gopura* with three openings and a vaulted roof with double frontons. The principal feature of interest at this temple is the Buddhist scenes on the frontons. They are some of the few that escaped defacement in the 15th century. The scenes depicted are: east, a reclining Buddha; south, a seated Buddha, which is especially beautiful in the mid-morning sun; north, a standing Buddha with his hand resting on an elephant.

CENTRAL SANCTUARY

Only the central sanctuary of Preah Palilay remains intact. The sandstone tower opens on four sides, each one with a porch. The tower stands on a base with three tiers intercepted by stairs on each side. The upper portion is collapsed and a truncated pyramid forms a cone which is filled with reused stones.

Phnom Penh's central market — a fine example of neo-classical design built by the French in 1933.

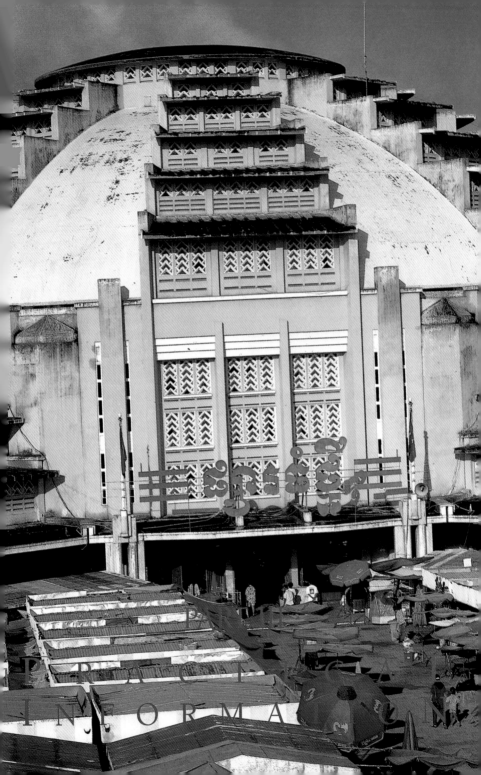

General

Cambodia is a constitutional monarchy with His Majesty Preah Bat Samdech Preah Norodom Sihanouk Varman as its head of state. Population is around 10.7 million, of which 90 per cent is ethnic Khmer and largely Theravada Buddhist. Khmer is the official language.

CLIMATE

Cambodia is suitable to visit year round because it lies in a tropical zone and the temperature remains fairly constant throughout the year. However, from late May or June to late October or early November daily rains can be expected. This makes going around the Angkor temples somewhat difficult because of muddy paths and slippery stones. The sandstone monuments, though, are truly beautiful after a rain storm. For those who are sensitive to the heat, Cambodia is slightly cooler from November to March, though to someone who is not accustomed to the heat and humidity of the tropics it will still feel very hot.

TIME

Cambodia Standard Time is seven hours ahead of Greenwich Mean Time. It is in the same time zone as Vietnam, Laos and Thailand.

CLOTHING

Lightweight, loose-fitting, cotton clothing is recommended and long-sleeved items should be included for protection from mosquitoes and the sun. It is not appropriate to wear very short shorts, nor for men to take off their shirts. Sturdy shoes with good support are recommended for visiting the temples. Hats are also essential.

CURRENCY

The unit of currency in Cambodia is the riel, but the US dollar and Thai baht are widely used throughout the country; small change, however, is usually given in riel. It is forbidden to take riels in or out of the country. Gold is also circulated in the markets. In an effort to wean people away from the use of American currency, a new range of notes and coins were introduced in March 1995. New notes in denominations of 1,000, 2,000, 5,000, 10,000, 20,000 and 100,000 were added to the existing notes of 500, 200 and 100. Riel coins are in denominations of 500, 200, 100 and 50.

There are no restrictions on the amount of foreign currency you can bring in to Cambodia, but any amount over US$10,000 must be declared. The most readily converted currencies are the: US dollar, Thai baht, French franc, Japanese yen, British pound, and the German mark. The value fluctuates, but as of July 1997, the rate was: 2,770 riels = US$1.

Payment for domestic air tickets, many hotels and restaurants in Phnom Penh, and almost everything in Siem Reap, must be paid for in cash. Some banks will give a cash advance with a credit card. Travellers cheques are not widely accepted.

VISAS

All foreign nationals entering Cambodia are required to have a visa. It can be issued by any royal Cambodian embassy or consulate, but the easiest place to get one is at the Immigration Counter at Pochentong Airport upon arrival in Phnom Pénh. Embassies are located in Canberra, Bangkok, Beijing, Prague, Havana, Bonn, Budapest, New Delhi, Tokyo, Pyongyang, Jakarta, Vientiane, Paris, Moscow, Washington DC, Sofia, Hanoi with a consulate in Ho Chi Minh City.

To apply for a visa you must have a passport valid for three months from the date of entry into Cambodia. If you are entering Cambodia by land a visa can be issued only at the checkpoint at Moc Bai, near the border between Cambodia and Vietnam. Regardless of where your visa is issued it allows a single journey and is valid for 30 days. You can apply for an extension at the Ministry of Interior in Phnom Penh (Norodom Boulevard, near Street 240). Visas currently cost US$20 per month.

TRAVEL TO CAMBODIA

Royal Air Cambodge, the national carrier of Cambodia, flies to and from all the international destinations listed below. In addition, there are direct, non-stop flights to Phnom Penh from: Bangkok (Thai Airways International); Ho Chi Minh (Vietnam Airways); Hong Kong (Dragon Air); Kuala Lumpur (Malaysian Airlines); Moscow (Aeroflot) Singapore (Silk Air); and Vientiane (Lao Aviation). Connecting flights are available to most parts of the world from these destinations.

Offices in Phnom Penh for the international airlines mentioned above are located at: Royal Air Cambodge (206A Norodom Boulevard, tel: 360 154); Aeroflot (Room 101, Allson Hotel, Monivong Boulevard, tel 362 008), Dragon Air (19 106 Street, tel: 427 665); Lao Aviation (58 Sihanouk Boulevard, tel: 426 563); Malaysia Airlines (ground floor, Diamond Hotel, 207 Monivong Boulevard, tel: 426 688); Silk Air (ground floor, Pailin Hotel, Monivong Boulevard, tel: 722 236); Thai Airways International (19 106 Street, tel: 722 335); Vietnam Airlines (35 Sihanouk Boulevard, tel: 427 426).

Pochentong Airport is the arrival and departure point in Phnom Penh for all international and domestic flights. It is located seven kilometres from the centre of the city. The official taxi service from the airport to central Phnom Penh costs about US$7. There is a US$15 exit tax for all travellers leaving Cambodia, regardless of nationality or age.

Travel Within Cambodia

It is possible to travel between Phnom Penh and Siem Reap by boat. Some may want to try the local ferries, but they are not geared to accommodate foreigners. Plan to take your own food and drink. There are now several fast boat services, which take about four hours, cost around US$25 and depart from near the Japanese Bridge (Chruoy Changvar) in Phnom Penh. Travel by boat to Siem Reap is possible only during certain times of the year when the water level is sufficient to allow the boats to navigate the course to the landing dock, located on a tributary to the Tonle Sap Lake. (The smaller variety operate all year round, but are much less comfortable.) These boats have, however, have been occasionally harrassed by fishermen. Travel by road between Phnom Penh and Siem Reap is not recommended for security reasons and because of the poor condition of the roads and bridges.

Domestic Flights

The route between Phnom Penh and Siem Reap is serviced by Royal Air Cambodge with about six flights a day depending on the demand. Because of the flight frequency it is possible to arrive in Phnom Penh and continue on to Siem Reap the same day. The flight takes approximately 35-45 minutes. The schedule for domestic flights is subject to change, so be sure to check the departure time. This can be done at the Royal Air Cambodge counter at the airport or at the main office in the city.

Tickets for domestic flights can be purchased from Royal Air Cambodge in Phnom Penh, at the airport or from Eurasie Travel (Pasteur Street, tel: 423 099). A round-trip ticket between Phnom Penh and Siem Reap is US$110. There is an airport tax of US$5 per person for each domestic flight, payable at the airport. There is also a weight limit of ten kilogrammes per person for baggage on each domestic flight. Overweight baggage is not expensive and not always checked.

Tipping

Tipping is not expected in Cambodia, but acknowledgement of services in cash is appreciated.

Vaccinations and Health

Vaccinations are not required, except cholera if you are arriving from an infected area. However, the following immunisations are recommended before travelling to Cambodia: typhoid, tetanus and hepatitis. Most travellers take precautions against malaria, but it is best to check with a doctor for the appropriate drugs to use against the mosquitoes prevalent in Cambodia. As prevention against malaria and dengue fever a mosquito repellent is essential: socks, trousers and a long-sleeved shirt, especially in the evening and early morning when mosquitoes are likely to be out, are

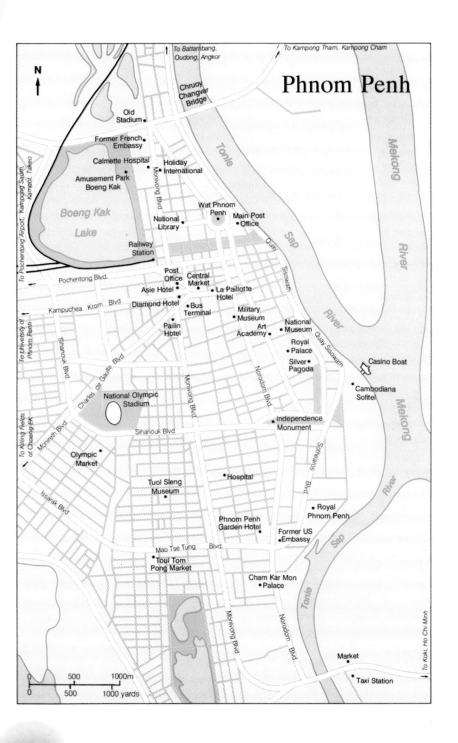

Phnom Penh

N

To Battambang,
Oudong, Angkor

To Kampong Tham, Kampong Cham

Chruoy
Changvar
Bridge

Old
Stadium

Former French
Embassy

Calmette Hospital

Holiday
International

Amusement Park
Boeng Kak

Tonle

Mekong River

Boeng Kak
Lake

Monivong Blvd.

Wat Phnom
Penh

National
Library

Main Post
Office

Sap

Quay Sisowath

Railway
Station

Pochentong Blvd.

Post
Office

Central
Market

Asie Hotel

La Paillotte
Hotel

Kampuchea Krom Blvd.

Diamond Hotel

Bus
Terminal

Military
Museum

Art
Academy

National
Museum

River

Pailin
Hotel

Royal
Palace

Silver
Pagoda

Quay Sisowath

Casino Boat

Cambodiana
Sofitel

Sihanouk Blvd.

Charles de Gaulle Blvd.

National Olympic
Stadium

Norodom Blvd.

Independence
Monument

Sihanouk Blvd.

Mekong

Olympic
Market

Tuol Sleng
Museum

Hospital

Sothearos Blvd.

Royal
Phnom Penh

River

Issarak Blvd.

Monireth Blvd.

Phnom Penh
Garden Hotel

Former US
Embassy

Mao Tse Tung Blvd.

Toul Tom
Pong Market

Monivong Blvd.

Cham Kar Mon
Palace

Sap

Tonle

To Pochentong Airport, Kampong Saom,
Kampot, Takeo

To University of
Phnom Penh

To Killing Fields
at Choeng Ek

Norodom Blvd.

To Koki, Ho Chi Minh

Market

Taxi Station

0   500   1000m
0   500   1000 yards

recommended. It is important to dress modestly and, for security reasons, wearing expensive or ostentatious jewellery is inadvisable.

Drink only bottled water in Cambodia. Purified water in sealed plastic bottles is readily available in hotels, restaurants, shops, street stalls, and even from vendors around the temples at Angkor. To avoid diarrhoea and more serious infections transmitted by unsanitary conditions, never eat peeled fruit or sliced vegetables sold by street vendors; and avoid all ice, either crushed or in cubes.

The tropical sun can be very strong and the heat overwhelming. Avoid being in the direct sun during the middle of the day. When you are outside, wear a hat and use sun block. It is important to apply a protective cream to exposed areas including the ears, nose and lips. Remember to re-apply sun block as it may wash off (even the waterproof brands) when you perspire.

CUSTOMS

Cambodia is primarily a Buddhist country and you should follow certain customs out of courtesy and respect for the religious practices. Visitors should remove their shoes before entering a modern temple if it contains a Buddha image. It is not necessary to observe this rule at the ruins of Angkor, as the temples are not actively used today. It is quite common to see monks around the ancient temples and they often like to practice their English with foreigners. A female, however, should never have any physical contact with a monk.

Respect the temples and keep in mind that they were once sacred places of worship and are still considered hallowed sanctuaries by Cambodians. As such, do not climb on stone images (not even for a photograph) and be particularly careful not to touch the head of a figure as this is considered the most sacred part of the body.

COMMUNICATIONS

The telephone services in Cambodia are improving all the time. IDD lines for overseas calls have been installed and pay phones are available in Phnom Penh near hotels and restaurants. Phone cards can be purchased from some hotels and restaurants in the capital or at the Angkor Business Centre, Ta Prohm Hotel, the Post Office and the Tourism Office. In Siem Reap, most hotels have a mobile phone which can be used for international telephone calls. The international phone code for Cambodia is 855; plus 23 for Phnom Penh. Telephone numbers change frequently in Cambodia due to the inadequate system, and calling into the country may prove frustrating. The postal service is very slow.

ELECTRICITY

Cambodia operates on 220-volt, 50 Hz. Blackouts occur often in Phnom Penh, but less frequently in Siem Reap. Most hotels and restaurants have back-up generators. It is recommended that you take a torch for power failures.

Phnom Penh

It is recommended you stay overnight in Phnom Penh as it has several points of interest. The main one for those going to Angkor is the National Museum which houses the most extensive and finest collection of Khmer art on public display anywhere in the world. The Cambodian capital has a population of over 800,000, and is very much a city in transition which gives a visible historical insight to the country's past.

HOTELS
The following is a selection of Phnom Penh hotels, bookings can be made on arrival at Pochentong airport.

DELUXE
The top end of the hotel market in Phnom Penh is limited, but improving.
Inter-Continental Regency Square, 296 Mao Tse Toung Boulevard, tel: 720 888; fax 720 885. Phnom Penh's newest and smartest hotel.
Juliana 16 152 Street, tel: 366 070. US$ 120-160.
Landmark 63 Monorom Boulevard, tel: 426 943; fax: 428 506. US$100 plus.
Royal Phnom Penh 26 Samdech Sothearos Boulevard, tel: 360 026; fax: 360 036. Several quality restaurants and most modern facilities. US$120.
Sharaton Cambodia 47 Street, tel/fax: 361 199. Relatively new property with swimming pool, business centre and nightclub. US$100-130.
Sofitel Cambodiana 313 Sisowath Quay, tel: 426 288; fax: 426 392. Popular riverside hotel with international facilities. US$120-170.
Hotel Le Royal is being restored and redeveloped by the Raffles Group and is scheduled to take its place as the premier hotel in Phnom Penh from August 1997.
Allson Hotel was due to close, re-opening later, at the time of going to press.

MID-PRICE
There is an abundance of places to stay in this bracket.
Asie 73 Street 136, tel: 427 826; fax 426 334. US$25-35.
Baccara 63 Street, tel: 720 755. US$20.
Beauty Inn 100 Sihanouk Boulevard, tel: 722 676; fax: 722 677. US$20-25.
Cathay 123-125, 110 Street, tel: 427 178; fax 426 303. US$20.
Diamond: 172-184 Monivong Boulevard, tel: 426 535; fax 426 535. US$40-80. One of the better establishments in this range.
Goldiana 10 282 Street, tel: 427 558. US$20-25.
Golden Eagle 256 Monivong Boulevard, tel 426 753. US$25-35.

Green 145 Norodom Boulevard, tel: 426 055; fax: 426 317. US$65-75
Hawaii 130 Street, tel/fax: 426 652. US$30-40.
Holiday International 84 Street, tel: 427 502; 427 401. US$50.
La Paillotte: 234 130 Street, tel: 722 151; fax: 426 513. US$25.
Lucky Inn 11 254 Street, tel/fax: 427 044. US$30-65.
Mekong Thmey 108 Street, tel: 424 556; fax 426 060. US$30-40.
Pailin 219 Monivong Boulevard, tel: 422 475; fax: 426 376. US$30-45.
Paris I 154 Street, tel: 426 724. US$40-50.
Phnom Penh Garden: 66 57 Street, tel: 427 258, fax: 427 345. US$60-80. Good facilities particularly restaurants.
Rama Inn 8-10 282 Street, tel/fax: 428 381, 425 667. US$35-42.
Singapore Monivong Boulevard, tel: 425 552; fax: 426 570. US$15-20.

BUDGET

There are scores of cheap price accommodation in the capital, particularly near the independence monument, central market, the river and Boeung Kak Lake.
Bert's 79 Sisowath Quay, tel: 015 916 411. US$5.
Capitol 14 182 Street, tel: 464 104. US$3-8.
Champs Elysees, 185, 63 Street, tel/fax: 427 268. US$15-20.
City Lotus 76 172 Street, tel 362 409. US$7-10.
Mittaheap 262 Monivong Boulevard, tel: 423 464; fax: 426 492. US$10.
Renakse opposite the Royal Palace, tel: 422 457; fax: 426 100. US$20.
Rex 99 Sihanouk Boulevard, tel: 724 344. US$12-15.
Tokyo 15 278 Street, tel: 427 048; fax: 422 836. US$15.

RESTAURANTS

There is a reasonable variety of local, regional and international cuisines available, most at affordable prices. Newer establishments, however, tend to open and close with regularity when they cannot meet the rent. Sisowath Quay is probably the main restaraunt area.
Ban Thai Thai. South of the independence monument, set in a garden, Thai-house style.
Casablanca Moroccan. On the corner of 84 Street and French Street.
FCCC Foreign Correspondents' Club of Cambodia with bar and restaurant overlooking the Tonle Sap-Mekong confluence. Open to non-members.
Hei Sei Japanese. On the street corner opposite the FCCC.
Kirirom Typical Khmer. In front of Wat Phnom on the river.
L'Amboise superior French restaurant with wine cellar in the Sofitel Cambodiana. One of the more expensive establishments in town.
La Paillotte Classic French. Very popular with the expatriate French community, on

the ground floor of the hotel of the same name.

La Troika Russian. On Norodom Boulevard near the independence monument. Vodka on tap.

Le Pacha French. Phnom Penh's power restaurant, but not overpriced at 193 208 Street near the independence monument.

Lilay Chinese. One of the best in the city, at 321 Kampuchea Krom Street.

Makara Khmer. Traditional-style eatery located at 87 Sihanouk Boulevard.

Mex Mexican. Next to the independence monument on Norodom Boulevard.

Ponlok Seafood, Chinese. Popular establishment on Sisowath Quay.

Royal Phnom Penh Quality hotel restaurant on Sothearos Boulevard.

BANKS
Asia Bank 86 Norodom Boulevard.
Bangkok Bank 26 Norodom Boulevard.
Banque Indosuez 77 Norodom Boulevard.
Cambodia Commercial Bank Junction of Pochentong and Monivong boulevards.
Cambodia Asia Bank 252 Monivong Boulevard.
Foreign Trade Bank of Cambodia 24 Norodom Boulevard.
National Bank of Cambodia Norodom Boulevard, near the Central Market.
Siam City Bank 79 Kampuchea Krom.
Singapore Banking Corporation 240 Street.
Standard Chartered Bank 95 Sihanouk Boulevard.
Thai Farmers Bank 114 Street.

TRANSPORT
Motos (usually 100cc Hondas) and taxis are available outside many of the capital's hotels and tourist spots.

USEFUL ADDRESSES
Access Medical Services 203 63 Street. Tel 015 912 100.
American Embassy 27 240 Street. Tel: 426 436, 426 810.
Assemblies of God 158 Norodom Boulevard.
Australian Embassy 11 254 Street. Tel: 426 000-1.
Canadian Embassy 11 254 Street. Tel: 426 000-1.
Church of Christ 21 294 Street.
DHL Worldwide Express 28 Monivong Boulevard. Tel: 426 931.
European Dental Clinic 195A Norodom Boulevard. Tel: 018 812 055, 362 656, 015 917 573.
Federal Express 19 109 Street. Tel: 426 391.

French Embassy 1 Monivong Boulevard. Tel: 430 020.
German Embassy 76-78 214 Street. Tel: 725 981.
Japanese Embassy 75 Norodom Boulvevard. Tel: 427 161-4.
National Library 92 Street.
Singapore Embassy Sofitel Cambodiana 313 Sisowath Boulevard. Tel: 426 288.
SOS-International Medical Center 83 Mao Tse Tung Boulevard. Tel: 015 912 765, 015 912 964, 015 916 685.
Thai Embassy 4 Monivong Boulevard. Tel: 426 182.
UPS Worldwide 134 Street. Tel: 366 324.
United Kingdom Embassy 27-29 75 Street. Tel: 427 124.

TOURIST HIGHLIGHTS

The Killing Fields The Choeng Ek extermination camp is located approximately 18 kilometres south-west of the capital. The English name originates from the famous Hollywood film, which highlighted the Khmer Rouge massacres. A perspex stupa has been erected to commemorate the more than 17,000 people who were executed.

National Museum Pre-Angkor and Angkor period sculpture are the main attractions, making a visit here before journeying to Siem Reap and afterwards an excellent idea. Much of the Khmer statuary has been placed here to protect it from looters at Angkor. Located close to the Royal Palace at the junction of 113 Street and 350 Street.

Royal Palace Strongly influenced by the Royal Palace in Bangkok, it is a surprise to many visitors to hear that this is a 20th century structure. The Chan Chhaya Pavilion, the Throne Hall of Prasat Tevea Vinichhay and the Silver Pagoda are some of the most important buildings. Phnom Penh's most attractive construction is situated on Saigon Boulevard.

Tuol Sleng This is where the Khmer Rouge interrogated and tortured its prisoners in Phnom Penh. The thousands of pictures on the walls of the victims are, perhaps, a much more stark revelation of the atrocities between 1975 and 1979 than Choeng Ek. Located west of Achar Mean Boulevard.

Wat Phnom Phnom Penh's oldest temple is said to hold the ashes of Ponhea Yat, the first king of the post-Angkor period of Cambodian history. Many of the capital's citizens come here to pray for protection before journeys, success in examinations and to help heal illness. Situated at the junction of Tou Samuth Boulevard and 47th Street in the north-east of the city.

Siem Reap

Capital of the province of the same name, this small, French colonial-style town is situated picturesquely along the banks of the Siem Reap River approximately seven

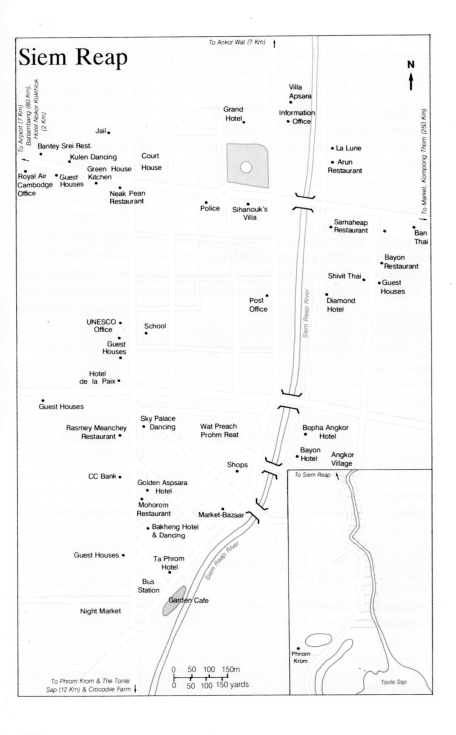

kilometres from the local airport.

HOTELS

A variety of accommodation is available in central Siem Reap, ranging from a few quality to moderate hotels and motels to guesthouses varying from modest to quite basic.

TOP END

Grand Hotel d'Angkor Recently taken over by the Raffles Group, the hotel is due to re-open in the third quarter of 1997 after renovation, and will be far and away Siem Reap's leading hotel with a full range of international-standard facilities.

Nokor Phnom Tel. 380 106; fax 380 033. US$55-65.

Nokor Kok Thlok New property on the airport road. Tel: 015 917 301. US$80-110.

Ta Prohm Riverside hotel in the centre of town (tel: 911783). $80-130.

MID-PRICE

Angkor Village Attractive Khmer house-style hotel very reasonably priced. But has only a few rooms and not all with air-con. Tel: 015 91 6048. US$45-60.

Banteay Srei Recent addition on the airport road at the start of the town. Tel: 015 913 839. US$50.

Bayon Opposite the new market. Tel: 015 911 769. US$30-50.

Diamond On Vithei Achasva Road near the river. Tel: 015 633 130. US$55-65.

Neak Pean Inn Close to the centre of town just off the airport road. Tel: 015 633 802. US$35-40.

Stung Siem Reap Centrally located. Tel: 963 682. US$20-30.

BUDGET

Golden Angkor. Near the centre of town just off the airport road. US$10-30. Tel: 015 632 537.

Kulen Airport road. US$20.

Mahogany Guest House Wat Bo Street. US$5.

Mom's Guest House Wat Bo Street. US$5-6.

Royal Villa US$20.

Sun Rise Guest House Wat Bo Street.

Vien Thmei US10-20.

RESTAURANTS

Some hotels have eating facilities, but there are reasonable local restaurants.

Banteay Srei On the airport road a special place for breakfast.

Bayon Near Mom's Guest House. Probably Siem Reap's most popular restaurant.
Chivit Thai Thai. Across from the Bayon.
Green House Kitchen Chinese, Thai, Khmer: opposite the Court House.
Little India Indian and Pakistani cuisine near the New Market and the Ta Prohm
Monorom near the Bakong Hotel.
Neak Pean opposite the Court House.
Only One French cuisine, opposite the Old Market.
Psar Chao Indian/ Pakistani cuisine near the Old Market.
Samaheap Khmer and western cuisine: on the river bank.
Samaki Khmer and western food: on the road to Angkor Wat.
Sunflower Thai and Khmer food: next to the Green House.
Zanzy Bar Western-style bar habituated by expatriates, with set menu on Saturday
nights.

BANKS

There are a few banks in Siem Reap where it is possible to change money. Otherwise
try the leading hotels.
Cambodian Commercial Bank Sivutha Street.
First Overseas Bank Mondol I Khum Svaydangkum.
Pacific Commercial Bank Sivutha Street.

TRANSPORT

A car and driver can be hired for US$20-30 a day, or a motorcycle with a driver for
US$5-8 a day. Some drivers double as guides to the temples.

PASSES

A pass to visit the temples is required and can be purchased at: Siem Reap Airport,
Angkor Tourism Information Office, the check-point before Angkor Wat; and the
Ministry of Tourism in Phnom Penh. You can buy a pass for one day, three days or
for one week. A pass is valid for all the sites of the Angkor area including Roluos and
Banteay Srei. The prices as of January 1997 are: one day US$20; three day US$40;
and four day to one week US$60. As Banteay Srei is now open to visitors there is an
additional US$30 to visit this temple to cover the increased security arrangements.

Appendix I
Comparative Chronology of the Khmer and Other Civilisations

BC
c 5000-0
CAM: early society
WEST: Stonehenge (2200-1700); Parthenon (447-433)

AD
0-100
SEA: Indianisation
IND: Sanci stupa; Amaravati stupa
CH: end of Western Han Dynasty
WEST: birth of Christ; Ptolemy's *Geography*; Colosseum (Rome) (72-80)

200
CAM: Funan
SEA: early state of Champa (200); Pyu kingdom (Burma) (250)
IND: Pallava Dynasty

300
SEA: Oc-Eo (Vietnam)
IND: Gupta Dynasty (320-600)
CH: Dunhuang Caves (336)

400
IND: wall-paintings at Ajanta; wall-paintings at Sigiriya (Sri Lanka)

500
CAM: Zhenla
IND: Ellura Caves
WEST: Hagia Sophia (Constantinople) (532-7)

600
CAM: Sambor Prei Kuk; Isanavarman I; Jayavarman I (645-81)

SEA: Dvaravati kingdom; Srivijaya dynasty (c 680-1287)
IND: Mamallapurmam temples (625-75)
CH: Tang dynasty (618-906)

700

CAM: Upper and Lower Zhenla
SEA: Sailendras dynasty (750); Borobudur (Java)
IND: Pala dynasty

800

CAM: Jayavarman II (802-50); Jayavarman III (850-77);
Indravarman I (877-89); Yasovarman I (893-c 900)
SEA: Pegu (880)
IND: temple of Kailasa at Ellura (800)
WEST: Charlemagne, Emperor of the West (800); Beginning of the
Norman invasions; first cathedral at Cologne (Germany) (873);
siege of Paris by the Normans (885)

900

CAM: Harshavarman (c 900-22); Isanavarman II (922-7); Jayavarman IV
(921-41); Harshavarman II (941-4); Rajendravarman (944-68);
Jayavarman V (968-1001)
IND: Chola Empire (900-1170); the Five Dynasties (907-60); Northern
Song Dynasty (960-1125)

1000

CAM: Udayadityavarman I (1001-2); Jayaviravarman (1002-11);
Suryavarman I (1002-50); Udayadityavarman II (1050-66);
Jayavarman VI (1080-1107)

WEST: conquest of Sicily by knights of Normandy (1010); St. Mark's,
Venice (1042-85); Westminster Abbey (1052-65); Norman conquest
of England (1066); Winchester Cathedral (1079); Durham Cathedral
(1096)

1100

CAM: Dharanindravarman I (1107-13); Suryavarman II (1113-c 1150);
Yasovarman II (1150-65); Tribhuvanadityavarman (1165-77);
Jayavarman VII (1181- c 1219)
SEA: Chams seize Angkor (1177)

IND: conquest of Northern India by Mongols (1192-6)
CH: southern Song Dynasty (1127-1276)
WEST: Notre-Dame de Paris (1163-1235); Oxford University (1167)

1200

CAM: Indravarman II (1220-43); Jayavarman VIII (c 1243-95)
SEA: Sukhothai kingdom (Thailand); Lan Na kingdom (Thailand)
CH: Yuan Dynasty (1270-1368); Mongol conquest of China; Zhou Daguan at Angkor (1296-7)
WEST: Magna Carta (1215); the Great Interregnum (1250-73); Marco Polo to the court of Kublai Khan (1271-95)

1300

CAM: Srindravarman (1300-7); Jayavarmadiparamesvara (1327-?)
SEA: Ayutthaya kingdom (1350-1767)
CH: Ming dynasty (1368-1644)
WEST: beginning of the Hundred Years' War (1337)

1400

CAM: Thais attack Angkor (1431)
CH: Imperial Palace and Temple of Heaven at Beijing (1421)

Appendix II
Chronology of the Monuments

NINTH CENTURY

Roluos:

879 –	Preah Ko
881 –	Bakong
893 –	Lolei

TENTH CENTURY

—	Bakheng
—	Phnom Krom
—	Phnom Bok
921 –	Prasat Kravan
947 –	Baksei Chamkrong
952 –	East Mebon
961 –	
967 –	
—	Kleangs (North and South)

11TH CENTURY

1000–1025	Ta Keo
—	Phimeanakas
1050-1066	Baphuon
—	West Mebon
—	West Baray

12TH-13TH CENTURY

1113-1150	Angkor Wat
1150 –	Chau Say Tevoda
1150 –	Thommanon
1150-1175	Banteay Samre
1186 –	Ta Prohm
—	Banteay Kdei
1190-1210	Neak Pean
1190-1210 –	Ta Som
1190-1210 –	Srah Srang
1190-1210 –	Angkor Thom
1190-1210 –	Bayon
1190-1210 –	Terrace of the Elephants
1190-1210 –	Terrace of the Leper King
—	Krol Ko
—	Preah Palilay
—	Prasat Suor Prats
1191 –	Preah Khan
—	Chapel of the Hospital

Appendix III
Chronology of the Cambodian Kings

Dates of Reign	Name of King	Posthumous Name	Monuments
802-850	Jayavarman II	Paramesvara	Kulen
854-877	Jayavarman III	Vishnuloka	
877-889	Indravarman II	Isvaraloka	Preah Ko, Bakong
889-910	Yasovarman I	Paramasivaloka	Lolei, Bakheng, Phnom Krom, Prasat Kravan
910-923	Hashavarman I	Rudraloka	
923-928	Isanavarman II	Paramarudraloka	
928-941	Jayavarman IV	Paramasivapada	Koh Ker
941-944	Harshavarman II	Vrahmaloka or Brahmaloka	
944-968	Rajendravarman	Sivaloka	Baksei Chamkrong, East Mebon, Preah Rup
968-1001	Jayavarman V	Paramasivaloka	
1001-1002?	Udayadityavarman I		
1002-1011?	Jayaviravarman		
1001-1050	Suryavarman I	Nirvanapala la	Ta Keo, Phimeanakas
1050-1066	Udayadityavarman II		Baphuon, West Mebon
1066-1089?	Harshavarman III	Sadasivapada	
1080-1113?	Jayavarman VI	Paramakaivalyapada	
1080-1113?	Dharanindravarman I	Paramanishkalapada	
1113-1150	Suryavarman I	Paramavishnuloka	Angkor Wat, Chau Say Tevoda, Thommanon, Banteay Samre
1150-1160	Dharanindravarman II	Paramanishkalapada	
1160-1165/6	Yasovarman II		

1181-1220?	Jayavarman VII	Mahaparamasangata?	Ta Prohm, Banteay Kdei, Neak Pean, Ta Som, Srah Srang, Angkor Thom, Bayon, Terrace of the Elephants, Terrace of the Leper King, Krol Ko, Preah Palilay? Preah Khan, Prasat Suor Prat
1220-1243	Indravarman III?		
1243-1295	Jayavarman VIII (abdicated)	Paramesvarapada	
1295-1308	Indravarman III?		
1300-1307?	Srindravarman (abdicated)		
1308-1327	Indrajayavarman		
1330-1353	Paramathakemaraja		
1371-?	Hou-eul-na		
1404	Samtac Pra Phaya		
1405	Samtac Chao Phaya Phing-ya		
1405-1409	Nippean-bat		
1409-1416	Lampong or Lampang Paramaja		
1416-1425	Sorijovong, Sorijong, or Lambang		
1425-1429	Barom Racha, or Gamkhat Ramadhapati		
1429-1431	Thommo-Soccorach, or Dharmasoka		
1432-?	Ponha Yat, or Gam Yat		

Further Reading

GENERAL BACKGROUND AND HISTORICAL

Briggs, Lawrence, 'The Ancient Khmer Empire', *Transactions of the American Philosophical Society*, Vol 41, Pt 1 (1951).

Chandler, David, *A History of Cambodia* (Westview Press, Boulder, Colorado, 1983; rev ed Colorado and Oxford, England, 1992, Silkworm Books, Chiang Mai, Thailand, 1993).

Chou Ta-Kuan (Zhou Daguan), *The Customs of Cambodia*, 2nd ed, Paul Pelliot, trans (The Siam Society, Bangkok, 1992).

Cœdès, George, *The Indianized States of Southeast Asia*, Susan Brown Cowing, trans (East-West Center Press, Honolulu, 1968).

Dagens, Bruno, *Angkor: Heart of an Asian Empire* (English translation, Harry N. Abrams, New York, 1995).

Mabbett, Ian and David Chandler, *The Khmers* (Blackwell, Oxford UK & Cambridge, USA, 1995).

White, Peter T, 'The Temples of Angkor, Ancient Glory in Stone', *National Geographic*, Vol 161, No 5, 1982, pp 552-589.

THE ART OF THE KHMERS

Boisselier, Jean, *Trends in Khmer Art*, Natasha Eilenberg, trans and ed (Cornell University, Studies on Southeast Asia, Ithaca, New York, 1989).

Cœdès, George, *Angkor: An Introduction*, Emily Floyd Gardiner, trans and ed (Oxford University Press, New York and Hong Kong, 1963).

Freeman, Michael, *A Golden Souvenir of Angkor* (Pacific Rim Press, Hong Kong, 1992).

Freeman, Michael and Roger Warner, *Angkor: The Hidden Glories* (Houghton Mifflin, Boston, 1990).

Giteau, Madeleine, *Khmer Sculpture and the Angkor Civilization* (Harry N Abrams, New York, 1965; Thames and Hudson, London, 1965).

Groslier, Bernard-Philippe & Jacques Arthaud, *Angkor, Art and Civilization* (rev ed Praeger, New York, 1966; Thames and Hudson, London, 1966).

Jacques, Claude, *Angkor* (Bordas, Paris, 1990) [French text]

Macdonald, Malcolm, *Angkor: and the Khmers* (Oxford University Press, London, 1987).

Mannikka, Eleanor, *Angkor Wat: Time, Space, and Kingship* (University of Hawai'i Press, Honolulu, 1996).

Rawson, Philip, *The Art of Southeast Asia, Cambodia Vietnam Thailand Laos Burma Java Bali* (Thames and Hudson, London, 1967; rep Asia Books, Bangkok, 1990).

Rooney, Dawn, *Khmer Ceramics* (Oxford University Press, Kuala Lumpur, Malaysia, 1984).

Travel, Personal Accounts

Lewis, Norman, *A Dragon Apparent: Travels in Cambodia, Laos and Vietnam* (rep Eland Books, London, 1982).

Madsen, Axel, Silk Roads: *The Asian Adventures of Clara & André Malraux* (I B Tauris, London, 1990).

Mouhot, M Henri, *Travels in the Central Parts of Indo-China (Siam), Cambodia, and Laos, During the Years 1858, 1859, and 1860*, 2 vols (John Murray, London, 1864; rep Oxford University Press, Singapore, 1989; rep White Lotus, Bangkok, 1986).

Thomson, John, *The Straits of Malacca, Siam and Indo-China Travels and Adventures of a Nineteenth-century Photographer* (Sampson Low, Marston, Low and Searle, London, 1875; rep Oxford University Press, Singapore, 1993).

Vincent, Frank, *The Land of the White Elephant: Sights and Scenes in South-East Asia 1871-1872*, (Harper & Brothers, New York, 1873; rep Oxford University Press, Singapore, 1988).

Footnotes

TITLE PAGE

1   P Jennerat de Beerski, *Angkor, Ruins in Cambodia* (Houghton Mifflin, Boston & New York, 1924), p 20.

INTRODUCTION

2   H Churchill Candee, *Angkor, The Magnificent, The Wonder City of Ancient Cambodia* (H F & G Witherby, London, 1925), p vii.

3   Lawrence Briggs 'The Ancient Khmer Empire', *Transactions of the American Philosophical Society*, 41, pt 1, 1951; Maurice Glaize, *Les Monuments du Groupe d'Angkor: Guide*, 3rd ed (A Maisonneuve, Paris, 1963).

GEOGRAPHY

4   Chou Ta-Kuan, *The Customs of Cambodia*, 2nd ed, Paul Pelliot, trans (The Siam Society, Bangkok, 1992), p 39.

5   *Ibid.*

HISTORICAL BACKGROUND

6   J P Carbonnel, 'Recent Data on the Cambodian Neolithic: The Problem of Cultural Continity in Southern Indochina', in *Early South East Asia, Essays in Archaeology, History and Historical Geography*, R B Smith and W Watson, eds (Oxford University Press, New York and Kuala Lumpur, 1979), pp 223–6.

7   *Ibid*, pp 224–5.

8   *Ibid*, p 14.

9   Claude Jacques, "'Funan', 'Zhenla': The Reality Concealed by these Chinese Views of Indochina', in *Early South East Asia, Essays in Archaeology, History and Historical Geography*, R B Smith and W Watson, eds, pp 371–9.

10   Lawrence Palmer Briggs, 'The Ancient Khmer Empire', *idem,* pp 67–8.

11   Michael Vickery, Cambodia after Angkor: the chronicular evidence for the fourteenth to sixteenth centuries, Ann Arbor, Michigan, University Microfilms, 1977 in *The Khmers*, Ian Mabbett and David Chandler, Oxford UK and Cambridge, USA, Blackwell, 1995, p 216.

12   Hugh Clifford, *Further India, Being the Story of Exploration from the Earliest Times in Burma, Malaya, Siam, and Indo-China* (Frederick A Stokes, New York, 1904, reprinted White Lotus, Bangkok, 1990), p 154.

13   Donatella Mazzeo and Chiara Silva Antonini, *Monuments of Civiilization, Ancient Cambodia* (Grosset and Dunlap, New York, 1978), p 181.

14   Clifford, pp 153–4.
15   Marcelo de Ribadeneira, 'History of the Philippines and Other Kingdoms', 17, Vol 1, Pt 2, Pacita Guevara Fernandez, trans (The Historical Conservation Society, Manila, 1970), p 441.
16   Clifford, p 154.
17   *ibid*, p 183.
18   DO King, 'Travels in Siam and Cambodia', *Journal of the Royal Geographical Society*, Vol 30, 1860, pp 177–182.

DAILY LIFE DURING THE KHMER EMPIRE
19   Chou Ta-Kuan, p 29.

RELIGION
20   For a detailed discussion of local spirits worshipped in Cambodia see *The Khmers*, Ian Mabbett and David Chandler, Oxford UK & Cambridge USA, Blackwell, 1995.
21   Herman Kulke, 'The Devaraja Cult', translated by IW Mabbett and JM Jacob, Ithaca, New York, Data Paper: Number 108, Southeast Asia Program, Department of Asian Studies, Cornell University, January 1978.
22   For an English translation, see *Reamker (Ramakerti)*, the Cambodian version of the *Ramayana*, translated by Judith M Jacob with the assistance of Kuoch Haksrea (Oriental Translation Fund, New Series, Vol. XLV, London: The Royal Asiatic Society), 1986.
23   *ibid*, pp 290–1.
24   G Groslier, Sculpture khmere, p 44 in 'Khmer Mythology' by C-H Marchal, p 205 in *Asiatic Mythology: A Detailed Description and Explanation of the Mythologies of All the Great Nations of Asia*, by J Hackin, Clement Huart, Raymonde Linossier H De Wilman-Grabowska, Charles-Henri Marchal, Henri Maspero, Serge Elisev, New York, Crescent Books, nd.

KHMER ART AND ARCHITECTURE OF THE ANGKOR PERIOD
25   Chou Ta-Kuan, p 2.

GROUP 1: ANGKOR WAT
26   H W Ponder, *Cambodian Glory: The Mystery of the Deserted Khmer Cities and their Vanquished Splendour: and a Description of Life in Cambodia Today*, London, Thornton Butterworth, 1936, p 316.
27   D H Dickason, *Wondrous Angkor*, (Kelly & Walsh, Shanghai, 1937), p 46.
28   H Churchill Candee, *Angkor: The Magnificent, The Wonder City of Ancient Cambodia*, p 71.

29   G Cœdés, *Angkor: An Introduction*, Emily Floyd Gardiner, trans and ed (Oxford University Press, New York and Hong Kong, 1963), p 40.

30   F Vincent, *The Land of the White Elephant: Sights and Scenes in South-East Asia 1871–1872*, (Oxford University Press, Singapore, rep, 1988), pp 209–11.

31   H Churchill Candee, *Angkor: The Magnificent, The Wonder City of Ancient Cambodia*, pp 68–9.

32   *Ibid*, p 25.

33   RJ Casey, *Four Faces of Siva: The Detective Story of a Vanished Race*, (George Harrap, London, 1929), p 200.

34   H Churchill Candee, *Angkor: The Magnificent, The Wonder City of Ancient Cambodia*, p 73.

35   Helen Churchill Candee, *Angkor: The Magnificent, The Wonder City of Ancient Cambodia*, p 68.

36   RJ Casey, *Four Faces of Siva: The Detective Story of a Vanished Race*, p 62.

37   Aymonier, trans, in *Textes Khmers*, 1878.

38   H Churchill Candee, *Angkor: The Magnificent, The Wonder City of Ancient Cambodia*, p 92.

39   O Sitwell, *Escape With Me! An Oriental Sketch-Book*, (Macmillan, London, 1940), p 91.

40   RJ Casey, *Four Faces of Siva: The Detective Story of a Vanished Race*, p 59.

Group 2: Angkor Thom

41   J Boisselier, 'The Symbolism of Angkor Thom', H H Subhadradis Diskul and V di Crocco trans, text of lecture given at the Siam Society on 17 November 1987, in Siam Society Newsletter, Vol 4, No 1, p 3.

42   Chou Ta-Kuan (Zhou Daguan), *The Customs of Cambodia*, p 2.

43   PJ de Beerski, *Angkor: Ruins in Cambodia*, p 52

Group 2: Terrace of the Elephants

44   PJ de Beerski, *Angkor: Ruins in Cambodia*, p 147.

45   *Ibid*, p 148.

Group 2: Terrace of the Leper King

46   PJ de Beerski, *Angkor: Ruins in Cambodia*, p 175.

Group 2: Baphuon

47   Chou Ta-Kuan (Zhou Daguan), *The Customs of Cambodia*, p 2.

Group 2: Bayon

48   H Churchill Candee, *Angkor: The Magnificent, The Wonder City of Ancient Cambodia*, p 126.

49   PJ de Beerski, *Angkor: Ruins in Cambodia*, p 124.

50   PJ de Beerski, *Angkor: Ruins in Cambodia*, p 125.

51   H Churchill Candee, *Angkor: The Magnificent, The Wonder City of Ancient Cambodia*, p 139.

52   H Churchill Candee, *Angkor: The Magnificent, The Wonder City of Ancient Cambodia*, p 141.

GROUP 3: PREAH KHAN

53   H Churchill Candee, *Angkor: The Magnificent, The Wonder City of Ancient Cambodia*, (HF&G Witherby, London, 1925), pp 274–81.

GROUP 3: NEAK PEAN

54   H Churchill Candee, *Angkor: The Magnificent, The Wonder City of Ancient Cambodia*, p 282.

55   In M Glaize, *Les Monuments du Groupe d'Angkor*, p 212.

GROUP 5: SRAH SRANG

56   PJ de Beerski, *Angkor: Ruins in Cambodia*, pp 189–90.

GROUP 5: BANTEAY KDEI

57   H Churchill Candee, *Angkor: The Magnificent, The Wonder City of Ancient Cambodia*, pp 249–50.

GROUP 5: EAST MEBON

58   H Churchill Candee, *Angkor: The Magnificent, The Wonder City of Ancient Cambodia*, p 269.

GROUP 6: TA PROHM

59   H Churchill Candee, *Angkor: The Magnificent, The Wonder City of Ancient Cambodia*, p 256.

60   HW Ponder, *Cambodian Glory: The Mystery of the Deserted Khmer Cities and their Vanished Splendour*, p 305.

61   G Cœdès, *Angkor: An Introduction* (Oxford University Press, Singapore, 2nd ed, 1990) p 96.

62   Rt Hon M MacDonald, *Angkor and the Khmers*, 4th ed, 1965, p 115.

63   RJ Casey, *Four Faces of Siva: The Detective Story of a Vanished Race*, p 181.

GROUP 6: CHAU SAY TEVODA

64   RJ Casey, *Four Faces of Siva: The Detective Story of a Vanished Race*, p 181.

Group 6: Baksei Chamkrong

65 HW Ponder, *Cambodian Glory: The Mystery of the Deserted Khmer Cities and their Vanished Splendour*, p 42.

Group 6: Phnom Bakheng

66 H Churchill Candee, *Angkor: The Magnificent, The Wonder City of Ancient Cambodia*, pp 217–18.

67 H W Ponder, *Cambodian Glory: The Mystery of the Deserted Khmer Cities and their Vanished Splendour*, p 72.

68 RJ Casey, *Four Faces of Siva: The Detective Story of a Vanished Race* , p 129.

69 H Mouhot, *Travels in the Central Parts of Indo-China (Siam), Cambodia, and Laos, During the Years 1858, 1859 and 1860*, 2 vols (John Murrray, London, 1864), Vol 1, pp 300–1.

Group 7: Banteay Srei

70 HW Ponder, *Cambodian Glory: The Mystery of the Deserted Khmer Cities and their Vanquished Splendour*, p 254.

71 M Glaize, *Les Monuments du Groupe d'Angkor: Guide*, p 230.

Group 10: Prasat Suor Prats

72 Chou Ta-Kuan (Zhou Daguan), *The Customs of Cambodia*, p 33.

73 Henri Mouhot, *Travels in the Central Parts of Indo-China (Siam), Cambodia and Laos*, p 8.

Glossary

Airavata A multi-headed elephant; Indra's mount

Amitabha The 'Father' Buddha in Mahayana Buddhism. Represented in Khmer art as a seated Buddha meditating; depicted on the headdress of a bodhisattva

Amrita The drink of immortality that was created by the Churning of the Ocean of Milk

Ananta see Vasuki

anastylosis A method of restoring a monument distinguished by often dismantling and, in theory, rebuilding the structure using the original methods and materials

Angkor (Kh) ('city or capital') An ancient capital in Cambodia that was the main centre of the Khmer Empire from AD 802 to 1432

Angkor Thom (Kh) The 'great' city built in the late 12th century by Jayavarman VII. It is located north of Angkor Wat with the temple of the Bayon at its centre

apsara A female divinity; heavenly dancer; celestial nymph

asura A demon with god-like power that represents the forces of evil and is the enemy of the gods

Avalokiteshvara ('the Lord who looks down from above') (see Lokesvara)

avatara ('descent') Refers to the descent of Vishnu in bodily form from heaven to be reincarnated on earth

Balarama The elder twin brother of Krishna; Vishnu's eighth avatara

baluster A short post or pillar in a series that supports a rail and forms a balustrade

Banteay (Kh) ('fortress') The name given to a temple with an enclosure wall

baray (Kh) ('lake') A large man-made body of water surrounded by banks of earth; reservoir

bas-relief A sculpture in low relief with the figures projecting less than half the true proportions from the background

bodhi tree An enlightenment tree so-named because the Buddha became enlightened while meditating under it

bodhisattva ('Enlightenment Being') In Mahayana Buddhism, a compassionate being who could become a Buddha, but postpones his nirvana and elects to stay on earth to help mankind achieve enlightenment

brahmin The priestly class in Vedism and Hinduism

Brahmanism The early religion of India that emanated from Vedism

Buddha (the) A being who has attained enlightenment.

Buddhism The Buddhist religion that adheres to the basic
principles of non-violence, compassion, and generous works

cakravartin A universal sovereign

Cambodia A country in south-east Asia bounded by Laos, Thailand, Vietnam and the Gulf of Thailand

causeway A raised road across a body of water

chakra The "wheel" of the Buddha symbolising immortality and power; solar-disc; a disc-like weapon of Vishnu.

Champa An ancient Indianised state and rival of the Khmer Empire. It was situated in an area corresponding approximately to present-day south and central Vietnam. It existed from the second century to the fifteenthth century

Chenla see Zhenla

corbel A method of spanning an opening used by the Khmers for vaults. It consists of an overlapping arrangement of stones, each course projecting one third beyond the one below

deva (feminine = devi) (devata = Sanskrit); A deity that is often a guardian

devaraja A cult instituted by Jayavarman II in AD 802 in Cambodia; based on the tenet that the king was an emanation of a god and would be reunited with that god upon death; usually represented in Khmer art as Shiva, symbolising the spiritual and royal essence of the Khmer king

dvarapala A guardian often standing and holding a club; frequently at the entrance to a temple

Dvaravati A Mon kingdom in Thailand from approximately the sixth or seventh century to the eleventh century

Funan A Chinese name for an ancient Indianised kingdom that seems to have been the predecessor to Angkor; located in the lower Mekong basin; although it existed in the first century AD, its zenith was the fifth century; in the seventh century it was eclipsed by the state of Zhenla

Garuda A mythical creature depicted in Khmer art with a human body and birdlike wings, legs and a thick curved beak with bulging eyes; his lower body is covered with feathers and he has the claws of an eagle; Vishnu's vehicle

gopura An elaborate gateway to a temple in south India; it serves as an entrance pavilion in enclosure walls around a temple; widely used in Khmer architecture

hamsa A sacred goose; Brahma's mount

Hanuman A mythical monkey from the *Ramayana*; chief of the army of monkeys

Hari-Hara ('Hari' = Vishnu; 'Hara' = Shiva) A deity who is a combination of these two gods and represents a synthesis of the two Hindu cults. The figure is depicted with Vishnu's tiara on one side and Shiva's plaited locks on the other and holding the main attributes of both gods

Hinayana Buddhism The 'Lesser Vehicle'; became the predominant religion in Cambodia in the 15th century; more commonly called Theravada Buddhism

Hinduism The religion and social system of the Hindus; popular in Cambodia particularly from the first century to the 12th century

Kailasa A mythical mountain in the Himalayas and the abode of Shiva.

kala A masklike creature with the characteristics of bulbous eyes, a human or lion's nose, two horns, clawlike hands and a grinning face

Kalkin see Vishnu

Khmer (Kh) The ancient indigenous people of Cambodia

Krishna A hero of the Hindu epic, *Mahabharata*, and one of the *avataras* of Vishnu

Laksmana The brother of Rama and a major character in the *Ramayana*

laterite A soil leeched of most of its silica abundant in Cambodia and north-eastern Thailand; characterised by a porous texture and a red colour; hardens on exposure to air; used as a building material, particularly for foundations of Khmer temples

linga A representation of the male organ of generation, a symbol of Shiva and his role in creation

lintel A crossbeam resting on two upright posts. On a Khmer temple the lintel is above the door or window opening, directly below the pediment

lokapala A protector of one of the eight directions of the earth in Hindu myths

Lokeshvara ('Lord of the World') The name is often used in Asia for the compassionate bodhisattva Avalokiteshvara

Mahabharata One of the great Indian epics. It describes a civil war in north India

Mahayana Buddhism The 'Greater Vehicle'; a school of Buddhism; flourished in Cambodia, particularly in the late 12th and early 13th centuries

Mandara A mythical mountain in the Himalayas that served as a pole for the Churning of the Ocean of Milk

makara A large sea animal with the body of a reptile and a big jaw and snout that is elongated into a trunk

Meru A mythical mountain at the centre of the Universe and home of the gods; the axis of the world around which the continents and the oceans are ordered

Mucilinda The *naga* king who sheltered the Buddha while he was meditating during a storm

naga A semi-divine being and a serpent-god of the waters who lives in the underworld beneath the earth or in the water; it is generally seven or nine-headed with a scaly body

Nandi 'The Happy One'; a white bull and the vehicle of Shiva

nirvana The 'Extinction' and final liberation from the cycle of rebirths; the goal of Buddhists

Pali A language derived from Vedic Sanskrit

pediment The triangular upper portion of a wall above the portico. Usually known as fronton at Angkor

phnom (Kh) 'hill or mountain'

pilaster A column used on the side of an open doorway that projects slightly from the wall

preah (Kh) 'Sacred, holy'

Prasat (Kh) 'Tower'

Rahu A demon depicted with a monster's head and no body; supposedly causes eclipes by seizing and swallowing the sun and moon

rakshasa A demon who lives in Lanka (Sri) with Ravana

Rama The hero of the *Ramayana*; the seventh *avataras* of Vishnu

Ramayana An Indian epic describing the story of Rama and Sita

Ravana King of the *rakshasas* depicted with ten heads and twenty arms. His abduction of Sita and battle against Rama are the essential parts of the *Ramayana*

rishi A Sanskrit term which refers to a sage, an ascetic, or a hermit. A *rishi* in Khmer art has a goatee and sits cross-legged in meditation

sakti The energy of a feminine deity who is regarded as the consort of the god

sampot (Kh) A Cambodian garment worn as a covering for the lower body

Sesa (see Vasuki)

Sita Rama's wife and heroine of the *Ramayana*

spean (Kh) 'bridge'

srah (Kh) 'pond'

srei (Kh) 'woman'

Sugriva The monkey king in the *Ramayana*

ta (Kh) 'ancestor'

Theravada Buddhism The 'Doctrine of the Elders' representing the traditional Pali heritage of early Buddhism (see Hinayana Buddhism)

Tonle Sap (Kh) ('sweet water') A freshwater sea in western Cambodia that is linked with the Mekong River by the Tonle Sap River

Upanisads Ancient religious texts from India

-varman (Kh) The 'protected', the victorious; the suffix is often attached to the names of Khmer kings

Vasuki The serpent upon which Vishnu reclines or sits. It also serves as a rope when the Ocean of Milk is churned by the gods and demons. It is sometimes called Ananta or Sesa

Vedas A group of hymns and prayers used by Indo-Aryans of northern India during the second millennium BC

wat A Siamese word meaning 'temple'

yaksha A male nature spirit and a deity who often serves as a guardian and has the characteristics of bulging eyes, fangs and a leering grin

yoni Vulva-shaped female symbol of creation and generation

Zhenla (Chenla) An ancient Chinese name for a state in Cambodia that existed from the sixth century to the eighth century

INDEX